D0754609

Love and Forgiveness for a More Just World

RELIGION, CULTURE, AND PUBLIC LIFE

FRONTISPIECE "The Calling of Saint Matthew" by Caravaggio (Michelangelo Merisi da). Contarini Chapel. S. Luigi dei Fracesi, Rome, Italy. Photo credit: Scala/Art Resource, NY.

LOVE and FORGIVENESS for a MORE JUST WORLD

EDITED BY
Hent de Vries and Nils F. Schott

Columbia University Press   *New York*

Columbia University Press
Publishers Since 1893
New York   Chichester, West Sussex
cup.columbia.edu
Copyright © 2015 Columbia University Press
All rights reserved
Library of Congress Cataloging-in-Publication Data
   Love and forgiveness for a more just world / edited by Hent de Vries and Nils F. Schott.
pages cm.—(Religion, culture, and public life)
   Includes index.
   ISBN 978-0-231-17022-2 (cloth: alk. paper)—ISBN 978-0-231-54012-4 (e-book)
   1. Love—Philosophy.   2. Forgiveness.   3. Conduct of life.   I. Vries, Hent de, joint editor.
   BD436.L6835 2015
   128'.46—dc23

                                                            2015007309

COVER IMAGE: Tsibi Geva, *Keffiyeh*, four parts, acrylic on canvas, 2010

COVER DESIGN: Julia Kushnirsky

References to Web sites (URLs) were accurate at the time of writing. Neither the author nor Columbia University Press is responsible for URLs that may have expired or changed since the manuscript was prepared.

CONTENTS

PREFACE AND ACKNOWLEDGMENTS

IN NOVEMBER 2010 Lawrence Sullivan asked one of us to be the chair of the Council of the Human Sciences at the Fetzer Institute, a private philanthropic foundation based in Kalamazoo, Michigan, established by broadcast pioneer John E. Fetzer (1901–1991). An earlier fruitful cooperation on the subject of so-called political theologies and public religions in the modern, postsecular world,[1] when Larry was director of the Center for the Study of World Religions (CSWR) at Harvard University, thus received a worthy follow-up as he took over as Fetzer's new president and CEO. "Join its efforts and do something you haven't done yet, potentially extending beyond the walls of academia and thinking in a different perspective and tone," seemed his surprising suggestion, as he himself signed up with a singular organization and even more daring mission that both seemed, well, off the beaten track.

The Council of the Human Sciences, one of approximately fifteen and consisting of a dozen prominent international members,[2] was sponsored as part of a multiyear project to "foster awareness of the power of love and forgiveness in the emerging global community." It was asked to disburse a significant annual sum of $550,000 and to help prepare a global gathering in Assisi, Italy, which took place in September 2012. The Council of the Human Sciences, for its part, sponsored a host of initiatives. It funded a radio soap opera in Arabic that focused on peace messaging for Palestinian youth in East Jerusalem, an Afghan women's poetry writing project, an arts project of the Sant Atizana Matenwa women's collective in a remote Haitian village, a comparative documentation project on social activism and service in Brazil, Cuba, and the United States (with special emphasis on the roles played by Dom Helder Câmara, a Brazilian bishop who worked for the poor and for human rights; Felix Varela, a Cuban priest who worked for peace and interreligious dialogue; and Dorothy Day, an American laywoman, activist, and peace builder who worked with the poor), and an innovative curriculum of the Fundación para la Reconciliación, allowing that organization to expand its program from Colombia into four more Latin American countries. And this list is far from complete.

The council further received a generous grant to organize one of two international humanities workshops on the very same topic. The first of these took place in June 2012 and the present volume contains some of the papers read and discussed on that occasion. An additional generous grant offered research assistance to further conceive an appropriate publication, bibliographic documentation and, if possible, a media archive that would capture some of the central intuitions and driving arguments behind the project as a whole.

In this context, we also received a grant to develop the concept and outline for a so-called Alternative Reality Game (ARG), tentatively called "A Serious Game," so as to reimagine what, paradoxically, might be called a "mobile canon" (Hent de Vries's concept) or also a "secular catechism" (Nils F. Schott's term). Building on an exemplary body of work using digital technologies for positive social change, our idea was to use interactive digital technology to highlight exemplars and foster greater awareness of the power of love and forgiveness. With that aim in mind, the Humanities Council convened by the Fetzer Institute partnered with a New York based production company, Jumping Pages, which brings out animated interactive apps for iPad and iPhones, to create a pilot for children ages five to ten that could serve as a model for further tools for worldwide instruction in the subject of love and forgiveness. This interactive digital platform would aim to engage children in problem solving and to develop their awareness of love and forgiveness in action in the world around them through a creative storyline and imaginative characters. Furthermore, the members of the development team for the app, led by Rania Ajami, would engage in a reflective process and document their experience while integrating the concepts of love and forgiveness into their work.

As we bring part of this overall project to a provisional close, we would like to thank several individuals without whose support and inspiration we could not have accomplished our tasks. In addition to thanking the Fetzer Institute for its hospitality and unique financial assistance, we would to express our gratitude, first of all, to Lawrence E. Sullivan, whose visionary leadership and calm confidence in our abilities to do something out of the ordinary never relinquished and motivates us to this day. Second, to Michelle Scheidt, our program coordinator at the Fetzer Council, whose gentle but firm competence and limitless kindness carried us each step of the way. Thanks also to Haleh Gafori, Segahl Avin, and Rania Ajami for allowing us to include their creations not only in this book but also on the Web site at Columbia University Press that accompanies it. We would like to express our thanks further to the *Revue de métaphysique et de morale*, for permission to translate an interview with Jean-Luc Marion, and to Éditions Galilée, Indiana University Press, and Routledge for allowing us to reprint the two texts by Jacques Derrida that, likewise, speak directly to our topic. We were also extremely fortunate to receive the truly generous gift of an original work of art for our book cover by the Israeli artist Tsibi Geva, entitled *Keffiyeh* (2010). Our deep gratitude, finally, to Wendy Lochner, Christine Dunbar, Philip Leventhal, and Susan Pensak, our editors at Columbia University Press, whose immediate and unrelenting faith in this challenging project, together with their remarkable efficiency, have made the work on this volume an exciting adventure and genuine pleasure.

New York, Paris, January 2015

NOTES

1. Hent de Vries and Lawrence E. Sullivan, eds., *Political Theologies: Public Religions in a Post-Secular World* (New York: Fordham University Press, 2006).
2. http://fetzer.org/work/projects/fetzer-advisory-coucil-humanities (last accessed December 10, 2014).

Love and Forgiveness for a More Just World

HUMAN ALERT

Concepts and Practices of Love and Forgiveness

Hent de Vries and Nils F. Schott

WHAT IS LOVE? WHAT FORGIVENESS? What, if anything, is their relationship? Historically and conceptually, as we will briefly sketch out, their origins and subsequent fates have been vastly divergent. And yet these terms and the realities—ideas, values, and affects, in short, the concepts and practices—they stand for have traveled parallel paths, just as they have often been associated, even to the point of confusion. Does love offer forgiveness? Does love require forgiveness in order to be what it is? Does one forgive out of love? Could one, precisely out of love, decide not to forgive? Can one forgive but not love? Is forgiveness a practical and pragmatic, perhaps even political or juridical concept, where love apparently is not? Or does love extend to a more than simply interpersonal level, captured also by other beings and things, groups and collectivities, nations and states, nature and cosmos?

Nothing here is self-evident. Add to this that there is nothing sentimental or moralistic, nothing rosy, really, about these notions, that indeed love is not a bed of roses and forgiving is anything but forgetting, and one is soon convinced that one has entered a deeply problematic terrain. What in everyday life and popular culture—almost across times and worldwide—seems to need no further explication and, in fact, finds no ulterior reason for its very existence, glory, and terror, is steeped in more complicated (at times, paradoxical, perhaps aporetic) relations of networks of meaning, configurations of force. And the latter, there is no doubt, inform, just as they are formed in and formed by, human practices, individual and collective, all of them guided by a profound sense of *alert*, by vigilant attentiveness and brisk action, but also by attunement to others, awareness of difference, and the patient cultivation of nascent relations, emergent communities.

While we are aware of the fact that love and forgiveness have alternative genealogies and modern narratives, we claim that what holds them together is—at minimum, perhaps, at most—this sense of alert. If there were any one key idea that we seek to convey with the following essays, it is this: our (need for) alertness toward love and forgiveness in their often downright painful ambiguity, their connection (historically, conceptually, and practically speaking) as well as their no less telling disconnect, here and there. After all, these notions are not simple synonyms, but find their distinctive meaning and force, precisely, in their complementarity and, at times, contrast and conflict, which makes them into what they are: the most distinctive, if ambiguous and problematic, conduits for our deeper-seated sense of *human alert*, first of all.

Love and forgiveness, then, are profoundly dated and culturally situated as well as specific, yet they find their common ground, if anywhere, in an essential humanlike feature, which is nothing natural, much less biological, per se. Their gratuitous character—quite literally, their for-nothing-ness—is their most basic feature. And any reduction of their "nature" to what they are not annuls our understanding and appreciation of the fundamental effect they have on the psyche of individuals and groups, collectives and nations, transnational communities and humanity, as realities we live by and as ideals we invoke when human strife goes well beyond them. Their force can only be described in its phenomenon (phenomenologically, as it were), just as it can only be analyzed in its putative content and contours (philosophically and psychoanalytically, as we will see). No explanation of ulterior or ultimate causes and their effects is of much help in the process of understanding the stakes of these concepts, let alone of their practices. Yet, regardless of their elusive, if persistent, character, they alert us. Or, more precisely, love and forgiveness are the precise responses to what might be called this human alert.

That said, there seems to be a simple truth that needs to be told: one can love and not forgive or, indeed, out of love, not forgive, decide not to forgive even where it would be opportune, what one does. There might be a greater difficulty, it might be a heavier task, to, precisely, not put things behind us, not to move on. For what else is forgiveness—like its virtual opposite, which is "to settle scores"—but to consider the wrongs of the past and present over and done with so as to no longer have to dwell on and suffer from them? Or would this itself be a caricature of the concept and practice in question? Is it the spirit in which one forgives, then, that makes all the difference? Without love no forgiveness, even if, as we said, one surely can love and not forgive?

Conversely, can one forgive, but not love, or even decide to forgive, but never love the one or all that one forgives and this in the name, precisely, of the one or ones that one loved to begin with? But then, there might be a greater difficulty and heavier task in loving beyond the one and ones that are loved. For what else is love—like its virtual opposite, which is impassioned hate—but to include all those worthy and unworthy of love, thus giving the concept, if not always practice, almost universal or, as we would now say, global and cosmic dimensions and more?[1]

Both love and forgiveness open and describe parallel and relatively independent paths that can be taken—in fact, we will suggest, cannot but be taken—for individual persons and social groups, religious communities as well as nations to, quite literally, find peace and peace of mind and heart. It is hard to imagine a flourishing life, subsisting institutions, and, indeed, global justice without invoking them (whether individually or in conjunction). Yet conflating their respective legacies, no matter how often they have been cited, mentioned, and used together or justified in one breath, serves no theoretical, much less any practical purpose.

Love and forgiveness, then, come in at least two analytical and phenomenological—if not necessarily empirical, much less natural—guises, each of them with their relevant vocabularies, images, gestures, traditions and canons. We can study their *concepts* and *practices*, all of which can be seen under different aspects. Roughly put, they reveal themselves genealogically, and they can be seen more or less generously or charitably. That is to say, we can take an outer or inner perspective on both ideas and notions, whether in isolation or woven into a larger tissue or network of philosophical thoughts and/or theological symbols, just as we can not only describe and reconstruct their social formation and function but also participate in and, hence, contribute to the very forms of life that embody them. But can we? Where such emphatic values and, at times, variables are at issue, can we really distinguish between these different points of view? Is it so much as possible and desirable to set concepts and practices, such as love and forgiveness, somewhat apart, suggesting they could at least *in principle*, if not always *in fact*, be differentiated? Is their association a mixed blessing, a gentle forgetting that love is sometimes unforgiving and that one may well forgive but not necessarily love?

Moreover, do love and forgiveness, separately and in conjunction, not also touch on—at times, switch into—their purported opposites, that is to say, into the perversion of love and/or hate or into the inability to forgive and move on? The most interesting—and this means also deeply troubling, if all too common—cases are, no doubt, those in which different shades of gray color the very phenomena in question. Instead of the "gray in gray" in which philosophy paints a world "grown old," as Georg Wilhelm Friedrich Hegel saw,[2] love and forgiveness manifest themselves according to a whole spectrum of modalities and amalgamations in which one emphasis can overtake—or fade into—another almost instantaneously and for no obvious reason. Examples abound.

Haleh Gafori's poem, "Orange Alert," which opens the volume, is a case in point, just as it sets the tone for the contemporary accentuation that love and forgiveness must necessarily—indeed, near fatefully, if not always jointly—operate in what the Fetzer Institute (in generously sponsoring the humanities symposium during which several of the essays collected here originated) has optimistically described as the "emerging global community." As Gafori, an Iranian American Brooklyn-based poet, aptly demonstrates, insinuating a simultaneously sensitive and raw voice into the governmental and broader cultural idiom of the post-9/11 world of the Pax Americana—almost overnight redefined in terms of a semipermanent "war on terror" and ever expanding surveillance apparatus ("when you see something, say something")—nothing is self-evident in the terminology of either the "global" or of "community." And the abruptness, and often numbing repetitiveness, with which worldwide events alter our global perception of things past, present, and future, while seemingly reinforcing an all-too-fatalistic sense of immanence, stasis, and closure, puts increasing pressure on the very concept of "emergence" as well.

The essays collected in *Love and Forgiveness for a More Just World* remind us that the category of "the human" (and what are often considered among the most human of actions, including acts of love and forgiveness) is, likewise, by no means self-evident. From the first encyclical, *Deus caritas est*, which the previous pope, Benedict XVI, issued within a year of his election, to the newly elected pope's chosen name, Francis I, reminiscent of the saint of Assisi—and condensing the striking phenomenon of a genuine Francis Effect from which our political leaders may well have to learn—to the more secular appropriations of love as a political category among post-Marxian theorists (who rightly see subterranean correspondences and resonances, sympathies and common causes, shared by protest movements geographical worlds apart), there is an increasing realization that the singular force of love eludes spatiotemporal coordinates or parameters and follows a logic and rhythm that is one of a kind (*sui generis*) and, indeed, in metaphysical parlance, its very own cause (*causa sui*), a cause out of the freedom that we retain or acquire no matter how much we are sealed off from the world and everything, everyone, in it. Paradoxically, love may not so much be the imperative of our times, but surely it is a strange, contingent necessity, its possible impossibility (or impossible possibility, depending on how we describe it in more philosophical, theological terms).

By the same token, from the invocation of forgiveness as one of the sole available responses to the havoc wrought by genocidal violence (for example, in the history of slavery, the Armenian catastrophe, the Holocaust, the aftermath of the genocides in Cambodia and Rwanda, ethnic cleansing in the former Yugoslavia with the Srebrenica massacre as its tragic culmination, and these may very well not be the only or last instances in human history); by the grave political injustices that followed in its wake or had different antecedents altogether (such as the legacy of racial discrimination and South African apartheid, the Palestinian Nakba that expelled and displaced an estimated seven hundred thousand inhabitants from their villages following the Israeli Declaration of Independence in 1948, but also the aftermath of European colonialism and repression of indigenous communities, not to mention the enormous and growing economic disparities worldwide); indeed, by no less intractable violations of a sexual nature (from the ongoing discriminations among genders and the denial of rights to the LGBT community to the rape and child abuse scandals that have plagued the Roman Catholic priesthood as well as other religious congregations, not to mention the much publicized sex scandals in which leading political figures seem to get themselves serially involved, from Bill Clinton to Anthony Weiner, and from Dominique Strauss-Kahn to Eliot Spitzer)—it seems that the transformative function and value of forgiveness is increasingly portrayed as the one remaining and instant solution, if not resolution, of the dramatic historical conflicts, racial and political injustices, and sexually inflected injuries widely at hand. Paradoxically, forgiveness may not so much be the imperative of our times, but surely it is a strange, contingent necessity, its possible impossibility (or impossible possibility, depending on how we describe it in more philosophical, theological terms).

Are the concepts and practices of love and forgiveness the instant solutions to—and, perhaps, partial resolutions of—unceasing horrors and predicaments that continue to surround us as the signs of the times, the writing on the wall of the prison house that, in all appearances, our psychic and political world has become? We spoke earlier of *instant* solutions because love and forgiveness are not only seen as *short-circuiting* and *substituting for* a more laborious process of potentially endless, indeed, infinite justification that no deliberation or reasonable compromise—however calibrated or even just—could ever negotiate and bring to an end, much less a consensus or closure; they are also considered to do whatever they do almost immediately. No matter how much effort working through the past incriminations leading up to—and following—their moment may take, love and forgiveness themselves operate and take effect *instantly*. We can grow in love, engage in a labor of love, and forgive ever more, but the actual act of love or forgiveness requires no time and no space—indeed, no reflective thought—to proceed or succeed. One sees the light or perceives the glimmer of hope at the end of a long tunnel of darkness quasi spontaneously, without a cause, with no reason given or needed. Love and forgiveness form the virtual—tangential, that is to say, far from firm but fleeting—points in time and space from which alone we can move forward. Figurally speaking, they are black holes, sometimes wormholes, from which no light, no weighty matter, emerges and into which everything disappears, yet allowing us only thus to speed toward alternative universes altogether, worlds in which nothing is impossible (by its very definition, origin or telos) per se. In that sense the concepts of love and forgiveness and the practices they suggest are, pragmatically speaking, *what is better for us to believe in*, even though we can cite no utilitarian considerations, no normative rules, no moral codes, and, a fortiori, no human knowledge interests on their behalf, to make their case. Much more than our need for survival, much else besides our well-understood self-interest—our *conatus essendi*, as Spinoza and, in his wake, Emmanuel Levinas aptly put it—can, ought, or will have to guide us here or there, where we plunge through the rabbit hole.

What is thus summoned and what summons us is not a worn-out remnant from a long-forgotten tradition that has lost relevance in all of its other aspects, but, on the contrary, the wider and deeper archive and apparatus whose integral meaning and global force or effect have become more and more apparent with the emergence of globalization. In an age of ever exponentially expanding economic markets and technological media, in which exchange and information, commerce and communication form the real currency of the day, novel approaches to old concepts and practices become more and more imperative or, as we said, contingently *necessary*. For good and for ill, such concepts and practices signal a revaluation of values we had deemed somewhat outmoded, if not downright obsolete, to our peril. In the present day and age, then, when their prospects seem weak and the world tends to spin out of control, with nowhere to go, love and forgiveness nonetheless name and trigger nothing short of an emancipatory option, an altogether different optics. It is the seemingly impossible possibility—or possible impossibility—of nothing less than a *total recall*, of seeing and setting things right. Its crucial importance we are only slowly beginning to fathom as well as appreciate, since it consists of nothing else than the growing realization that we "can be the 'anachronistic' contemporary of a past or future 'generation,'"[3] as Jacques Derrida put it in his last interview, *Learning to Live Finally*. It reveals the surprising "fact"—a "fact of reason" (as Immanuel Kant called it) and a "total social fact" (as Marcel Mauss surmised)—that we can effectively reclaim our absolute past: "a past" of which William Faulkner had once aptly written that not only it "is not dead. In fact, it's not even past."[4]

THE ESSAYS COLLECTED in this volume, together with the aforementioned opening poem, entitled "Orange Alert," the short film *You Shall Know No Grief,* and *Maggie and Her Magical Glasses*, the children's game or iPad app, both of them discussed in this introduction—all revolve around the question of love and forgiveness, addressing their moral urgency, conceptual rigor, and practical necessity. More specifically, they address what we described earlier as the seemingly *impossible possibility* of love and of forgiveness as well as their no less apparent *possible impossibility* in historical and political, theological and philosophical, literary and psychoanalytic terms, with an occasional excursion into the registers of so-called speech act theory, ordinary language and its performative utterances, and quite a few examples drawn from literature and the visual arts.

Such exploration, Jean-Luc Marion suggests in a recent interview, comes down to first allowing and then investigating, perhaps, "the impossibility of impossibility" and thereby, philosophically speaking, to opening a whole "new frontier" of thought and of practice. What seems thinkable and what, as we say, seems to work in more practical terms may very well not seem thinkable or workable upon first or second reflection. After all, "one of the characteristics of the possible is that you cannot distinguish it from the impossible. And it is absolutely consistent to say that."[5] Indeed, saying the contrary—turning the possible and the impossible into contraries—is, precisely, to propose a metaphysical foundation, an a priori principle, on the basis of which such a distinction could be made and, hence, to wall off our experience from all the "counterexperiences" to which it could yet be *alerted* (and to which it can and should alert others, witnesses and bystanders, in turn). Not to see this and say so as well as act upon it is also to forget that there are "certitudes," which are, technically speaking, "negative" in that they lack any determining (rational) ground and remain irreducible to any preceding or ulterior (metaphysical, physical, or psychological) cause. Siding with Ludwig Wittgenstein on this very point, Marion states this explicitly: "our deepest certitudes have no reason."[6]

Yet this, of course, is precisely the reason why any declaration or act of love or forgiveness can easily be suspected of being not it, whether not quite being it or being its opposite: a parody or mere posturing. Of such negation and betrayal we can never be certain. Indeed, we have no criteriological or otherwise normative means, standards, or conventions to establish that we are dealing with the real thing (genuine love, true forgiveness) rather than its counterfeit (and what would that be, exactly?). The very talk of instant love or instant forgiveness captures this potential duplicity effectively. Just as historical faith or religious belief go hand in hand with at least the possibility of idolatry or blasphemy, so also love and forgiveness—their very concept and practice—may well be a sham. This risk cannot be avoided and may well be a chance for their notions and gestures to work unexpectedly. But whether they do so or not will never be easy to tell.

To cite an example from the spectacle of contemporary American electoral politics: When Huma Abedin, longtime aide to Hilary Clinton and spouse of former congressman and candidate in the 2013 campaign for mayor of New York City Anthony Weiner, made a stunning appearance during a press conference publicly stating that she loved and had forgiven her husband for having had online affairs with "six to ten" women, was she sincere and serious (clearly saddened, she definitely appeared that way) or merely pulling a page from the textbook of the "Clinton school of forgiveness" according to which "power is more important than dignity," as one conservative commentator instantly and cynically commented?[7] Was she laying the foundation for her own future career (as Hilary Clinton, in her role as First Lady, had done before her) and assuming she might not salvage—or even want to rescue—her husband's prospects? Or was she simply attempting to "move forward," putting a difficult chapter in her private life behind her? Heaven knows, and perhaps not even. But does this uncertainty mean that the invocation of the concept and practice of love and forgiveness was inappropriate or irrelevant in this context and for that very reason? Nothing seems further from the truth, this much we know. Fallibility, like deniability, the very possibility of parody and perversion, no matter how sincerely or seriously one talks the talk and walks the walk, belong to the essence—or, should we say, heart—of the thing. Our criteria, as Stanley Cavell put it in *The Claim of Reason*, can and will often "disappoint" us.

To give yet another example, one might mention the quasi-perennial search for a future for an embattled Israel whose military successes come at a price, as is made painfully clear by Segahl Avin's 2010 prize-winning short film *You Shall Know No Grief*.[8] This seemingly Sci-Fi-inspired film imagining a not too distant future powerfully evokes a political situation in which the question of love and forgiveness is more urgent and ambiguous, not to mention parodied and perverted, than ever before. Starting from a fictive scenario that plays itself out in 2015 (the explicit caption with this early date is itself somewhat of a provocation in light of the events unfolding) in which the Israeli Defense Force has just conquered unspecified post-Soviet Muslim republics with "no casualties" on its side, the film beautifully captures the unexpected homecoming of one of the soldiers named Mike. A return without a return,

FIGURE 0.1. Still from "You Shall Know No Grief" by Segahl Avin.

really, since Mike (or what is left and/or has been made of him) is no longer quite there. Rather, he is too perfectly present, in an indestructible iron body in which the spirit, no matter how often faint smiles are attempted, and simple human gestures all too quickly, all too automatically, mimicked, seems either broken or just simply absent.[9]

As the parents, especially the father, sense that something's different ("Are you OK?" "Is everything all right?"), the prodigal son ("I'm your son," "I'm your son," "I'm YOUR son") responds, at first, almost mechanically, soullessly, raising more and more suspicions, something only the mother ("It's so great to see you, my love") chooses to fully ignore at the outset, perhaps all along. Unless, of course, she knows something that we, as spectators, like the father, do not. Mothers, the film intimates, have something to do with love and forgiveness—perhaps, a greater strength, a different weakness—that fathers and mere bystanders have not. For one thing, the mother does not need to see and empirically test (an inquisitive look into the shower, a violent experiment at the table). She merely walks out and is the first to accept, to welcome the prodigal son back into her love, if ever this love slightly doubted or hesitated (which we, as viewers, have all reason to believe it did not).

When father and son find themselves alone at the lunch table, the first ("Who are you?" "Who are you?") shockingly jabs a fork in the hand of the latter, causing no harm for all we can tell. The father thus sub-

FIGURE 0.2. Still from "You Shall Know No Grief" by Segahl Avin.

jects the son to a disturbing *experimentum crucis*, seeking to determine whether the other (the "other mind") is an automaton or the loved living being. As the son pulls the fork out of his hand without blinking, a squeaking metal sound revealing the artificial makeup or makeover of his reinforced arms, the two get up and join the mother outside. Has the son, who by all appearances is the very same as the person whom the parents longed to return safe and sound, come home as the one (and, we are led to believe, the one and only child) they so dearly loved? Or is he, indeed, an automaton, an army's machine, a latter-day Robocop, a replacement whose real body and soul were sacrificed either in battle or even before (the singing of a shared song into which the father lures him being the final giveaway, a failed Turing test for parental lineage, as it were)? Should one be grateful for his survival in some form or other—undisturbed by the subtle niceties of the so-called philosophy of mind with its modern musings about personal identity, puzzles of other mind skepticism, and its obsession with humanoids, androids, robots, avatars, etc.—and, perhaps, *forgive* the military apparatus and its unbridled imperialism that saved Mike as such (as a quasi immortal who, at least, will cause *no more grief* to the family that, perhaps, all too easily and far from lovingly, gave him up to an unforgiving fate, in the first place)? Should an army be "strong and moral" in that it "returns its soldiers from battles" *at any price* (inoculating them against the pains and

FIGURE 0.3. Still from "You Shall Know No Grief" by Segahl Avin.

qualms of love and forgiveness, which seem to require both a soul and a body)? Can one still or yet again love and forgive Mike for what he has, clearly, become? Can or must one love or forgive a military apparatus that sends sons and soldiers into painless battles that can serve no meaningful purpose of peace or security (such as quickly defeating and occupying the fictive post-Soviet Islamic republics, far from one's own geographical borders, without even the semblance of any justification in terms of self-defense, let alone international law or sound political instinct)?

In addition to suggesting that it is better not to deprive oneself of the possibility of grief, the film wisely leaves all these questions open and allows us to imagine a dystopian future—again, perhaps, not so far off—in which they ought to be raised. We'll know neither love nor forgiveness without pain and, again, without grief, the film seems to suggest with an insistent inversion of its unloving and unforgiving title (its "You shall" perversely conflating the idiom of biblical commandments with present-day military imperatives), no matter what modern army generals "promise" or deliver to us with the best and worst of intentions, namely, to leave no one behind, to inflict harm while suffering no harm in return. Love and forgiveness, their very concepts and practices, function only where and when their, inevitable, grief is not avoided but acknowledged and, in this sense, "known." And to say this is not only a matter of logical consequence or empirical observation but the normative injunction ("You shall") written all over them.

ONE FURTHER WAY OF ADDRESSING these matters needs to be mentioned before we turn to the essays collected in this volume, especially now, at the present juncture in time, and in light of this project's original formulation (i.e., the Fetzer Institute's mission in question), namely to "foster love and forgiveness in the emerging global community." No matter how much one would need to question the temporal and spatial (here geographical) concept of "emergence" as well as the practices of so-called globalization, this much is clear: any genuine account of love and forgiveness, indeed, any lesson or instruction to be drawn and insisted upon (and what else could "fostering" mean?), would now call for new genres and methods of exposition, in sync with the new media technologies of information and communication that have grown markets and commerce as well as social networks and, in so doing, have become more and more available and dominant in recent decennia, notably in the lives of the youngest among us. Here progressive tendencies and potential compete with their regressive counterparts, each step along the way, click by click, bit by bit.

In the field of digital gaming, some creative developers stand out for their commitment to social change, and their work develops technology that is both fun and engaging, immersive and smart, while promoting positive values and socially responsible behaviors. Whereas many interactive apps, video games, and online gaming platforms use simulations of war and violence to appeal to young people, often to detrimental—numbing moral and psychological effect—the aforementioned *serious gamers* have invented a body of work that uses digital media for prosocial development that is no less entertaining (if that is the word) but far more educational, informative, and, indeed, formative. What has emerged is a whole series of alternative thought experiments and imaginative variations that now serve as countercultural, technologically mediated, spiritual exercises, nothing less. Several of these serious games that developed out of computer simulations pioneered in the medical and military fields, on the one hand, and massively multiplayer online games, on the other, have been inspiring in this context as well. The wider availability of hardware and the spread of mobile technology, which were the basis for the development of apps, have also led to applications of serious games in fields such as diplomacy and policy planning, medical treatment and public health, and have had wide appeal in the fields of primary, secondary, and higher education. Examples include Asi Barak's *Games for Change* group and the *Greater Than Games* lab at Duke University with Katherine Hayles and Tim Lenoir as pioneering leaders.[10]

The potential of the serious game approach is particularly apparent where what is known in game theory as the prisoner's dilemma—the question whether to back down, cooperate, or stay silent (the very key to breaking through stalemates and gridlocks)—is concerned in a new and more than simply game-theoretical or formal mathematical light. Exploring the affective, moral, and emotional possibilities and potentialities opened up and triggered by love and forgiveness for, say, *backing down without losing, being prudent without, therefore, being weak* in practical yet hypothetical ("fictive") situations that are compellingly visualized and narrated is the strength par excellence of these digital platforms. The whole concept and practice of modeling strategic and tactical situations takes on a whole other—speculative and spiritual, yet also mundane and visceral—dimension that is deeply and pragmatically significant. What the games in question offer is not so much Big Data, but, on the contrary, Little Data, as they emblematize and miniaturize conceptual and practical choices that impose themselves more and more, albeit now unaided by the grand narratives, the ideological dogmas and moral certitudes of past generations. Exercises in noncriteriological thinking, they present us with phenomenological descriptions whose density and intensity should somehow speak for themselves.

In collaboration with the app development company Jumping Pages and its founder Rania Ajami, an iPad app for children, based on the character Maggie and her magical glasses, was developed as one of the projects sponsored by Fetzer's Council of the Humanities. Maggie's story is told through the interactive pages of a digital book, allowing children to touch, move, and experience the sounds and images of Maggie's world. In the story line, Maggie's special glasses allow her to see everything around her through a lens of love and forgiveness. Each episode features Maggie using her magical glasses to tackle a problem or resolve a conflict, moving difficult situations toward love and forgiveness, if not always with the explicit use of these concepts and, definitely, in an original redesign of their better-known practices.

FIGURE 0.4. Still from the application "Maggie and Her Magical Glasses" by Jumping Pages.

The character thus brought to life goes on a journey, faces obstacles, and learns about the power of love and forgiveness in different situations: at home, at school, among neighbors. The extra dimension of interactivity aims to help with the learning process and pull the child that "plays," views, and reads it into the story, providing it with a serious game, something greater than a game, that is nonetheless good fun. In the words of the development team at Jumping Pages:

> In the world of Maggie and her magical glasses, there's always a different way of seeing things. When we first meet Maggie, our heroine, she's being picked on by the meanest kid in school because of her thick glasses. He grabs them and stomps on them, smashing them to pieces. Maggie trudges home to the house she shares with her dad, an absent-minded inventor who spends most of his time in his workshop building a forgiveness machine that's never quite finished. He fixes Maggie's glasses with some spare parts from the machine. Maggie goes back to school vowing to confront the bully, who she finds picking on another kid. But instead of getting mad, when she looks at the bully through her new glasses something magical happens—she sees that he bullies because his parents bully him, and she forgives him. She makes peace between the bully and his new victim and helps the bully by coaching

him for a history test, as it's her best subject. The episode ends, as each one will, with Maggie telling us about a little example of love and forgiveness from history. In each episode Maggie will use her magical glasses to tackle a problem or resolve a conflict, guiding the fighting parties towards love and forgiveness. Suddenly, everywhere she looks, there are people who need her help. From feuding families and warring neighbors to the law, courts and politics—who knows where Maggie's glasses will lead her next? They could even go global!

A little lesson in love and forgiveness thus learned (in the bullying episode and beyond) might well be that these concepts and practices do not require that we respond to others, including those who may have harmed us, measure for measure, eye for eye, until all harms have been evened out, in principle or in fact (which no conceivable or practicable idea of justice—or doing justice—can ever realize in any possible world). A further lesson might be that the greatest strength in social interaction may lie in adopting an altogether different attitude and expectation, namely that of a weak but no less tenacious force for the good or the better. Put differently, Maggie learns that she can change the rules of the "game" that is human, social, and eventually political life by introducing new and more liberating ways and forms of living with others. Yet the upshot of her story is that the "rules" of the serious game of love and forgiveness thus envisioned cannot be stated in general and abstract terms but only exemplified case by case, one episode at a time, step by step, bit by bit. Hence the importance of the individual stories, making the case, each time differently, but ultimately with the same overall point (its generic and strangely generative "truth," if one may say so).

ALL THE ESSAYS that make up the present collection provide further examples of past and current religious and spiritual, political and existential situations that have called for love and forgiveness to intervene, to answer their call so as to cut through the Gordian knots that societal strife and psychic pressures have stitched in the web of historical and ontological immanence, war and violence, closed and static mindsets, including the seemingly unbreakable nexus of determining causes and their proportionate effects, which cynically predict that there can be nothing new under the sun, no pages turned, no beginnings made, no future to speak of. Every single contributor offers a different perspective on the empirical and phenomenological givens that would otherwise be unalterable in their metaphysical makeup.

Love and forgiveness, then—not unlike miracles, belief in miracles, and the deeds of so-called miracle workers—each represent escape hatches from empirical impasse and moral fatigue. They summon, as we said earlier, a "fact of reason," as Kant might have said, a "total social fact," as Mauss would have added, that when realized (i.e., clearly seen and faithfully followed up), in *total recall*, changes everything all at once, revealing all theological predestination, every historical and psychological determinism—no matter how many serious, accumulated reasons and other, imperiling facts these may further rely on—to be mystically and metaphysically, but also speculatively, hypothetically, and pragmatically, profoundly *contingent*, that is to say, *reversible* or, at the very least, *perfectible*, not the last word.

Paradoxically, the apparent necessity to love and forgive—and this, in our day and age of global economic markets and technological media, of exponentially growing forms of commerce and communication, more than ever before—is that they show that all is not said and done when all determinable facts, established with the help of epistemic and other normative criteria, seem to suggest so. In other words, they inexplicably and, often, unjustifiably reveal that things might just as well be or come to be seen altogether otherwise, short-circuited and rerouted, as it were. Love and forgiveness, called for at any given moment of time and at every imaginable place on the globe, thus give all things and every being a first or second chance to be or become what they might have been all along, indeed, what they may not even need to "be" (foregoing ontological grounding, categories, possibilities, and the like). It is in this, and in nothing else, that they—the concepts and practices of love and forgiveness and everything they stand for—find their redeeming, indeed, transformative quality. The essays collected in this volume are *alert* to this impossible possibility or possible impossibility of what it means to be *human*, tracing its contours in wide variety of philosophical and theological, psychological and political, literary and visual registers.

JEAN-LUC MARION's ESSAY "What Love Knows" is a succinct exposition of the transformative effect of love, an effect it shares with that of forgiveness, as he has amply argued in different contexts. Conceiving of love phenomenologically as an "erotic reduction," Marion argues that love, far from being merely a passion, is first of all a point of view. It operates a profound displacement in our experience of space, time, and self. Love, in his view, is never a question of give and take. Love always comes first; it is not an exchange, but a gift. This idea of the gift is also the central notion underlying Marion's description and analysis of forgiveness. Arguing that in any situation of giving the giver is forgotten, he shows that and how the act of forgiveness is the simple (but by no means obvious or easy) act of giving *again*, of not insisting on reciprocity, the *do ut des*, the measure for measure. It is to maintain the gift *as* gift since, in only so doing, the gift "opens up a completely different world" at the furthest remove from the one dominated by the omnipresent economy of market exchanges, of commerce and communication in which bits of information make it from one end to another, instantaneously, following algorithms specifically designed for transmission and storage, of exchanges and substitutions in terms of the digital 0 and 1. Such mediated and mediatized banking and brokering, of futures and derivatives, keep scores, take stock. Love and forgiveness do not.

In a companion piece, entitled "Unpower" and for the first time translated as well as reproduced here, Marion responds to questions addressing the question of power—arguably the mantra and obsession of postwar French philosophy, up to this day—only to argue that the very concept and practice of power as we have inherited it seems, like its all too abstract negation of "powerlessness," to be a metaphysical holdover whose very premises we need not accept. If we want to come to a better understanding of the political—of the very domain in which, in Marion's words, modern egos are staged—and in particular of the alternative practices that seek to go beyond so-called power politics of the powers that be (including, one must assume, their so-called soft power of diplomatic and symbolical persuasion of the public opinion, broadly defined), then we have to abandon the oppositional logic of power and counter-powers (however non-violent and seemingly idyllic these latter may be at first glance). Instead one must develop a conception and practice of what Marion suggestively—and, in an unmistakable and surprising psychoanalytic register—calls "unpower" (*impouvoir*).[11] Such a concept and its presumed practice has important political ramifications that would need to be spelled out in much further detail, just as it would seem to have significant juridical reverberations as well. Levinas spoke of the "curvature of social space."

Detecting a "rampant confusion of the wrong deed with the wrong-doer," Regina Schwartz sets out to sketch the assumptions made in considering revenge and retribution to be acts of justice, chief among them the idea that it is possible to measure harm (and thus to repair it by restitution as if nothing had happened). Yet, as Schwartz demonstrates in a suggestive reading of the "antirevenge tragedy" *Hamlet*, "revenge cannot correct an injury. "With *King Lear*, she argues, it is possible to take a further step: "forgiveness is not only offered as an alternative to revenge . . . [it] is tied to recognition, or the rediscovery of love." And it is the "biblical Shakespeare" of *Measure for Measure* and *The Tempest*, she writes, who manages to "join . . . justice to love."

Leora Batnitzky's contribution takes parallel key principles in Judaism and Calvinism as a foil for developing a conception of the intricate links between love and law. Conjugating this relationship in a series of direct comparisons, she shows that the spirit and the letter of the law, divine grace and human practice, sin and forgiveness are inextricably linked. The demands made by God's love and by its human expression, the law, are impossible to fulfill, but for that very reason solicit and enable forgiveness as an act of love. There is, according to the Jewish tradition Batnitzky draws on, in "all human beings" a fundamental love of "what is theirs." To love, then, would be to take the universal view in the most particular situation—that is to say, *to include*—and to forgive would be to move from particular victimhood back to where love can again be given—that is to say, *to (re)integrate*.

In a discussion of a teaching manual by St. Augustine, Nils F. Schott shows how in the back and forth of questions and answers, in pronouncing sermons and listening to the response they elicit, obstacles to love are removed and a community is instituted. Yet there is no guarantee that even the most skillful combination of encouragements and admonishments, of love and fear, will ever succeed, and Augustine is just as aware of the central importance of alertness to the needs of others as he is to the possibility that love is refused and forgiveness is needed.

Two contributions from practitioners and theorists of psychoanalysis develop the idea that forgiveness, in particular, is a fundamental aspect of our relation to others and to ourselves. Picking up on the work of Melanie Klein and her followers, Orna Ophir urges us to understand *both* love and forgiveness as *processes* that can only be successful (albeit never conclusive) if we confront evil not so much in its manifest and external forms (that is to say, evils done such as wrongs, harms, injuries, traumata, etc.) but above all the evil in ourselves. Despite the dearth of psychoanalytic literature on the topic, forgiveness, according to Ophir, is of immediate relevance to a wide range of psychoanalytic concerns. Through and beyond these therapeutic and theoretical concerns, as a recent example from postrevolutionary Libya she discusses powerfully demonstrates, a psychoanalytic approach helps us to understand how it may be possible to break the vicious cycle of violence and countervio-lence. Furthermore, a meticulous reconstruction of Klein's argument leads Ophir to articulate the concept of a "lifelong work" of love and forgiveness, which she conceives of as the interminable work of repara-tion by which we overcome our tendency to split ourselves and our world into good and bad, saints and sinners (a tendency that inevitably follows pain and frustration).

Albert Mason, too, comments on the lack of literature on forgive-ness in his field, accordingly expanding his field of vision to include the traumata of the last one hundred years as well as the precepts of the world's great religions. From this wider perspective, Mason develops a comprehensive notion of forgiveness that sees it not only as fundamen-tal to the relationship of the analyst to the patient but also to the rela-tionships we entertain with others and with ourselves. In the end, "re-ality itself needs to be forgiven, because it cannot possibly live up to our delusional expectations." And we, in turn, need to forgive (reality) be-cause without renouncing retribution there cannot be a future without violence. Like the healing of physical wounds, forgiveness is a "vital need" that reverses the processes of dehumanization and exclusion that make atrocities and lesser violence possible in the first place.

Jacques Derrida's short remark on love, excerpted from a series of interviews, highlights the central importance of the question of love to philosophy. First, he insists, love cannot be talked about in general terms; second, he says that love (like philosophy in its original conception and practice) is always already split between a "who" (i.e., a singularity) and a "what" (i.e., the characteristics shared with others), which is where the first betrayal of love may already reside.

It is this latter distinction that also plays a major role in Derrida's reflections on forgiveness. Who can/may ask/grant forgiveness of whom and for what? In outlining the preconditions of a "hyperbolical ethics," that is to say, an ethics beyond a tradition that has (had to) come to an end—namely that of the possibility of the impossible forgiving of the unforgivable—Derrida raises and redirects many of the questions addressed throughout this volume. Centrally, he is concerned with questioning the (im)morality of forgiveness, the fear that forgiving may lead to forgetting, the reciprocity of forgiveness asked for and forgiveness granted, and seeks to find a way to think together forgiveness and reparation, law and punishment. The suspension of lawfulness or reciprocity crucial to the gift is also a question of an abandonment of measure, and Derrida's—and our—question thus becomes whether forgiveness can even be said to be of the order of the human or whether, as Vladimir Jankélévitch, invoked here by Derrida, had provocatively asserted, there are "unexpiable" crimes that cannot be forgiven because they go beyond the human scale, because they are, literally, crimes against humanity (unable to be forgiven by any human or by the sum total of humans, in their very humanity, at their most human).

In their assertion of the centrality of love and forgiveness to philosophy and in particular to the way in which they shed light on the very concept and limits of "the human" as such, Derrida's reflections occupy a central position in this volume. They alert us to the multiple dangers we (necessarily) face when we love and seek love, forgive and seek forgiveness, use their concepts, engage in their practices. Derrida's texts thus offer ways to both summarize and problematize many of the insights presented in the preceding essays, just as they emphasize the kind of dilemmas and aporias explored in further detail by the next essays in the volume.

Sari Nusseibeh addresses a kind of suspension, namely by introducing the extrarational power of love by way of the music of Umm Kulthoum. He goes on to cite recent interventions in the public sphere that see love as an "insuperable" power. Yet if love is so powerful, he asks, then how is it that it seems to be perpetually sidelined, powerless, in public affairs? Juxtaposing the theories of Ibn Khaldoun and Thomas Hobbes, Nusseibeh argues that our contemporary view of the political is predicated on a notion of self-love that is but another word for fear. To follow Ibn Khaldoun instead would be to take the revolutionary step of replacing fear of others with love for others at the very basis of human interaction. Heeding the objection that, in world affairs, peace is mostly negative, the result of fear, Nusseibeh draws on the work of Harry Frankfurt to argue that in fear and self-love either love or the self is lost:

we love what we love with others. And this, despite the fact that much of the same can be said about hate, is, precisely, the extrarational point at which, each time anew, new relationships and thereby—extrapolating beyond the others one knows and loves already—a new politics can be built, step by step.

Hent de Vries, finally, returns to Marion's work on love and revisits some of its central premises, while zooming in on the specific nature of the utterance—here called "passionate"—that names its opening gesture, the speech act "I love you." Recalling that love, in the guise of the erotic reduction, is central to Marion's very notion of philosophy, he both situates the latter's discussion in a wider historical, theological, literary, and visual context and emphasizes a key point argued in "What Love Knows" and implicit throughout the other essays in this volume as well. Love, as Marion conceives of it, is absolutely prior to thought and action and cannot be reduced to any of the categories (whether those regarding "objects" or "beings") that habitually describe our thinking and doing. Far from being self-evident or reminiscent of a long forgotten era, the interventions of the "passionate utterance" of love as well as the "impossible possibility" of forgiveness, along with their multiple, unresolved, and perhaps irresolvable consequences, their irreducible concepts and practices, raise questions and matters of the utmost urgency in the pragmatically defined contexts we necessarily, if always contingently, encounter (as we do things and humans). Their apparent lack of definition and their non-criteriological use are not their perennial weakness, but their paradoxical strength: the sole motor behind their endless passion and uncontrollable force.

The essays collected in this volume invite us to be *alert* to these and other questions and trace out alternative paths for responding to them as much as this is *humanly* possible.

NOTES

1. As an interesting sign of the times, the columnist David Brooks, in a recent contribution to the *New York Times* entitled "Love and Gravity" (November 20, 2014), reviews Christopher Nolan's new "epic movie" *Interstellar*, claiming that it overcomes Hollywood's obsession with romantic love and sex and, instead, explores "the slightly different kinds of love, *from generation to generation, and across time and space.*" Paramount Pictures and Warner Brothers Pictures reprinted the review in a page-wide advertisement for the film (November 28, 2014) under the heading

"Love is the most powerful thing in the universe." One need not, perhaps, commit to the whole concept of "quantum entanglement," inspired by the work of physicist Kip Thorne, nor assume that people in different times and spaces, like distant particles, interact and "react in the same way at the same time to the same things" (as if this is what love does or requires) and yet can appreciate Nolan's quasi-theological, quasi-mystical film, including much that it gestures toward.

2. Hegel's expression *Grau in Grau* can be found in the "Vorrede," the preface, to his *Grundlinien der Philosophie des Rechts*. G. W. F. Hegel, *Elements of the Philosophy of Right*, ed. Alan Wood, trans. H. B. Nisbet (Cambridge: Cambridge University Press, 1991), 23.

3. Jacques Derrida, *Learning to Live Finally: An Interview with Jean Birnbaum*, trans. Pascale-Anne Brault and Michael Naas (Hoboken: Melville House, 2007), 27.

4. The words "The past is not dead. In fact, it's not even past," can be found in William Faulkner's *Requiem for a Nun*. Barack Obama cites and varies them in his speech "A More Perfect Union," held in Philadelphia on March 18, 2008: "As William Faulkner once wrote, 'The past isn't dead and buried. In fact, it isn't even past.'" See also Barack Obama, *Dreams from My Father: A Story of Race and Inheritance* (New York: Three Rivers, 2004), x, where Obama evokes Faulkner in the context of a reference to the events of 9/11 in which "the world [is] fractured": "What I do know is that history returned that day with a vengeance; that, in fact, as Faulkner reminds us, the past is never dead and buried—it isn't even past. This collective history, this past, directly touches my own."

5. Tarek R. Dika, "An Interview with Jean-Luc Marion," in Tarek R. Dika and Chris W. Hackett, eds., *Quiet Powers of the Possible: Interviews in Contemporary French Phenomenology* (New York: Fordham University Press, 2015).

6. Ibid.

7. Adam Weiss quoted in Hadas Gold, "Critics: Huma Abedin Following Hillary Clinton Plan," *Politico*, July 24, 2013, http://www.politico.com/story/2013/07/anthony-weiner-huma-abedin-clinton-94708.html (last accessed, July 27, 2013).

8. https://www.youtube.com/watch?v=4esCcxxQe7s (last accessed March 29, 2014).

9. There are the (in retrospect strangely ominous) opening lines of an Israeli song he doesn't remember or no longer quite "gets":

DAD: "Do you remember what we used to sing on our way to Uncle Aaron?
"I have a song that upsets people . . . "
And you used to answer . . . ?
MOM: "I have an Uncle who fixes people"
SON: "I have an Uncle who fixes people" (*repeated five times*).

10. See http://www.gamesforchange.org and http://sites.fhi.duke.edu/greaterthangames/ (last accessed March 28, 2014).

11. On psychoanalysis, see Jean-Luc Marion, *La rigueur des choses: Entretiens avec Dan Arbib* (Paris: Flammarion, 2012), 254–58.

ORANGE ALERT

Haleh Liza Gafori

We're on orange alert again I hear
as we cross the East River
and the winter sun beams its blinding white light
across the jagged surface of the water.
Orange alert?
So am I to be on the lookout now
for a suitcase that ticks, for a turbaned man,
a veiled woman, a shoulder belt of rockets?
Shall I suspect all Mohammeds today?
Or shall I envision my escape through the office hall, the bathroom
    window,
through the shaken streets as ash rains down
and my morning coffee gets cold?

I am so tired of terror!

Orange alert, really?
How about a russet alert?
A coral alert, a sienna alert,
a burnt ochre, vermilion alert,
a salmon, pumpkin, persimmon alert,

a rust carrot apricot alert, a saffron alert!

Give me a saffron alert!

Take me to the rugged mountains of Iran and let's get down on our
    knees and pluck the saffron threads from purple crocuses that
    paint a belt out to the blue sea!

Let's stand over a burlap sack stuffed with it and inhale its aroma of
    honey, hay, and steel

Saffron alert!

Give me one glimpse of the powdery grains the color of flames,

of my great grandmother's mortar and pestle they stained a luminous
    yellow,

of Cleopatra's tinted bathwater,

or the saffron robes of Buddhist monks meditating as the first sliver of
    sun appears on the horizon

Saffron, the color of illumination!

Give me a saffron alert!

Or give me an orange alert, but make it a citrus alert!

Naval, Valencia, Satsuma, Blood—

glowing spheres of trapped sunlight I hold in my palm,

their yielding skin and the fragrant spray of summer wakes me
    through the winter.

Desert lime, clementines, tangerine, citron,

tangelo, pomelo, bergamot, mandarin—

the juice is dripping down my fingers!

This is a citrus alert!

And if tomorrow is a red alert,

then make it a ruby alert, a pomegranate alert, a full-bodied Bordeaux
    alert, a blood alert!

Our blood, this magical medium pumping through us,

brimming with iron atoms that were once inside the core stars—

iron atoms that were once shooting across the cosmos, now inside our
    blood, delivering oxygen to our muscles, minds, and hearts even
    while we're sleeping!

Alert me to the magic of our blood!

This is a red alert!

But red alert is maximum terror alert they say again and again
So what am I to do now?
Shall I avoid all close quarters, elevators, buses, and subways?
Shall I walk over two bridges to get to work?
Or shall I stay at home, lock the door, sit on the sofa and consider the
    tears of a child six thousand miles away, just orphaned
Streaks of red dripping down an Afghani man's arm,
Streaks of red dripping down an American soldier's arm,
Children sleepwalking in bodies rigid with trauma
This is a red alert!
For who experiencing such agony wouldn't consider revenge?

Red alert, orange alert, human alert
Under that veil, a woman
Under that turban, that cap, that beard
Under that skin the color of pyramids, the color of sand dunes, the
    color of lions is a soul
And under that ink-blue business suit walking up the bone-white
    stairs of the Capitol is a soul
And under that U.S. army camouflage the color of my skin is a soul!

Alert me, alert us to this possibility
as we cross the sacred, wretched, swirling river

2

WHAT LOVE KNOWS

Jean-Luc Marion

I HAVE BEEN ASKED to say some few words about the concept of love and how it can lead to a concept of forgiveness. I shall try to do that by addressing the following points:

- love and the question of space
- love and the question of time
- love and the question of self and
- the question of reciprocity,

in order to then make some final points about forgiveness.

I

I think the great obstacle to any approach to the question of love lies in the common assumption that we understand very well what it means to love and to be loved. We assume this because we rely on the modern understanding of love, which is the experience of love as a passion. From the point of view of the history of Western philosophy, from the point of view of human subjectivity from, let's say, Descartes to the twentieth century, we love the way we suffer from a disease. The literary presentation of love was exactly that of a disease. When you read Proust or

Stendhal, among the French authors, for example, you see that to be in a situation of loving means that free will is suspended, that you go through the stages of "I love you" and a crisis, which lead you to a conclusion that—whether positive or negative, that makes no real difference—was not decided by you. The idea is that love is an excruciating joy or an exciting pain, but it is not, in any case, decided by us—like a disease. This idea prevents us from understanding that love is a question of knowledge. The situation of love means that by loving we shall understand things around us in a different way and understand new information or understand new connections in this information than we would do otherwise. Love is not a passion; it is a point of view.

I think that there is a kind of erotic reduction. Reduction, in phenomenology, is the operation by which you put into brackets some assumption usually made about the state of the world around us and focus on what is really given. Let's say we think of the noise made by the water in a fountain. In the natural attitude, from the point of view of classical empiricism, when asked, what do you hear, they would say, I hear sound of a certain frequency, on a certain place on the decibel scale, etc. In fact, that is not true, that is an abstraction. What we hear is a fountain. In most cases, what we perceive is not a sound; it is the thing itself. When we are in the street, we do not perceive sounds, we not only perceive the sound of this or that machine, but we hear a car, say, and can even identify a particular model of car. So we very often have to make a reduction to really understand what is experienced. And that is also the case when we are in love, when we are talking about the erotic phenomenon. It is another way of experiencing the world. Let's take three dimensions of the erotic reduction.

II

The first is about the experience of space. In the natural life, which is both a metaphysical situation and a scientific situation, we perceive space starting from a zero point. The point zero, the center, is the place where the observer is, where I am. Objective knowledge consists in always understanding how far away the event is from the center of the observer, who I am. And if I am not in fact the observer, I can imagine myself to be in the observer's central position. So I am always in the observer's zero point, I am always *here*, and everything else is always *there*, including the other. The other is being described precisely as being away from me. While I can perfectly well imagine that we exchange positions, I will in that case again be at the center, even if that center is somewhere else.

In the erotic reduction, however, I discover that wherever I may go I shall never again be the center. The center of any experience is the beloved. The beloved being is the one from whom I am away. I feel myself to be away from the center. In other words, the only question is, where is the center? The center is not where I am; it is where he or she stands whom I would like to get to first when I arrive somewhere. The center is *never* again me, myself. And this is a very troubling experience because it is the experience of being out of the center for the first time; what I really am is no longer with me. I am reunited with myself only when I am in the same place as another. That other being, according to a paradox of St. Augustine's, is more intimately myself than I am myself. If I want to be with me, I have to be somewhere else than the place where I am. I have to be where he or she is. And so I am away from myself.

III

We have the same experience of reduction in the case of time.

In ordinary time, in the time of everyday life, we have a very paradoxical but common experience of time: time is past, present, and future. Future and present time expand indefinitely, with this one reservation that things do not really exist when they are in the past or the future, things really only exist when they stay in the present. Unfortunately, the present itself does not last for very long; strictly speaking it does not last at all. The present remains present only for an instant, i.e., for a nothing. This is the paradox. Anything only exists when it remains in the present, but the present does not remain. I am the only one who is always present to himself. In ordinary life, when I think something, it is in the present, and things have to go through this moment for them to be. I can decide what is happening right now, what is present and what exactly I am experiencing at this time.

In the erotic situation, in turn, my experience of time is completely modified because I can stay here in the present and just say, nothing is happening. Nothing is happening. What do I mean? Of course, things *do* happen. I am doing things, you are doing things, so things are happening. Nevertheless, I say, nothing has happened yet. Why? Because for me, now, what presence means is the last manifestation of the attention paid to me by him or her, by the significant other. Thus nothing is happening; the last time something happened, the last time something was present was the last time she or he called, and the next moment, the next time that will be present will be the next time that she or he calls or comes. That is what is present, although it may be past or to come. If I stick to what is happening right now from my point of view, nothing is happening, if it is not happening from the other, as it were. So the past and the future now can be the place of the real present, and the present the place where nothing happens. So we have an irregular time, that is, an irregular succession of events, which keep to themselves although they are yet to happen in the future or have already happened in the past, which are the real owners, so to speak, of the present.

IV

This is an essential decentering of articulation, that is to say: the self cannot establish itself. The *ego cogito*, the *I think therefore I am*, cannot be performed anymore. This is a very special situation because we are not all spontaneously followers of Descartes, but we do what Descartes said: we are what we think, we *are* insofar as and each time we think . . . what? Our self. Even if this perception remains empty, it is the essential act of experiencing my existence through the easiest act to perform, which is the act of thinking. In the erotic reduction, the fact of obtaining certitude about my existence through the performance of thinking stops being obvious enough to give me the absolute certainty that I am. I need much more to have the assurance, so to speak, the security that I really am. I need not to think myself or to reach my existence through the act of thinking (whatever I may think). What I need is to be thought by someone else. It's only when I'm thought, when I'm the focus of the attention of one special other, that I am. Von Baader used to say that instead of *ego cogito ergo sum*, one should say *ego cogitor ergo sum, I am insofar as I am thought*, and not *insofar as I think*.[1]

To be is to be identified, acknowledged by an ego that is another ego than mine. I am not thought by myself, I am thought by someone else, so therefore I am: that is the erotic situation. Which is very strange.

Because, in the erotic situation, you can, for instance, find yourself at a party where the room is crowded with people and you can still very well say, *I am alone, there is no one.* Because there is only one who is entitled to make you alive, to identify you, and if that other does not show up, you are alone. This does not make sense, because socially you are connected. But you *are* not if you are not seen or thought by *that* one. There is thus a crisis of the ego, of the ego in the most traditional phenomenological understanding, at stake in the erotic situation. And I suggest that the experience of being in love is not a subjective, psychological experience, that it is a global modification in the perception of the whole world, which includes reversing the situation of the ego. There is still a first principle, the ego, but it is not a self-sustaining first principle. And there is an original heteronomy of the self over against the original autonomy of the ego in Descartes and in all modern philosophy. The global modification of the world in this situation is that in the erotic reduction the ego is never [mine]. I am exempt from the situation of autonomy. And this may be intricately linked to the experience of inequality, to the crisis of reciprocity.

V

In many discussions of love and in all philanthropic behavior, so to speak (humanitarian policy, the gift, etc.), there is a deep misunderstanding. We imagine that we are still in the situation of love. But love is not an expansion of reciprocity, exchange, economy, justice, and so on. Love, to some extent, implies the suspension of any form of equality. Many of the difficulties in the classical discussions of the gift stem from the fact that we always imagine that the gift succeeds when it can be reciprocated. A gift should be followed by a gift back in order for us to be in a situation of love, fraternity etc. That is the classical conception of the gift (Marcel Mauss's conception, criticized by Derrida): the gift is about the countergift. What is peace? It is a countergift to a first gift. Reciprocity is very often seen as a sign of a settled situation, reestablishing some kind of unity, which in turn gives rise to a form of peace.

But in love we are in a completely different situation. In love we experience a radical inequality that will never be balanced out, erased, or deestablished. There is always an anteriority, and that anteriority will last. This is the experience of the fact that love begins (if you take the simplest situation of two partners) when one partner begins to love the other even if the other will not return that love, even if the other is not aware of being loved, even if the other does not want to be loved, even if the other does not exist yet.

This is characteristic of the lover. Don Giovanni, and we have no reason to distrust him at that moment, starts to love any woman earlier than this woman is aware that she could be loved. By his decision to act as if he were in love, he creates not only his own love but her love. In the Jewish-Christian view of the relationship between God and humankind, you have the same thing. God and Don Giovanni decided to love without reason and being the first. The point, this anteriority, is made very clear by the fact that what God loves does not yet exist. It exists as a consequence.

We begin to love in a complete disequilibrium. And the reason for that is that there will never be any average agreement after that. That is, if I decide to love first and find myself loved as well, this does not mean that we establish a fair exchange. It means that the other establishes, of his own initiative and from his own point of view, the same uneven relationship that I started first. The inequality is repeated in different ways, but it is not suppressed. Love remains completely free because you have no claim to a priori conditions, there is no claim to reciprocity as a precondition for beginning to love. The infinite power of love is based on the principle that there is no prerequisite to love. To love, there is no need to be loved. You can love someone who does not love you, does not know you, someone who to some extent does not exist yet or does not exist anymore or simply does not exist. What distinguishes, to use a different terminology, the erotic reduction from any other attitude is that there are no conditions of possibility attached to it.

VI

This explains why, and this will be my last point, forgiveness, like the erotic reduction, can be seen as an action and as a very powerful action indeed. What is forgiveness? There are, I think, a number of common misunderstandings about forgiveness. You might imagine that to forgive is to forget. But we know that it is perhaps impossible to forget. And it would be unfair. So, how far forgiveness has something to do with justice, that is, under what conditions it is possible for the victim to forgive, to what extent it is possible for others to accept forgiveness from the victim and thus to free the perpetrator, is by no means a settled question. The common understanding of forgiveness is so imprecise that you can use it—in the name of justice and with good reason—against forgiveness.

So let's try to come to a different understanding of forgiveness. I would like to suggest that to understand forgiveness we have to understand the gift. To forgive is a variation of the gift, which is the erotic reduction. And what is specific to the gift is that when the giver gives something to the givee, the movement of giving, already achieved, will concentrate only on the side of the givee, on the thing given, on the result of the giving, and the movement of the gift and the giver will to some extent fade away and be blurred by the obvious presence of what is given. When you give something to someone and that someone really needs what you give, thus, if you are right to give at that moment and if you do the right thing, the more you do the right thing and the more the givee is needy, the less time he will waste in thanking you, the giver. He will just look at the thing given, and he is right. Even if he refrains from consuming the gift too quickly and pays attention to the giver, everyone will in fact focus on the thing given, which, so to speak, becomes the star of the show, and the giver will in every case fade out. The fate of the gift is that the gift gives away the giver. And you cannot escape it—it is the experience of paternity, for example.

The giver has to disappear. This is not due to ingratitude on the part of the givee. If the giver didn't disappear, remaining present, supervising everything, it would create a situation of confusion, power struggles, incest. The giver has to disappear. The result is that the giver and the process of giving itself can be completely overlooked. We may have the impression that it was part of the economy, a fair exchange—or an unfair exchange—but not a gift. And we could even say that a large part of what we call the global economy, the net of exchange and reciprocity, is an illusion because everything begins with the gift and ends up in the economy of the ideal exchange.

The economy of exchange appears in the exact measure in which the gift, the process of the gift, disappears. And there is a process tied to the extension of the economy, of going from the gift to something initially foreign to it, to an economy of production and exchange. Large parts of the private sphere have become public through its economization, and the gift has disappeared for the sake of what is economic. You'll find, for example, an increasing number of television ads for specialized seniors' housing, i.e., for helping the elderly shift from the situation of the gift in the family to the economy of hospitalization. Or think of the generalization of the new insurance system, which is to some extent a substitution of personal care with an economic interpretation of how you should treat people.

So how can we keep the gift alive? That is, what is forgiveness? To forgive is not to erase the fact that, willingly or not, the giver was not seen, was forgotten, that the givee, willingly or not, could not avoid being and remaining ungrateful toward the giver. To forgive is not to forget that. It is for the giver to give again what he gave the first time, what was neglected, became invisible, was not accepted, was not celebrated as such, was not recognized. The giver can do two things: either say, *Well, my gift was not well received, I was not praised, I was not seen as the giver, so I decide that I shall never do that again and, if possible, I shall take back my gift or, in any case, nullify my gift by destroying it or asking for payback.* This, I think, is the usual and, I would say, the fair way to react. And there is the other way, which is to say: *OK, my gift was not received as such, and, in fact, it should not, it could not be received as such. But I keep my gift as it was given and, to make this clear, I give it again.* So regiving the gift is, in fact, to give it forever for the first time.[2]

What we have here is a logic in which reciprocity is never restored, and this inequality is forever a consequence of the uncompromised heteronomy of the erotic reduction. Love and forgiveness are not an economic exchange, but a way of opening up a completely different world.

NOTES

This chapter transcribes a lecture given at the Fetzer Humanities Symposium on June 4, 2012.

1. Franz von Baader, *Vorlesungen über speculative Dogmatik*, in *Sämtliche Werke*, ed. Franz von Hoffmann et al. (Aalen: Scientia, 1963), 8:339.
2. The best example is Abraham's nonsacrifice, because Isaac was a gift. Abraham and Sarah had been unable to have children anymore. It is unfair on the part of Abraham and Sarah to celebrate the birth of Isaac as *their* child. In making Isaac their own son, they do not regard him as a gift. So when God claims the life of the son, he is after all just claiming his property, since he has the right to any firstborn of Israel (in this case, literally). And Abraham got the point. At the moment

of the gift being reopened and seen again by Abraham, what is this "again"? It is not the death of Isaac—God says, *I've seen that you obey God*, but Abraham has done nothing, he has not sacrificed his son. What has he done? The answer, clearly, is that he has seen the giver again, which is what was claimed, what was asked for. To forgive is to give back and is to see, forever, the giver.

3

UNPOWER

An Interview with Hugues Choplin

Jean-Luc Marion

HUGUES CHOPLIN: I would like to submit to you a hypothesis and a question. The hypothesis may be put as follows: contemporary French philosophy is defined by its inventiveness when it comes to power [*pouvoir*], more precisely, to *authority* and *force* [*puissance*]. The guiding question for this conversation would then be: in what sense can your research lead beyond this contemporary regime of power, either in the form of authority or of force?

JEAN-LUC MARION: The first thing to say is that all the terms of your question—power, authority, force—belong directly to the vocabulary of metaphysics. In the same way, the question you raised earlier [about measuring the call against power in terms of weakness and strength] presupposes, in the very way the question is put, that it has to be possible for the call to be qualified, be it as strong, be it as weak. The question that asks only if the call reverses just the "force of subjectivity" is a question that turns back on itself. It presupposes not only that the relationship that plays itself out between the call and the one who hears the call is a relationship of an object to a subject. It also presupposes (and, incidentally, with perfect coherence) that this relationship can and must express itself in terms of power, as a relation of strength or of forces. Yet we can show that the relationship (if it is a relationship in the sense of the category of relation) of the givee to the call does not replicate the relationship between subject and object because here the categories of power and effective power are in fact inoperative.

Let me note, first, that we cannot assume that the call acts on the givee by virtue of a superior effective power and force, which has the givee receive the call in a situation of passivity and powerlessness. I'm well aware that the call is often described this way. But such a description is not appropriate to the phenomenon of the call such as it is really taking place. For what we see there instead is a weakness of the call in the face of the strength of the givee: the call in fact depends on the one who hears or, more precisely, on the one who takes it on himself and for himself by consenting to hear it and respond to it (and thus also by being able sovereignly to refuse it). For, by itself, the call most of the time only manages to be denied a hearing, to be stifled in indifference, or to be shattered in hostility. In fact, the call not only becomes effective in but only becomes audible to the one who is well disposed to hearing it. It thus depends on the strength and power of the response to which it finds itself to be essentially relative, if not alienated.

At least two decisions testify to this power to respond or, rather and primarily, to listen. First, it depends on the one who can respond to decide whether or not there is a call (and not, instead, a pure silence, an indefinite brouhaha, an insignificant shout, or an invocation to someone other than myself) such that, even if I'm wrong in one way or another, it is always up to me to decide how effective (if at all) the call is. Second, it is also up to me, if I respond to the call, to name—in my response and in my behavior—the content, the implications, even the consequences of the call. If the call sheds its anonymity and finally seeks to mean something, I alone can name it explicitly and effectively. The call speaks and is named according to what my response gives to understand.

In consequence, the call can be described as powerlessness itself, exposed to the arbitrariness of the power of the respondent, just as well as, perhaps even better than, it can be described as overpowering power. If, therefore, the opposition between the force of the call and the weakness of the response can so easily turn into the inverse dependence of the call on the strength of the respondent, how can we not conclude that the oppositions between force and weakness, potentiality and actuality, power and submission, etc. (which all derive from Aristotelian, i.e., metaphysical categories) become indifferent or, rather, inoperable and nonpertinent in this context? This, incidentally, is the conclusion you yourself reach when you suggest that "the call would be . . . all the stronger for its anonymity," which is to say that, although it is anonymous (in fact, *because* it remains so), the call would be valid—the term *strong* is inappropriate. This is the contrary of how one would put it in a metaphysical vocabulary where, precisely for there to be a power and for it to be exercised, the call is above all required to leave its anonymity behind. The call, however, is precisely characterized by *not* saying "I," but instead by letting the *you* take the risk of saying—*is this for me?*

And you go on, rightly, to ask: "Does the love it calls for not rather lead us to disqualify the pertinence of the couple force—weakness? Does not the call as such, in this sense, mark a certain indifference toward power stakes?" Quite obviously so. When the lover resolves as such to love first without the least certainty that he is the first, when he says, "here I am," is this decision to be seen as a strength or as a weakness? One could say either. Here the greatest power—since it will be up to him to decide to get the love plot going, to, in a way, constitute an other as an other who is desired—coincides with the greatest weakness. The decision is nothing less than the decision whether to suspend reciprocity, that is, in fact, to suspend the principle of identity and even to act without sufficient reason, in short: whether to dispense with nothing less than the two principles of metaphysics. What more perfect situation of unpower could one imagine? Maintaining or reintroducing the problem of power (and of powerlessness)—to my mind, essentially a metaphysical problem—in a mediation on the call becomes absolutely untenable.

My question with regard to your question thus becomes: when we speak of politics, power, strength, powerlessness, are we not necessarily caught up in the political dimension of philosophy and thus in the divisions of metaphysics? It would be astonishing if, among all the branches of metaphysics (ontology, logic, rational theology, psychology, cosmology), which, in a certain sense, are all subjected to the end of metaphysics, which have all been—and still are—subjected to a radical destruction, it should be political philosophy that alone remains as it was, unchangeable and unquestioned. That would mean that the concepts of political philosophy, power, for example, would still invariably be applicable. To be frank, I sometimes wonder by what right I am asked, time and again, the question of power. Would this question be the one exception to the deconstruction of the discourse of metaphysics (which, by the way, it has so powerfully claimed in its entirety as its heritage)? If everyone thinks they can and must, in all domains, deconstruct and overcome metaphysics (as if there were nothing easier and more pleasurable), why is there such an effort not only to exempt the vocabulary of political philosophy but even, on the part of some, an effort to operate this so-called overcoming according to the very terms of political philosophy? Shouldn't we admit what is obvious, namely that the project of theorizing the organization, distribution, and equilibrium (as democratic as you would like it to be) of *powers* manifests the last incarnation of metaphysics, thus of *nihilism*? Shouldn't we, at least, suspect that the primacy of politics ("Politics first!" was, after all, Maurras's rallying cry,[1] but it was shared by all revolutionary doctrines of the last century) derives from the authority of metaphysics, which has not been questioned in this domain? If one pretends that political philosophy is exempt from the demise of metaphysics, one should seek to liberate political philosophy from the metaphysical principles that govern it—the principle of identity and the principle of sufficient reason. I sometimes think that no liberalism, no republicanism, and no communitarianism has so much as suspected that one must and one can ask that question—and that, therefore, the blindest of metaphysical conservatisms controls their alleged innovations.

H. C.: Your research thus indicates an indifference to the question of power. What importance do you ascribe to that indifference?

J.-L. M.: At the very least, it is, if I may say so, an active indifference, since admitting the unquestioned primacy of the question of power seems to me, when it comes to philosophy, a failure of deconstruction and, when it comes to theology, a perseverance of idolatry. Questioning this primacy instead of adapting (and thus admitting) it, not immediately disputing the organization of power (which comes and goes, constantly watching out for itself) but conceiving of being suspicious toward it: that remains a different path for thought, a parallel, tradition of radical protest. At the very moment that politics establishes itself as a branch of metaphysics, at the two turns of the seventeenth century (the crucial century of modernity), in Hobbes, Spinoza, Rousseau, there are also thinkers who disqualify the primacy of power in politics and even of politics in metaphysics: Montaigne, for example, Pascal, obviously, Descartes above all, even Locke in his involuntarily paradoxical way. And if one had to place Nietzsche in a tradition, it would be this one. Or Chateaubriand, a man of the Ancien Régime, an aristocrat, a staunch Catholic, who rejects the Terror because he is the first to understand it and who *therefore* also rejects Bonaparte's rational dictatorship just as much as he rejects the irrational Restoration of the Bourbon monarchy. Their standpoint never depended on a political decision, and this eventually allows them to make extraordinary political judgments.

Take de Gaulle, for example: his position as a real political giant is due to his *not* being interested in the question of power, in its theory, in preserving it at all costs. He exercised power in a way few have managed to do precisely because he went against the order of power. He owed his almost miraculous, his, as it were, somnambulant resistance to all ideology, including and above all the ideology of the social class he came from, and his ability to embody an absolute opposition to Pétain's (as well as to Lenin's) ideology, to his original stepping out of the primacy of the political.

Ideology, which is but the precise name of the metaphysical primacy of politics when it accomplishes the metaphysical project, does not constitute a true foundation. A true foundation certainly does not consist of a slab of concrete placed on the ground, which appears to be very solid, but can, ultimately must, crumble under its own weight at the very moment those in the know, the experts, the theoreticians expect it the least. Thus the Berlin Wall yielded to the pressure of people who did not engage in politics (thinkers, writers, workers, believers, people who didn't organize, in short: reality).

H. C.: This kind of "pressure," in your view, is neither a resistance nor a nonviolence, which remains captive to the regime of power. How, then, would you characterize it?

J.-L. M.: We do indeed have to be careful when it comes to certain modes of political attitude or political action that only appear to exempt themselves from the exercise of power. The exercise of nonviolence, for example, remains inscribed in face-to-face confrontation, that is, in a dialectic of recognition. That one of the parties renounces violence or armed force only means that this disarmament itself retains enough strength for the armed gaze to yield to the unarmed gaze—which has happened throughout history, including in modern history. Admirable as this attitude may at times appear, it remains a struggle for recognition, a confrontation of the weak and the strong in which the weak, too, deploy a force that inscribes itself in the balance of power, among other (military, economic, etc.) forces. In this sense and not at all paradoxically, nonviolence, no more than terrorism, is not an exception from the logic of power. Besides, experience even shows that individuals may transition imperceptibly from one to the other (and back). In the same way, a solemn relinquishing of power, too, can turn out to be a subtle and highly efficient form of exercising power: think of calling for referenda or of manipulations from behind the scenes of visible power—there's no dearth of examples. Nonpower belongs essentially to the logic of power and often to the very exercise of power.

What possibilities, then, remain thinkable? If we admit that the question of power (of strength, of efficiency, and of production) is a question of causality, we admit that it belongs to metaphysics and thus to the principle of sufficient reason. It would therefore make no sense to question the primacy of this question unless we try (at least try) to question the metaphysical horizon of the principle of reason. Any attempt that aims for less will only lead, at best, to adaptation and, more often, to more or less voluntary illusions. But what does it mean to question the question of the principle of reason? Here, it seems to me, we may risk introducing the concept (but is it a concept?) of unpower.

Unpower is neither a counterpower nor even an absence of power; it is that which intervenes when the description of a phenomenon can or even must dispense with the concept of power because this concept turns out to be inoperable in practice. I've outlined the example of the relationship between call and response where, if we absolutely must employ the concept of power, power can be attributed alternatively to one or the other precisely because it is appropriate to neither of them. But contemporary philosophy doesn't suffer from a shortage of remarkable examples of such an inapplicability of the concept of power. These examples—nonetheless and par excellence—are of phenomena that belong to the sphere of exchanges between egos, be it an exchange between two or between more than two parties: the face, substitution, responsibility, the gift (abandon, forgiveness), hospitality, the promise (and other pragmatic uses of speech), and, of course, all facets of the erotic phenomenon.

In these and many other cases, the question is not one of renouncing or justifying power but simply one of admitting that we no longer have any use for it. If by chance one set out to reintroduce it, for example in the interest of not being fooled, of reestablishing a rigorous (sufficient) reason, of objectifying and guaranteeing, etc., one would in fact suppress the phenomena at issue and, at best, replace them with other phenomena under the same names—names that are thus rendered equivocal. Unpower does not begin where one opposes power but where the rational pertinence of the concept of power comes to an end, namely in the description of phenomena that stage egos.

I'm well aware that these indications remain very programmatic and rather taunting—like the question of the end of metaphysics, which is constantly sketched (and constantly comes back). Yet that it is difficult and that it is a program is not enough to disqualify it—quite the contrary.

NOTES

This is our translation of a text first published as Jean-Luc Marion, "L'impouvoir," *Revue de métaphysique et de morale* 4, no. 60 (2008): 439–45, copyright © 2008 PUF.

1. Charles Maurras (1868–1952), reactionary author and politician, leader of the Action Française, and theoretician of a "complete nationalism."

4

REVENGE, FORGIVENESS, AND LOVE

Regina M. Schwartz

He who fights with monsters should look to it that he himself does not become a monster.

—Nietzsche, *Beyond Good and Evil*

Love talks with better knowledge, and knowledge with dearer love.

—Shakespeare, *Measure for Measure*

SOMETIMES, JUSTICE IS AN IDEA that people use to hurt other people. They inflict harm to "satisfy" justice, an odd metaphor suggesting that justice may be hungry and need to be fed some juicy morsels, "satisfied." Nietzsche wrote that high-sounding talk about justice may be only a cover for vindictiveness.

> These cellar rodents full of vengefulness and hatred—what have they made of revenge and hatred? Have you heard these words uttered? If you trusted simply to their words, would you suspect you were among men of ressentiment? . . . [his interlocutor responds] I understand; I'll open my ears again (oh! Oh! Oh! And close my nose). Now I can really hear what they have been saying all along: "We good men—we are the just—what they desire they call, not retaliation, but 'the triumph of justice'; what they hate is not their enemy, no! they hate 'injustice' . . ."[1]

Even Kant says, "We like to flatter ourselves with the false claim to a more noble motive, but in fact we can never, even by the strictest examination, completely plumb the depths of the secret incentives of our actions."[2] The kind of justice that would be satisfied by harming another is justice as retribution, and the satisfaction of such justice is achieved by punishment.

What are the chief arguments for retribution? One of the most persistent is that, if someone injures another, the injurer deserves to be punished. There seems to be a widespread intuition that just as those who do good should be rewarded, so those who do harm should be punished. But why? On what grounds? It turns out that such intuitions rest on surprisingly little grounding. Those who support the idea that we should punish wrongdoers, hurt the hurters, often argue that this desire for retribution is foundational; that is, it needs no further explanation. They describe it as "natural." But without a plausible reason for hurting the injurer, it is not possible to justify.

Just as high-sounding talk of justice may only mask revenge, so high-sounding talk of just punishment often masks responses in excess of the crime. Why do we punish so hard and so much? Rage is partly responsible, as well as the culture's ready confusion between wrongful acts and the wrongdoers, which stems from our understanding of the human person. Our criminal justice system is built on the anthropology that humans are freely choosing moral agents. Understanding criminality as taking place in a realm of freedom is part of the liberal fiction. Its forbear is Kant, who believes the moral law must be followed independent of social context or inclination, that infractions of it must be punished according to the iniquity. His fury is directed not against the wrongdoer so much as against the injury to the moral order itself. Hence, for the sake of justice, he endorses merciless retribution. Kant's bloodthirsty passages on retribution are in his *Metaphysical Elements of Justice*: "Judicial punishment can never be used merely as a means to promote some other good for the criminal himself or for civil society, but instead it must in all cases be imposed on him only on the ground that he has committed a crime." After all, criminals freely choose to do wrong.

But to what extent is this freedom of choice a fiction? As a noted legal scholar writes, "It is no secret that certain social conditions are 'crimogenic'—that those born to poverty and discrimination are far more likely to offend than those who are raised in or achieve high economic or social status."[3] Nonetheless, "the criminal law system does little to discern how social disadvantage may constrain choice or to think about moral desert in light of social disadvantage."[4] Under the regime of justice that claims to adjudicate right and wrong, some behaviors—regardless of social disadvantages—are considered just wrong.

Bad behavior, bad person. There is rampant confusion of the wrong deed with the wrongdoer.

Many theories of retribution rely not only on the intuition that an injurer deserves punishment but also that moral life is measurable; therefore each injury has a measurable compensation. Theories of retribution often assert that while punishment is deserved, it must be in proportion to the wrong. This is supposed to correct the excesses wrought by rage. Proportionality can either be in kind (literally, an eye for an eye) or it can be symbolic, usually monetary. (The rabbis concluded that *lex talionis* had to be a metaphor, that the intention was surely to pay back in proportion to the injury.) In addition to the language of desert, then, retribution theories are chock-full of the language of proportionality. Kant said that punishment should be proportional to the moral iniquity, the act and the motive, the "inner viciousness." In such thinking punishment becomes even a principle of fairness.[5] Hegel said that criminals have a "right" to punishment, that it demonstrates that we respect them as responsible beings. Again, that respect is grounded on their ostensible freedom of will.

Proportional thinking about punishment is coupled with an emphasis on distribution. In Aristotle's theory of retribution, the judge is the equalizer who takes something away from the injurer and gives it to the injured to equalize. But injury is not a "good" to be distributed or measured out in fair quantity. Incredibly enough, Aristotle—the master of categorization—seems to have made an enormous category mistake. For him, the distribution of harm works the same way as the distribution of goods. That is, he applied distributive justice to wrongs. Aristotle's hope, like Kant's, was that by spreading the injury around—making the victim into a victimizer and returning harm with harm—he could set the moral order aright. But punishment, which often is justified as correcting an imbalance, does not in fact correct harm. It only adds more harm. As Plato's Socrates forcefully maintained, injuries are harms to be avoided. Hence, any addition to injury results only in further harm, not in the restoration of any order.

If the theory of retribution is based on the inchoate idea that one should be punished because it is "deserved," this is easily countered by the conviction that no one "deserves" to have harm done to him. It is a bizarre idea of wrongdoing that imagines "balancing" harm in any way to correct injury instead of doubling injuries. As Martin Luther King

Jr. repeatedly cautioned, "An evil deed is not redeemed by an evil deed." For him, violence is immoral because it thrives on hatred rather than love. He added "Violence is impractical because it is a descending spiral ending in destruction for all. It is immoral because it seeks to humiliate the opponent rather than win his understanding. It seeks to annihilate rather than convert. Violence ends up defeating itself. It creates bitterness in the survivors and brutality in the destroyers." The consequences of retribution seem to argue against it more powerfully than for it. John Milton writes that "revenge, at first though sweet, bitter ere long back on itself recoils,"[6] expressing the observation that the punisher ultimately punishes himself. Again, this is brilliantly anticipated by Plato. If commonplace ancient ideas about justice were preoccupied with retribution, Plato turned this on its head: "It is never just to harm anyone," for our goal is to cultivate virtue, and men "become worse in human virtue when they are harmed."[7] They become even worse when they do harm.

How can Plato's insight differ so markedly from the intuitions of those who uphold retribution? His notion of justice does not imagine paying back either goods or harms, protecting contracts and transactions. Instead, for him, the purpose of justice is to order the soul and the city to achieve their highest aims. His goal is understood as seeking a just order, and so his central metaphor for improving the character of persons is improving their health. No physician would treat an injury with another injury. Plato, unlike so many others in his day—and ours—does not buy into the idea that justice requires a concept of reciprocity.

But Aristotle gained far more influence: ever since Aristotle, most theories of retribution think of harm distributively, imagining harm as measurable, and endorsing the concept that payment should be in proportion to the crime. They also describe this distribution of harm as a principle of fairness. This has led to such remarkable theories as Richard Posner's *Economics of Justice*,[8] which even assigns an economic value to rape. But as the bizarre idea of paying for rape so forcefully demonstrates, injury is not a good to be distributed, it is not a good to be measured in fair quantities and made equitable for the moral order to be restored. Rather, injuring someone, inflicting harm on another, is a violation of the moral order; hence duplicating it only makes it doubly violated. Imagine raping the rapist.

Other arguments, more attentive to the consequences than the motives of retribution, focus on deterrence. Punishment—rather, fear of punishment—is supposed to be an important motivation for doing the right thing. The assumption is behavioral, that we can offer rewards and punishments, goads and checks, to regulate behavior. Hardly anyone accepts that this is effective, however, as the statistics seem to concur that even the worst punishment, capital punishment, does not act as a deterrent. Furthermore, such a manipulative version of human nature does not embrace human dignity as its chief virtue. Even the most committed behaviorists have found that people respond better to encouragement than to punishment, so that children are now to be raised with affirmations, and withholding them is powerful enough to serve as a disciplining warning.

Efforts have been made to distinguish retribution from revenge. According to Robert Nozick, retribution is done for a wrong, not an injury. Retribution sets a limit to punishment, whereas revenge is endless. Retribution involves satisfaction for justice being done, whereas the satisfaction of revenge comes from hurting another, and retribution is governed by general standards while revenge is governed by private ones. Retribution is impersonal, with the agent having no personal tie to the injurer, whereas revenge is deeply personal.

Intentionality plays a key role in his understanding of retribution: Nozick describes the "complicated structure" of retribution, "wherein something intentionally is produced in another with the intention that he realize why it was produced and that he realize he was intended to realize all this."[9] But if the intention is for an intention to be understood as such, what retribution is doing, above all, is *communicating*—sending a message that is vital to be received. With punishment, this communication is done in an "unwelcome way." Here is the first glitch in his theory: if the goal of communication is to be understood, this "unwelcome way" is likely to defeat the success of the communication. Messages that are delivered with doing harm are very likely to be resisted.

Nozick argues that, by retribution, "someone is shown something by being presented it directly. If an act is wrong because of what it does to someone else, the most powerful way to show him what it does is to do the same to him." Here a second problem with his thinking emerges, for such logic would play out in a way that is patently absurd: if one is maimed for life by a gunshot wound, the offender would also need to be maimed for life. If someone is robbed, the offender needs to be robbed. Surely, doubling an offense in order to "directly" communicate does not teach anything: it only harms (Plato's insight). Nozick asserts, "The hope of retributive matching punishment is that the wrongdoer will realize his act was wrong when someone shows him that it was wrong and means it."[10] But if this is how moral education is achieved—by demonstrations of wrongdoing—then we are all in serious trouble! As Novick himself notes (without taking in the lesson), "Many child-batterers were themselves battered children; their defect is not ignorance of what it is like to be battered."[11]

Finally, Nozick argues, "the wrongdoer has become disconnected from correct values, and the purpose of punishment is to 're-connect' him. It is not that this connection is a desired further effect of punishment: the act of retributive punishment itself effects this connection."[12] While his diagnosis of a disconnect makes some sense, his conclusion again defies logic. Harming cannot teach that it is wrong to harm. When he is harmed in this way, the victim only receives a moralized version of the same injury he inflicted. To tell him that his injury was wrong but ours is right (because it is retributive) makes no cognitive or experiential sense. There is a good reason why we do not teach children not to bite by biting them.

Still, as Nozick astutely discerned, the close companion of retribution is revenge. The emotions associated with it are hatred and rage, and, because these are notably difficult to control, retribution has a tendency to slide into vengeance. Moreover, vengeance is notably given to spiraling into further vengeance. The codes of vengeance that characterized feuding societies instituted this spiral: an injury had to be "paid pack with interest." But the economic metaphor is misleading, for there was no substitution of monetary payment for injuries to one's person or one's honor: the injurer and his kin were visited with a bloody response.

IN *HAMLET*, Shakespeare has written a sustained rumination on the problem of retribution, and it is not an endorsement. Retribution ensues in a blood bath, a stage strewn with bodies in the end, and, unlike Thomas Kyd's *Spanish Tragedy*, where revenge is imagined as satisfying justice, nothing is righted. Violence spreads like a contagion, and the guiltless—Polonius, Ophelia, and Laertes—die with the guilty. This was noted forcefully as early as 1765, when the great critic Samuel Johnson wrote: "The poet is accused of having shown little regard to poetical justice, and may be charged with equal neglect of poetical probability. The apparition left the regions of the dead to little purpose; the revenge which he demands is not obtained but by the death of him that was required to take it; and the gratification which would arise from the destruction of an usurper and a murderer, is abated by the untimely death of Ophelia."

For Johnson, the ending of *Hamlet* is both improbable and unjust. Hamlet kills Polonius unintentionally, and his son Laertes kills Hamlet. In this way the cause and effect of revenge are disjoined, and the persons involved are substituted. There is no such thing as correcting justice. Revenge cannot correct an injury: the parties to the injury are changed—the young Hamlet is not the elder Hamlet. Revenge cannot correct an injury: the injuries are only compounded, intentionally, to Claudius, and unintentionally—to Ophelia, Polonius, Laertes, Gertrude, and Hamlet. "Revenge . . . bitter upon itself soon recoils." This lack of a just resolution makes Hamlet's extended uncertainty about taking revenge far more profound than simply that of the caution of a detective ferreting out the truth of events. Hamlet's famous hesitation reflects uncertainty about a deeper truth, about the uncertainty of revenge as a moral code. In the end, *Hamlet*, the greatest revenge tragedy in English drama, is an antirevenge tragedy.

> Horatio: [G]ive order that these bodies
> High on a stage be placed to the view;
> And let me speak to th' yet unknowing world
> How these things came about: so shall you hear
> Of carnal, bloody, and unnatural acts,
> Of accidental judgments, casual slaughters,
> Of deaths put on by cunning and for no cause,
> And in this upshot purposes mistook
> Fall'n on th' inventors' heads: All this can I
> Truly deliver.
> (5.2.351)

Throughout, Hamlet underscores the enormity of the burden of revenge, the futility of the violence, and the impossibility of correcting injustice, for the passage of time means that one cannot go back and rectify the past. Over and over the play stresses that its temporal context is eternity. The ghost comes from beyond the grave to seek revenge.

Hamlet would kill himself, but the torments he imagines of an afterlife stop him. Gertrude must not be punished by Hamlet but by Heaven. The fate of Ophelia's body and soul is at risk due to her unlawful suicide, requiring that her death be mercifully interpreted as an accident in order for her to have a Christian burial. Hamlet himself says repeatedly that the dead are the lucky ones, and, in the end, his soul is wished to heaven: "Goodnight, sweet Prince, may flights of angels sing thee to thy rest." The yawning of an immeasurable time, then, is the context for both crime and punishment.

In such eternal time, neither the deed nor the retribution can be comprehended within the living duration of justice. Instead, injuries and their rectification become as insignificant as life, a passing shadow. The graveyard scene performs this message of the futility of life; in it the imperial greatness of Alexander has become dust to stuff up a bunghole. Gazing at the skull of the jester who has now lost his laughter, "poor Yorick," Hamlet reflects that his mother could put an inch of paint on her face and still end up a bare skull. Her vain dissembling will be defeated as surely as the ambitions of an emperor and the jests of a clown. *Mutatus mundi.*

> Alas, poor Yorick! I knew him, Horatio: a fellow
> of infinite jest, of most excellent fancy: he hath
> borne me on his back a thousand times; and now, how
> abhorred in my imagination it is! my gorge rims at
> it. Here hung those lips that I have kissed I know
> not how oft. Where be your gibes now? your
> gambols? your songs? your flashes of merriment,
> that were wont to set the table on a roar? Not one
> now, to mock your own grinning? quite chap-fallen?
> Now get you to my lady's chamber, and tell her, let
> her paint an inch thick, to this favour she must
> come; make her laugh at that.

From the perspective of the graveyard, justice does not fare well. The great and the mean, the righteous and criminal, the generous and the miserly, the good and the evil, are all leveled. The futility of legal justice is further exposed explicitly as he ruminates on the skull of a lawyer.

There's another: why, may not that be the skull
of a lawyer? Where be his quiddities now—his quillets,
his cases, his tenures, and his tricks? why does he suffer
this mad knave now to knock him about the sconce with
a dirty shovel, and will not tell him of his action of
battery? Hum! This fellow might be in's time a great
buyer of land, with his statutes, his recognizances, his
fines, his double vouchers, his recoveries. To have his
fine pate full of fine dirt! Will vouchers vouch him no
more of his purchases and doubles than the length and
breadth of a pair of indentures? The very conveyances
of his lands will hardly lie in this box, and must
th' inheritor himself have no more, ha?
(5.1.93–105)

Echoes of the injustice of Hamlet losing his inheritance abound: he
stresses that all of the means of securing the transfer of land, of inheritance (conveyances, vouchers and double vouchers, recoveries) are futile.
All of the deeds that secure land transfer could scarcely fit in the coffin,
and yet the inheritor—the lawyer, who has taken possession of rather
than inherited lands—has no more land than his grave. A passion for
justice suggests that life has purpose and meaning. But the impossible
demand made to Hamlet to correct the past, in the form of the request
to avenge, inspires not a passion for a just order, but futility. The crime—
that Hamlet's father was murdered by his brother—*cannot* be undone.

Not only eternity, but its opposite, the moment, the present instant,
also haunts the play, doubling the futility of revenge. The moment, once
past, cannot be revisited; events that happen and can neither be anticipated nor changed. "If it be, 'tis not to come. If it be not to come, it will
be now. If it be not now, yet it will come": lines that are often plausibly
interpreted as referring to the moment of death—for Horatio is here
worried about Hamlet accepting a duel with Laertes—have a wider range
of meaning (5.2.199). Once any event occurs, it is not "to come." And if
it is not in the future, it is now. The ghost who visits from the afterlife
impossibly insists on Hamlet addressing the now:

Now, Hamlet, hear:
'Tis given out that, sleeping in my orchard,

> A serpent stung me;
> … but know, thou noble youth,
> The serpent that did sting thy father's life
> Now wears his crown.

The term *now* intones like a bell throughout the play, even putting now in conflict with eternity.

> Hamlet: Now might I do it pat, now he is praying;
> And now I'll do't. And so he goes to heaven;
> *And so am I revenged. That would be scann'd:*
> A villain kills my father; and for that,
> I, his sole son, do this same villain send
> To heaven.

Hamlet foregoes the opportunity to kill the murderous king when he comes upon him praying, for he would not send his soul to heaven, but then we learn that his prayers were hollow so that Hamlet missed his chance. Revenge depends upon certain knowledge, but this is impossible. While the play within the play is asked to grant that certainty, and the King starts and leaves, troublingly, the dumb show evinces no reaction from him. But the scene raises not only the troubling question of knowledge, which must be absolutely certain for retribution to make sense, it also suggests that revenge cannot be complete for another reason: any revenge in this life is not assured in an afterlife.

In the final act of *Hamlet*, the poisoned sword intended for Hamlet wounds Laertes; the poisoned cup intended for Hamlet kills his mother; and when Hamlet uses those instruments to kill Claudius, we are left feeling that the original command to avenge his father is only carried out circumstantially. It does not feel like revenge offers a just punishment to an injurer, but that instead it works haphazardly, wielding a clumsy sword that cuts down the innocent with the guilty. Shakespeare persistently depicts a ruined moral order as madness. Sanity requires not just reason, but the right reason of thinking justly, of living justly. Revenge becomes a form of madness—not only assuming the calculated feigning of madness that Hamlet dons, but also a rage that, seizing Hamlet, distorts his love for Ophelia, leads him to kill the guiltless Polonius, and ultimately destroys his engagement with the world.

In the midst of this profound critique of revenge, something else is offered: a rebuke. The ghost forbids Hamlet to harm his mother, leaving her punishment to God. Hamlet is expressly forbidden the classical path, the one Orestes takes in Aeschylus's trilogy, killing his mother to avenge his father's murder, or the path of Nero, who had his mother Agrippina murdered for poisoning her husband and living with her brother.

> Ghost: If thou hast nature in thee bear it not,
> Let not the royal bed of Denmark be
> A couch for luxury and damned incest.
> But howsomever thou pursues this act
> Taint not thy mind nor let they soul contrive
> Against thy mother aught; leave her to heaven
> And to those thorns that in her bosom lodge
> To prick and sting her.
> (1.5.81–88)

While Hamlet may leave his mother's punishment to heaven, he takes her moral education upon himself as his duty, deliberately substituting his rebuke (*shent* is the past participle of the archaic verb *shend*, to rebuke or scold) for bloodletting. He wills that his soul would never consent to executing a punishment beyond the rebuke.

We don't know for certain—are not told explicitly—that this queen has gone to her husband's brother's bed before her husband was slain, but the enormous fault attributed to her, by both the ghost and Hamlet, makes it difficult to imagine that her only sin is marrying too soon. A betrayal is suggested, a lack of fidelity. It is "most unnatural" (3.4.38): murder may not be the only offense.

> 'Tis now the very witching time of night,
> When churchyards yawn and hell itself breaks out
> Contagion to this world. Now could I drink hot blood,
> And do such bitter business as the day
> Would quake to look on. Soft, now to my mother.
> O heart, lose not thy nature. Let not ever
> The soul of Nero enter this firm bosom—
> Let me be cruel, not unnatural:
> I will speak daggers to her, but use none.

My tongue and soul in this be hypocrites.
How in my words somever she be shent,
To give them seals never my soul consent!
(3.2.378–89)

Speaking daggers but using none, Hamlet rebukes his mother, naming her offense as a crime against the natural moral order, against love, against virtue, against judgment.

After all, it is not so surprising that *Hamlet* does not endorse revenge. The play reflects an Elizabethan Christian ethos that makes revenge not only unsavory but sinful.[13] "The primary argument against revenge, therefore, was that the revenger endangered his own soul. No matter how righteous a man might think his motives, the act of revenge would inevitably make him as evil as his injurer in the eyes of God," explains scholar Eleanor Prosser. And she quotes the sermon of the highly regarded divine, Edwin Sandys, among many others: "In so going about to revenge evill, we shew our selves to be evill, and, while we will punish, and revenge another mans folly, we double, and augment our owne folly." The Christian antirevenge code had such widespread influence that "the average spectator at a revenge play was caught in an ethical dilemma—a dilemma, to put it most simply, between what he believed and what he felt."[14]

But we need not assume that theatrical productions only *reflected* an already forged ethos against revenge. We have every reason to believe that a popular drama like *Hamlet* helped to forge that ethos. And *Hamlet* is not an isolated instance: throughout the corpus of Shakespeare, revenge is suspect. In *Othello*, Shakespeare provocatively joins the urge to revenge to madness. Ultimately, Othello's delusion deepens into madness expressed in his perverse vow: "Arise, black vengeance, from the hollow hell! / Yield up, O love, thy crown and hearted throne / To tyrannous hate!" (3.3.447–49). In *Romeo and Juliet* the code of vengeance destroys the young lovers.[15] In *Troilus and Cressida* revenge "is the nurse of barbarism and irrational frenzy."[16] And in *King Lear*, as in *Othello*, the onset of Lear's madness coincides with his vow of vengeance. While Lear begins by praying for patience toward his unkind daughters, he gives himself up to rage—and to madness:

No, you unnatural hags
I will have such revenges on you both,

That all the world shall—I will do such things,—
What they are, yet I know not; but they shall be
The terrors of the earth.

(2.4.281–85)

Shakespeare's plays not only condemn revenge. They endorse forgiveness, even—especially—when one is seized by fury.

Though with their high wrongs I am struck to the quick,
Yet with my nobler reason 'gainst my fury
Do I take part: the rarer action is
In virtue than in vengeance.

(*The Tempest*, 5.1.25–28)

In Shakespeare, forgiveness is not only offered as an alternative to revenge. It holds much more: forgiveness is tied to recognition or the rediscovery of love. Piero Boitani has written eloquently about recognition in Shakespeare as virtually constituting his gospel: "The Good News that Shakespeare's last plays bring to us is that we can reach happiness on earth, and that this can be true 'eternal life.' To be reunited with one's loved ones, to rediscover them and recognize them, constitutes happiness: nothing more than this, but equally nothing less."[17] This reaches exquisite intensity in the recognition scene between Lear and Cordelia, in which the once-banished Cordelia now asks for Lear's blessing and the suffering Lear awakens from madness and begs her forgiveness: "O! Look upon me, Sir, / And hold your hand in benediction o'er me. / No, Sir, you must not kneel" (4.7.58–60). Boitani comments: "'Forget and forgive,' Lear will shortly implore. Recognition thus means, in the instant between past, present, and future, a new awareness, an opening of the mind towards the other, which contrasts with Lear's previous falling in on himself. That earlier kind of knowledge was the all-too-human wisdom of madness: this present knowledge, which is forged by the earlier one through a wheel of fire, is communion; it is a fully human wisdom sublimed and purified by acceptance."[18]

Why is love regarded as the highest human value in some cultural sectors and not even on the map in others? Make no mistake, for many thinkers in many times, love is the very purpose of life. Leviticus in the Hebrew Bible, Jesus in the New Testament, Socrates in the *Symposium*,

Aquinas in the *Summa Theologica*, Shakespeare in *Romeo and Juliet* and *King Lear*: for each of them, love defines us as human. And love is not only our core self, it is also the goal of all of life's experiences. From *La Bohème* to the Beatles ("All You Need Is Love"), from *Sabrina* to *Star Wars*, from *Antigone* to *Anna Karenina*, the arts underscore the priority of love. And, yet, in my office where several bookshelves are devoted to books on theories of justice, not one has a chapter on love. Justice is deemed a political, public concern, while love is personal and private. There is an exception: the books on religion are full of it, and there love comes in different names depending on who is loving and how they are loving: *caritas*, *agape*, *eros*, divine love, neighbor love. In these books, love is preeminently public—it is social glue—furthermore, it is tantamount to justice.

Shakespeare's understanding of justice flows not only from classical conventions but also from the biblical tradition, where forgiveness enables just restorations of an injured social order and where love is bound to justice. His compelling dramatic expressions of the religious understanding of justice help to explain the enormous cultural currency of his work. Audiences resonate unconsciously to his understanding of justice, not only condemning his villains (Iago in *Othello*, Edmund in *King Lear*) and embracing his heroes (the forgiving Cordelia, the principled Juliet) but sharing the conflicts in values (Hamlet's revenge) and then suffering or rejoicing in the outcome. What defines comedy is the restoration of the right order, the just order. Even in his romantic comedies, like *As You Like It* or *Twelfth Night*, what satisfies is the disentanglement of the wrong partners and the mutual recognition of the right ones. Throughout the comedies, the marital order, the *ordo amoris*, must be right for the social order to be just. What constitutes a "tragedy" is not only its conclusion of sadness, but the specific sadness felt at the triumph of injustice—with the murders of Desdemona and Cordelia, not only are innocent people destroyed, but goodness itself seems defeated.

FORGIVENESS

What is forgiveness? Most definitions are negative: it is *not* succumbing to resentment, vindictiveness, or the desire to punish. The Greek *aphesis* suggests letting go; the Latin *ignoscere* suggests overlooking or not knowing. Forgiveness has been described as a change in inner feeling more than an action. This is defined as "the overcoming, on moral grounds, of the intense negative reactive attitudes that are quite naturally occasioned when one has been harmed by another."[19] The "vindictive passions" to be overcome include "resentment, anger, hatred, and the desire for revenge." But forgiveness is not always understood as overcoming resentment—sometimes forgiveness takes place *even as* we resent, as it does for the Renaissance thinker Montaigne.

> He that through a naturall facilitie and genuine mildnesse should neglect or contemne injuries received, should no doubt performe a rare action, and worthy commendation; but he who being toucht and stung to the quicke with any wrong or offence received, should arme himself with reason against this furiously blind desire of revenge, and in the end after a great conflict yeeld himselfe master over it, should doutlesse doe much more. . . . The first should doe well, the other vertuously: the one action might be termed Goodnesse, the other Vertue.[20]

Similarly, for Shakespeare's Prospero, the "greater virtue" requires reason triumphing over anger rather than simply responding to injury with stoic calm of mind.

Forgiveness also includes a positive meaning, derived from its Old English etymology *forgiefan: giefan* (to give) and *for-* (completely), that is, extreme giving. What is given, granted is acknowledgment of the wrongdoer's remorse and an opportunity for restoration in a disrupted relationship. This is extreme giving. In this sense forgiveness suggests more than simply overcoming resentment or reasoning beyond a will to punish. Forgiveness adds the positive goal of restoration.

Forgiveness is not a unilateral act. It involves two: it is a response to apology. Nor is it an isolated act: it is part of a process that includes the acknowledgment of wrongdoing, remorse, and apology from the perpetrator and the response of forgiveness from the injured. Without such recognition of wrongdoing and without such remorse, forgiveness would have no meaning: it would be an empty gesture. With them forgiveness is performative, that is, the very act of forgiveness not only *acknowledges* the restoration of the moral order, it *restores* the right moral order.

Forgiveness—not revenge—occupies the front and center of the Western religious response to wrongdoing. It is the goal, the telos of the response to injury or iniquity. Religious traditions may offer different paths to that goal. The sacrament of penance in the Christian Middle Ages offered a public testimony of restitution, after confession and contrition, and these were the prerequisites for forgiveness. In medieval Judaism the wrongdoer's change of heart enabled a sincere apology; there were standards to discern this, and this change of heart was the precondition for forgiveness. Are there cases when a wrong is unforgivable? In the Jewish tradition forgiveness is only impossible when a wrongdoer cannot or will not sincerely repent.

The tradition views forgiveness as comprised of two interrelated duties—the duty of the offender to seek forgiveness is primary and unconditional, while the duty to grant it is conditional upon the offender's having fulfilled her prior duty. Thus, one has a duty to forgive only if the offender has sincerely repented and sought reconciliation. Where the individual involved is reticent to acknowledge the harm done, one has a further obligation to rebuke the sinner in order to prompt that person to repentance. On the other hand, one does not have a duty to forgive if the person will not or cannot repent, for this entails overlooking or minimizing sinful behavior. Apart from this condition, however, the duty to forgive is unlimited with respect to the offense committed. "God's willingness to forgive, while conditional upon the sinner's repentance, is unlimited with respect to the severity of the sin."[21] And that divine forgiveness is the model for human forgiveness.[22]

In radical cases forgiveness is prior to apology—in Jewish and Christian thought, God the Father forgives or Christ forgives, but even this is not quite unilateral. The forgiveness is still in a dialogue with the apology; only here the recognition and apology come after rather than before, and forgiveness is even more radically performative, for, instead of being prompted by apology, it prompts recognition of wrongdoing and remorse.

In the biblical traditions, God is depicted neither as a judge nor an executor of righteous wrath, but as, above all, forgiving. This may seem surprising, but divine justice is persistently joined to forgiveness: "The Lord, the Lord, a god compassionate and gracious, long-suffering, ever constant and true, maintaining constancy to thousands, forgiving iniquity, rebellion, and sin and not sweeping the guilty clean away" (Exodus 34:6–7). In biblical prophecy, the restoration of the very relationship between God and Israel is enabled by forgiveness: "'Return, faithless

Israel,' says the Lord. 'I will not look on you in anger, for I am merciful,' says the Lord" (Jeremiah 3:12). In the following fascinating passage, God is both forgiver and forgiven, granting clemency and apologizing. God has the "change of heart" that Israel should have, on behalf of her, and he has that remorse for even considering responding to her with fury/ revenge.

> How can I give you up, Ephraim,
> How surrender you, Israel . . .
> My heart is changed within me,
> My remorse kindles already.
> I will not let loose my fury,
> I will not turn round and destroy Ephraim.
> (Hosea 11:8–9)

For the philosopher and Talmudic commentator Emmanuel Levinas, justice itself must flow from charity and answer to charity, the true source of justice. Simply put, "Love must always watch over justice."[23] He rejects a simply negative justice, one that only limits violence. In that vein, critics often speak of the relative weakness of "human rights" law as stemming from this negative understanding of justice, one that protects against violence but fails to promote human flourishing. Instead, Levinas urges a positive vision of justice that springs from charity. His clearest enunciation follows: "Justice itself is born of charity. They can seem alien when they are presented as successive stages; in reality, they are inseparable and simultaneous, unless one is on a desert island,"[24] that is, unless no reciprocal giving, including acknowledgment of injuring, apology, and forgiveness obtain there.

This understanding of justice born of charity is delineated forcefully in the Hebrew Bible. While Amos speaks of punishing the Israelites for their failure to follow the law, for their failure to be responsible for the poor, for the widow, orphan, and stranger—their failure to extend charity—Jeremiah speaks of forgiveness: "They have found pardon in the wilderness, / those who have survived the sword. / Israel is marching to his rest" (Jeremiah 31:1–2). God affirms his love: "I have loved you with an everlasting love, so I am constant in my affection for you. I build you once more; you shall be rebuilt, virgin of Israel. / Adorned once more, and with your tambourines, you will go out dancing gaily." Something new will happen according to the prophet: a wife will return to her husband.

The brief book of Jonah distills this portrayal of divine forgiveness powerfully. It opens with the divine judgment against Nineveh, the capital of the evil empire that sent Israel into exile—and the wickedest city on the earth. God's initial response to their evil is to threaten them through a dire message sent by his prophet Jonah: "Go to Nineveh, the great city, and inform them that their wickedness has become known to me" (1:2). But then, in a witty parody of the prophets who vehemently denounce evil and proclaim punishment, the book of Jonah describes a very *unwilling* prophet who is sent to denounce the city and its inhabitants.[25] Yet he does not merely object to his commission, he runs in the opposite direction!—boarding a ship to Tarshish instead of Nineveh. Thereafter, ironies redound. The sailors are foreigners who do not worship Yahweh, but when a great storm comes up, they ask Jonah to call on his God (not theirs), and when they learn that he is trying to escape from his God ("who made the sea and the land"!) they themselves call upon Yahweh before they throw Jonah overboard. When the sea grows calm, they immediately offer sacrifices and pray to Yahweh. The sailors are more pious than the prophet.

The message of the Lord will not go undelivered. Comically, "Yahweh had appointed that a great fish" should be there to swallow Jonah when he is thrown overboard. And this fish will transport him to shores of Nineveh! "The word of the Lord was addressed a second time to Jonah: 'Up!' he said, 'Go to Nineveh, the great city, and preach to them as I told you' (3:1). Jonah makes a day's journey into the city (it takes three days) and says (you can almost imagine a whisper in the outskirts), "in forty days Nineveh is going to be destroyed." Some warning! When the biblical prophets warn that Israel will be destroyed if it does not reform, they are not heeded, and this is why dire prophetic warnings—of exile and destruction and defeat by Israel's enemies—often become predictions.

Against this conventional deaf ear to the prophetic warnings is the case of Nineveh, whose repentance is improbably immediate and complete, extending from the greatest to the least of its inhabitants: "And the people of Nineveh believed in God." A repentant king issues a proclamation for thoroughgoing repentance: "Men and beasts, herds and flocks, are to taste nothing; they must not eat, they must not drink water. All are to put on sackcloth and ashes and call on God with all their might; and let everyone renounce his evil behavior and the wicked things he has done." God saw their efforts "and God relented; he did not inflict on them the disaster he threatened."

Several conclusions emerge. First, even the wickedest city on earth can reform. Second, repentance is the precondition for the divine pardoning of Nineveh. Third, the reason God gives for accepting this repentance, for not destroying even the wickedest city, is that it is his creation. In this parody of strict retributive prophetic justice, divine forgiveness responds so readily to the repentance of Nineveh that the forgiveness almost seems to have prompted it. Again, this is how divine forgiveness works in Aquinas: it prompts repentance, and that is the reason God forgives man even before his repentance—while humans forgive one another only after repentance.

The drama of repentance and forgiveness is not over. Jonah himself is filled with righteous wrath and furious with this course of events. He is the portrait of the retributivist who wants the wrongdoers punished "because they deserve it." God, according to Jonah, is too soft-hearted: "That was why I fled to Tarshish: I knew that you were a God of love and compassion, slow to anger, rich is graciousness, relenting from evil. So now, Yahweh, please take away my life for I may as well be dead as go on living." Jonah the retributivist cannot bear living in a world where the wicked are not punished. But God, confronting Jonah's will to punish the deserving, asks him a core ethical question, twice: "are you right to be so angry" at my forgiveness? The question works in two ways: exposing Jonah's motive of anger—is it right to be angry?—and questioning the value of the response that anger prompts—is it right to punish? To teach Jonah a lesson, God appoints a plant to grow to shade Jonah from the scorching heat and then kills it. Jonah's dismay prompts a lesson: "You are only upset about a plant which cost you no labor, which you did not make grow, which sprouted in a night and has perished in a night. And am I not to feel sorry for Nineveh, the great city, in which there are more than a hundred and thirty thousand people who cannot tell their right hand from their left, to say nothing of all the animals?" Jonah, the son of Amittai, is the son of Truth (the Hebrew root *a-m-t* signifies truth), and Jonah does not want to be made a liar. But his righteousness is wrong. Jonah means dove, alluding to surviving the flood at the time of Noah, where the appearance of a dove signals the newly found dry land. There and here, the divine purpose is not wrathful obliteration for wrongdoing, but the survival of the creation.

The book of Jonah offers one answer to the question: What is a just response to wrongdoing that is watched over by love? But it narrates the divine response. What about the human response to wrongdoing? The passage in the Bible that enjoins us to love the neighbor as ourselves also says you shall not take vengeance against him and, further, that you shall not bear a grudge against him. Even vindictive feelings are anathema: "You shall not hate your brother in your heart; you shall surely rebuke your neighbor, and not bear sin because of him. You shall not take vengeance, nor bear a grudge against your neighbor . . . but you shall love your neighbor as yourself" (Leviticus 19:17–18). The injunctions against vengeance, against hating, and even against bearing a grudge, and alongside the command to love the neighbor, have a notably odd companion, one that seems to not fit: "You shall surely rebuke your neighbor." Why? What purpose could rebuke serve? The Jewish philosopher Maimonides offers an answer, and does so in the context of commenting upon the love command of Leviticus:

> When a man sins against another, the injured party should not hate the offender and keep silent . . . his duty is to inform the offender and say to him, "Why did you do this to me? Why did you sin against me in this matter?" And thus it is said, "You shall surely rebuke your neighbor" (Lev 19:17). If one observes that a person committed a sin or walks in a way that is not good, *it is a duty to bring the erring man back to the right path* and point out to him that he is wronging himself by his evil courses . . . If the offender repents and pleads for forgiveness, he should be forgiven.[26]

This idea of rebuke sounds foreign to modern ears. It can either suggest a version of social policing—images of Calvin's Geneva come to mind—or an ineffectual response to wrongdoing, one soft on crime. How can a rebuke really stop an offender? Furthermore, how can one possibly intervene to offer correction without infringing another's rights? "Coercion for a person's own good or coercion for the perceived general long range moral good of society are in most cases to be ruled out" of our legal codes.[27] Indeed, interfering with someone can only be justified in the most extreme cases.[28] Whatever rebuke is, it is another way: neither retribution, nor is it forgetting the crime. It is part of the process of forgiveness.

In Rabbinic Judaism, forgiveness is

> closely related to another duty, one especially incumbent on the injured party, namely, to chastise the wrongdoer if that person is unaware of the wrong committed. . . . This encourages the wrongdoer to repent, and hence to improve his moral character, and it saves others from being subjected to a similar offense. But rebuking also places a significant role on forgiveness. It highlights the fact that the act of forgiveness that follows this rebuke is NOT designed to minimize the offense or worse, to make believe that it did not occur. Quite the opposite is the case. It is because the offense and its effects are very significant to the parties involved that forgiveness is called for. . . . Forgiveness is meant to call attention to the morally objectionable nature of the offense at the same time that it facilitates a bridging of the gap that this offense has created.[29]

A rebuke to the perpetrator is restorative for the one who has gone astray from the principles regarded as just in the community, as well as restorative for the victim, who is thereafter not forced to sustain the insult of wrongdoing unrecognized. In not leaving the offense unrecognized, rebuke also restores justice for the community. Rebuke and forgiveness, rather than ignoring the culpability of the offender, are designed to make it explicit. Finally, does a rebuke satisfy justice itself? It is more likely that, rather than satisfy a pregiven justice, as punishment purports to do by distributing harm, rebuke—perhaps like forgiveness—creates justice. In the activity of rebuke, right and wrong are given expression and definition. Justice comes into being.

Maimonides understood rebuke, apology, and forgiveness as reconstituting an impaired social moral order. This is why he insisted on seeking forgiveness from the dead, to prevent a "standing injustice," as Dan Philpott astutely terms it, from prevailing. Maimonides says that if we committed a sin against someone who died and have not asked their forgiveness we must assemble ten people, which stands for the community, and go to the grave and say, "I have sinned against the Lord and this individual." An interpersonal offense implies a sin against God or, in secular terms, against the moral order. *This means seeking forgiveness from someone is also seeking to repair the moral order.* The contemporary philosopher, Raimond Gaita, concurs on the importance of manifesting guilt and shame, which "often express acknowledgement of collective responsibility, sometimes directly for the wrongs done, but more often to those who were wrongs by our political ancestors. It amounts to the acknowledgement that we are rightly called to a communal responsiveness to those who are the victims of wrongdoing or the wrongdoing of those who preceded us."[30]

Another biblical narrative offers further insight into this process of rebuke, apology, and forgiveness engendering justice: the story of Joseph in the book of Genesis. Joseph's brothers, envious of his special standing with his father and his ambitions, throw him into a pit intending to murder him. But, unbeknownst to them, he survives, is sold into Egypt by traders passing by, and even prospers there. He becomes Pharaoh's right-hand man, his vizier, and saves all of Egypt from a terrible famine through his prudent economic policy. Then, one day, he finds himself confronting his once-scheming brothers. They have traveled from their famine-ridden home in Israel to Egypt to ask for food and they do not recognize, in the official before them, the brother they had tried to murder. What ensues is not simply punishment, nor ready forgiveness, but a severe rebuke as part of an agonizingly prolonged recognition scene. Joseph begins by speaking harshly to his brothers, accusing them of being spies, holds them in custody, but then gives them grain and puts money in their sacks. He demands that the brothers seeking food go home first and come back with their adored youngest brother and then, when they do, he insists that they leave him as a hostage in exchange for grain. He is thereby forcing them to give away another brother, the one now most beloved by their father. At this, "They said to one another, 'Truly we are being called to account for our brother. We saw his misery of soul when he begged our mercy, but we did not listen to him, and now this misery has come home to us' . . . *They did not know that Joseph understood, because there was an interpreter between them.* He left them and wept. Then he went back to them and spoke to them. Of their number he took Simeon and had him bound while they looked on" (Genesis 42:21, my emphasis).

In this extraordinary narrative, Joseph is simultaneously suffering and inflicting pain —leaving to weep and binding Simeon as a prisoner before his brothers' eyes. Like Hamlet's play within the play, by means of this reenactment, Joseph is bringing their crime, of abandoning a brother, to their attention, evoking a confession they do not know they are giving, for there was an interpreter between them, and they do not know Joseph understands—making it all the more authentic. The performed and internal remorse are harmonized completely here, because "there was an interpreter between them." The figure of the translator enables the truth to appear, liberating the brothers' confession from instrumentality. Joseph understands all, but he is not yet finished.

The rebuke is prolonged and multifaceted: next, he plants a silver cup in his youngest brother's sack and accuses him of thievery. The life of Joseph's full brother Benjamin (the other child of Rachel) is now imperiled. How do the once-murderous brothers respond to the threat posed to this favorite? Now, another brother, Judah—one of the ringleaders who abandoned Joseph, rises to the eloquent defense of Benjamin.

> You said, if your youngest brother does not come down with you, you will not be admitted to my presence again. . . . So your servant our father said to us, "you know that my wife bore me two children. When one left me, I said the he must have been torn to pieces. And I have not seen him to this day. If you take this one from me too and any harm comes to him, you will send me down to Sheol with my white head bowed in misery." If I go to your servant my father now, and we have not the boy with us, he will die as soon as he sees the boy is not with us, for his heart is bound up with him.
>
> (Genesis 44:23–30)

That's not all: Judah then offers himself in place of the loved boy. All the violence and jealousy the brothers had for the favored Joseph has now been transformed. Judah, once the perpetrator of injury, now sacrifices himself before allowing another brother to be captured. With the lesson learned, Joseph finally reveals his identity to his shocked brothers, and then they rebuke themselves for their wrongdoing, apologize, and he forgives them: "I am your brother Joseph whom you sold into Egypt. But now, do not grieve, do not reproach yourselves for having sold me here, since God sent me before you to preserve your lives" (Genesis 45:5–6). Both Joseph's rebuke of his brothers and Hamlet's rebuke of Gertrude, however harsh, are depicted, in the end, as acts of love.

Like so many of Shakespeare's plays, *The Tempest* is also preoccupied with justice. The background is another heinous injustice. As Joseph was abandoned to die by his brothers, so, in *The Tempest*, the throne of Milan has been usurped by Prospero's brother who had ruthlessly put Prospero out to sea to die with his young daughter. More plots of treachery and betrayal take place in the time of the play: a plot to murder the king of Naples by his brother and a plot by Calaban, Stephano, and Trinculo to murder Prospero and take over the island. Prospero must not only abort the new treachery and right the old wrongs, he must also dispense justice. Astonishingly, this is imagined in the play not as the work of the court or of private feuding but as the creative work of the theater. Prospero is the master artist who creates a world through his vision and the magic of conjuring, i.e., theater. The made world will be made just. Now that the villains are in Prospero's power, he is tempted to punish his brother Alonso for his misdeeds—"bountiful fortune / (Now, my dear lady) hath mine enemies brought to this shore" (1.2.179–80); "At this hour / Lies at my mercy all my enemies" (4.1.263–4). But instead he creates the conditions that will induce his enemy to experience remorse: the presumed loss of his own son. It works: Alonso interprets his devastating loss as the payment for his own dreadful crime of casting Prospero and his daughter out to sea.

> Alonso: O, it is monstrous, monstrous!
> Methought the billows spoke and told me of it;
> The winds did sing it to me, and the thunder—
> That deep and dreadful organpipe—pronounced
> The name of Prosper. It did bass my trespass.
> Therefore my son i'th'ooze is bedded, and
> I'll seek him deeper than e'er plummet sounded,
> And with him there lie mudded.
> (3.3.95–102)

Miranda responds to the suffering of Alonso and his companions in the tempest with the seemingly natural sympathy of one who has never known harm—"O I have suffered with those that I saw suffer" (1.2.5–6)—and even Prospero's sprite Ariel feels sympathy for the suffering. But the sterner Prospero, meting out justice, only recovers such sympathy when his victimizers have shown remorse. He seeks apology, penitence, and to correct the standing wrong—not vengeance. "Hast thou, [Ariel] which art but air, a touch, a feeling / Of their afflictions, and shall not myself / (One of their kind, that relish all as sharply, / Passion as thy) be kindlier moved than thou art?" Revenge is not Prospero's purpose; justice is.

> Though with their high wrongs I am struck to th'quick,
> Yet with my nobler reason 'gainst my fury
> Do I take part. The rarer action is
> In virtue than in vengeance.
> (5.1.25–28)

> They being penitent,
> The sole drift of my purpose doth extend
> Not a frown further.
> (5.1.28–30)

His sole purpose is their penitence, not a frown further. Once that is achieved, Prospero forgives, and with that restoration he is willing to abjure his staff, abdicate his godlike magic powers, and give up the need to conjure a just world (5.1. 21–24).

The contrast between judgment and mercy is also taken up explicitly in Shakespeare's *Measure for Measure*, where the strictest sentences are handed down from a judge who is not just and a law that is not just. Here, a virtually Kantian respect for the universal priority of the law is voiced by the corrupt Angelo, who is intent upon killing Claudio for consummating his marriage before the contract is complete, a technicality:

> Angelo: It is the law, not I condemn your brother:
> Were he my kinsman, brother, or my son,
> It should be thus with him: he must die tomorrow. . . .
> Isabella: Yet show some pity.
> Angelo: I show it most of all when I show justice;
> For then I pity those I do not know,
> Which a dismiss'd offence would after gall;

And do him right that, answering one foul wrong,
Lives not to act another.

(2.2.80–105)

Angelo's overstrict scruples collapse into hypocrisy when he propositions Claudio's sister, a novitiate. All the wrongs have to be righted by the duke, who, disguised as a monk, learns of Angelo's reign of terror. But while setting the order straight does include confessions and contrition, it does not include doling out punishments. Instead, the punitive Angelo is supplanted by the merciful duke, who forgives all.

IN THE BIBLE and in the biblical Shakespeare, then, rebuke is joined to forgiveness, justice to love. Why does the religious tradition value forgiveness so highly when the legal/political system minimizes its value? The law presumes not only the right but the duty to punish: it does not ask whether it should punish, but who, when, how, and how much. In the legal literature there are four justifications for punishment:

- Retribution: punishment is needed because it is deserved. This means only such punishment as is proportional to the harm. This concept of punishment includes repaying for some advantage someone has stolen.
- Incapacitation: to keep the criminal from doing further harm. This includes both the specific (the harms that criminal could commit) and the general (the harms other potential criminals could inflict on society). The effort is to control dangerous antisocial conduct.
- Expression: punishment expresses the community's commitment to the norms that were violated.
- Rehabilitation: the function of punishment is only to teach, to educate.

But, of late, the first justification is by far the one most invoked. Impulses to rehabilitate have given way to a climate of retribution. Forgiveness is not even on the radar screen.

How could our "corrective" system be more responsive to the moral value of forgiveness, one so strong in the Western cultural imaginary?

In biblical traditions, desert seems to be swept away as a criterion for punishment. If God did not continually forgive his creation, there would be no creation. For Luther, if God punished all sinners, there would be no one left. Instead, forgiveness is an outpouring of love precisely to one who does not deserve it. Forgiveness is a free gift, an act of grace; no one has a "right" to be forgiven. Forgiveness exceeds desert as love exceeds desert. And, in the religious tradition, human forgiveness is enjoined to imitate this exceeding forgiveness attributed to God.

Jesus engaged in a polemical attack on what Nicholas Wolterstorff calls "the reciprocity code," the assumption that good should be reciprocated with good and evil with evil. "Love your enemies, do good to those who hate you, bless those who curse you, pray for those who abuse you" (Luke 6:27–28). His most radical formulation includes loving the enemy: "You have learned that they were told, 'Eye for eye, tooth for tooth.' But what I tell you is this: Do not set yourself against the man who wrongs you . . . You have heard that they were told, 'Love your neighbor, hate your enemy.' But what I tell you is this: Love your enemy and pray for your persecutors: only so can you be children of your heavenly father, who makes the sun rise on the good and the bad alike, and sends the rain on the honest and dishonest" (Matthew 5:38–39 and 43–45).[31] Why are these biblical teachings, carried forward so effectively in Shakespearean drama and embraced by generations of theatergoers (if not believers) left behind when we enter the legal/political realm? The concept of the human person as worthy, as possessed of ineradicable dignity, as capable of caring, loving, forges a completely different ethos than that flowing from the image of the competitive, brutish, warring human that dominates political thought. But surely that anthropology of innate human violence is self-perpetuating. After all, those who harm are harming themselves. Conversely, the anthropology of loving humans can achieve not only healing for the injured but far more: the radical gift of forgiveness.

NOTES

This essay is drawn from my forthcoming book, "Justice: What's Love (and Shakespeare) Got to Do with It?"

1. Friederich Nietzsche, *On the Genealogy of Morals*, trans. Walter Kaufmann (New York: Vintage, 1989), 48.

2. Immanuel Kant, *Grounding for the Metaphysics of Morals,* trans. James Wesley Ellington (Indianapolis: Hackett, 1993), 19.

3. Carol S. Steiker, "Murphy on Mercy: A Prudential Reconsideration," *Criminal Justice Ethics* 27, no. 2 (Summer-Fall 2008): 45–54, here 49.

4. Ibid.

5. Herbert Morris, "Persons and Punishments" (1968), in *On Guilt and Innocence: Essays in Legal Philosophy and Moral Psychology* (Berkeley: University of California Press, 1976).

6. Milton, *Paradise Lost* 9, ll. 171–72.

7. *Republic* 335e.

8. Richard Posner, *Economics of Justice* (Cambridge: Harvard University Press, 1981).

9. Robert Nozick, *Philosophical Explanations* (Cambridge: Harvard University Press, 1981), 370.

10. Ibid., 372.

11. Ibid., 373.

12. Ibid., 374.

13. Eleanor Prosser, *Hamlet and Revenge* (Stanford: Stanford University Press, 1967), 5.

14. Ibid., 4.

15. Prosser convincingly shows how the scene in *Henry V,* which many regard as retributive—in which Henry doles out his punishments to those who plotted to murder their king (2.2.12–181)—is the opposite: Henry exacts repentance from his plotters, thankfulness that their purposes have been prevented, and joy in their contrition.

16. Prosser, *Hamlet and Revenge,* 82.

17. Piero Boitani, *The Gospel According to Shakespeare,* trans Vittorio Montemaggi and Rachel Jacoff (Notre Dame: University of Notre Dame Press, 2013), 8.

18. Ibid., 36.

19. Jeffrie G. Murphy, *Getting Even: Forgiveness and Its Limits* (New York: Oxford University Press, 2003), 13.

20. Michel de Montaigne, *Essays,* book 2, section 11.

21. Louis E. Newman, *Past Imperatives: Studies in the History and Theory of Jewish Ethics* (Albany: SUNY Press, 1998), 94.

22. Ibid., 45.

23. Emmanuel Levinas, *Entre Nous: On Thinking-of-the-Other,* trans. Michael B. Smith and Barbara Harshav (New York: Columbia University Press, 1998), 108.

24. Ibid., 107.

25. It turns out that unwillingness characterizes all of the major prophets after all, beginning with Moses, who all demur when they are given an assignment to deliver the bad news. "But I am slow of speech," claims the hesitant Moses; "but I do not know how to speak, I am only a child," says the demurring Jeremiah; "I am lost for I am a man of unclean lips," complains the reluctant Isaiah.

26. Newman, *Past Imperatives,* 90 (my emphasis).

27. Jeffrie Murphy, "Legal Moralism and Retribution Revisited," in *The Proceedings and Addresses of the American Philosophical Association* 80, no. 2 (November 2006): 45–62, here 46.

28. Compare Murphy, *Getting Even*, 46.

29. Newman, *Past Imperatives*, 90.

30. Raimond Gaita, *A Common Humanity: Thinking About Love and Truth and Justice* (New York: Routledge, 2000), 87.

31. This does not prevent Christ from feeling moral indignation against wrong. See also Matthew 5:29–30 and 23:33, Luke 13:1–5.

5

LOVE AND LAW

Some Thoughts on Judaism and Calvinism

Leora Batnitzky

MY TITLE IS "LOVE AND LAW." In the contexts of the histories of Judaism and Christianity, it would be easy to interpret love as a stand-in for Christianity and law as a stand-in for Judaism. Love and Law would then mean Christianity and Judaism and if we understand the phrase *love and law* in this way, love and law might easily become love or law—or Christianity *or* Judaism. Yet when thinking about Calvinism and Judaism these dichotomies do not pertain. Both Calvinism and Judaism emphasize love *and* law. So I begin by stressing the conjunction, the *and,* and not the disjunction, an *or,* in my title.

Throughout this chapter, I describe Calvinism and Judaism in very general terms. Undoubtedly, this will lead to some oversimplification, but I hope nevertheless to paint a broad picture of the issues at stake in thinking about the relation between Judaism and Calvinism. The chapter has two sections. In the first section I consider seven striking parallels between Judaism and Calvinism. In the second section I argue that where Judaism and Calvinism differ is not on their views of God's nature (which are rather similar) but instead on their views of human nature. In the conclusion of the chapter, I briefly consider the implications of this difference for thinking about Abraham Kuyper's "common grace."

Dichotomies between "spirit and flesh" or between "faith and works" in which the former represent Christianity and the latter Judaism, are familiar ones, especially for the intellectual inheritors of Luther's reading of Paul (which pretty much means all of us). Let us recall Luther's preface to Romans, of which he writes that it is "the most important piece of the New Testament [and] purest Gospel." On Luther's reading of Paul, "the law increases sin . . . a person becomes more and more an enemy of the law the more it demands of him what he can't possibly do."[1] In his commentary on Galatians, Luther continues: "Paul sets here the spirit against the flesh. . . . Flesh . . . is here taken for the very righteousness and wisdom of the flesh, and the judgment of reason, which seeks to be justified by the law . . . Paul says therefore . . . if you will so end in the flesh, that is to say, follow the righteousness of the law, and forsake the spirit, as you have begun, then know you, that all your glory and affiance which you have in God is in vain."[2]

Yet neither Calvinism nor Judaism affirms a dichotomy between love and law or between spirit and flesh in the way that Luther has come to be read. Calvin's relation to Luther is, of course, a complicated subject, but, at the very least, in writing about Galatians, Calvin offers a different reading of law: "When Saint Paul said that the Law was given because of transgression, it came not in his mind to rehearse all the fruit and profit which the Law bringeth with it: for (as I have already said) it serveth also for our instruction, that we might learn to discern between good and evil, and again it quickeneth us up, as though God should give us strokes with the spur, to make us apply ourselves the more diligently unto him."[3] Law, for Calvin, allows human beings to "strive continually" and "to advance day by day." In his *Lectures on Calvinism*, Kuyper accentuates the interplay between gospel and law and between the old covenant and the new one. In Kuyper's words, "for the Calvinist, all ethical study is based on the Law of Sinai, not as though at the time the moral world-order began to be fixed, but to honor the Law of Sinai, as the divinely authentic summary of that original moral law which God wrote in the heart of man, at his creation. . . . "[4]

Just as Calvinism does not reject law in order to affirm spirit, so too Judaism does not reject spirit for the letter of the law. To offer just a few, very basic examples: Jews are commanded by the Torah not to follow the commandments but to live by them (*v'chai bahem*). The first lines of the Jewish creed, the Shema, make the interconnection between spirit and letter or love and law absolutely clear: "Hear O Israel. The Lord your God, the Lord is one. You shall love the Lord your God with all your heart and with all your soul and with all your might. And these words that I command you today shall be in your heart." These words are recited by observant Jews upon waking in the morning and before going to sleep at night. These words are also an integral part of the daily morning and evening liturgies. All of which is to say that the affirmation of love and law are at the very center of the Jewish tradition.

Now Judaism is of course an interpretive tradition. The Torah (or the law) encompasses both "the written Torah" (*Torah she b'chtav*) and "the oral Torah" (*Torah she b'al peh*), or the letter and the spirit. Rabbinic Judaism considers those who reject the spirit for the letter heretics, an issue that played itself out during the Middle Ages in controversies between rabbinic authorities (including Maimonides) and Karaite Jews who adhered only to the letter of the written law.

In their interactions with their Lutheran interlocutors, German Jewish thinkers were especially sensitive to the accusation that Judaism was synonymous with the dead letter of law. Clearly having Paul's statement in mind that "the written code kills, but the Spirit gives life" (2 Corinthians 3:6), the eighteenth-century German Jewish philosopher Moses Mendelssohn, the father of modern Jewish thought, defined Jewish law as follows: "The ceremonial law itself is a kind of living script, rousing the mind and heart, full of meaning, never ceasing to inspire contemplation and to provide the occasion and opportunity for oral instruction."[5] In a very different intellectual environment, a contemporary of Mendelssohn's, Rabbi Chaim of Volozin, one of the great Lithuanian rabbis of the eighteenth century, expresses the same idea in different terms. Likening rabbinic commentary to "hot embers," Rabbi Chaim writes that "the embers light up when one blows upon them; the intensity of the flame that thus comes to life depends on the length of breath of the person who interprets."[6]

The view that Judaism adheres to the dead letter is often accompanied by the assumption that Jews believe that by adhering to the dead letter of the law they are saved (or justified). Let us recall Luther's statement that "Paul sets here the spirit against the flesh. . . . Flesh . . . is here taken for the very righteousness and wisdom of the flesh, and the judgment of reason, which seeks to be justified by the law." However, Jews do not believe that the law justifies them. Rather, from a Jewish theological perspective, God's grace precedes law. It is in fact as a result of God's grace that the Jewish people received the law.

Recent historical scholarship on Paul helps us to appreciate another way in which Judaism and Calvinism both differ from the accepted reading of Luther's view of justification. In his now well-known article of 1961, "The Apostle Paul and the Introspective Conscience of the West," the former dean of Harvard Divinity School and the former bishop of Stockholm, Krister Stendahl, rejects the common view that the Apostle Paul opposed the law. Stendahl sees the responsibility for misunderstandings of Paul's view of the law as lying "with the great hero of what has been called 'Pauline Christianity,' i.e., with Martin Luther." Luther, Stendahl argues, anachronistically privileged the introspective conscience of the individual over and against the question of membership in God's covenant. According to Stendahl, "we look in vain for a statement in which Paul would speak about himself as an actual sinner." Stendahl reformulates Luther's conception of justification—"In Romans the principle of justification by faith is a principle of mission."[7] This means, in the words of the Anglican bishop, N. T. Wright, that "'justification' is not about 'how I get saved' but 'how I am declared to be a member of God's people.'"[8] A grace/law dichotomy makes sense neither for Jewish theology nor for Calvinist theology. Grace and law, or better, grace and practice, are inextricably linked, which means that justification is fundamentally social and not individual.

This brings us to another affinity between Judaism and Calvinism: neither is a religion, at least not in the sense that the father of liberal Protestant theology, Friederich Schleiermacher, understands religion. Schleiermacher, who was, of course, a Lutheran, holds that "religion maintains its own sphere and its own character only by completely removing itself from the sphere and character of speculation as well as from that of praxis."[9] Samson Raphael Hirsch, the nineteenth-century founder of what today is called modern Orthodoxy, explicitly rejects this account of religion for Judaism:

> Judaism is not a religion, the synagogue is not a church, and the Rabbi is not a priest. Judaism is not a mere adjunct to life: it comprises all of life. To be a Jew is not a mere part, it is the sum total of our task in life.

To be a Jew in the synagogue and the kitchen, in the field and the warehouse, in the office and the pulpit, as father and mother, as servant and master, as man and as citizen, with one's thought, in word and in deed, in enjoyment and privation, with the needle and the graving-tool, with the pen and the chisel—that is what it means to be a Jew. An entire life supported by the Divine idea and lived and brought to fulfillment according to divine will.[10]

Kuyper emphasizes this very same point with respect to Calvinism. He writes that the Calvinist

does not hold to religion, with its dogmatics, as a separate entity, and then place his moral life with its ethics as a second entity alongside of religion, but he holds to religion as placing him in the presence of God Himself, Who thereby imbues him with His divine will. Love and adoration are, to Calvin, themselves the motives of every spiritual activity, and thus the fear of God is imparted to the whole of life as a reality—into the family, and into society, into science and art, into personal life, and into the political career. A redeemed man who in all things and in all the choice of life is controlled solely by the most searching and heart-stirring reverence for a God who is ever present to his consciousness.[11]

Part and parcel of Kuyper's rejection of a Schleiermachian definition of religion is his insistence on what he calls "the organic bond between generations." This bond, Kuyper maintains, must be understood in terms of the church's covenantal relationship with God. Kuyper writes:

It is perfectly true that the church is the "gathering of believers" and that however broadly this term is applied, it has no room for unbelievers or non-believers. But the confession of the Covenant, which in turn is bound up with the organic bond between generations, gives rise to tangible difficulty here. If one adopts a Pelagian posture, holds exclusively to the existence of individual persons, and posits that only those who personally profess Christ as their Savior belong in the church, one indeed has the means of determining who does and who does not belong to the church—but one also comes into immediate conflict with the Covenant, with the bond between generations, and hence with the practice of child baptism. If, on the other hand, one is convinced on the basis of Scripture (1) that the covenant idea may not be abandoned, (2) that the bond between believers and their offspring is a holy organic connection which must be strictly honored and (3) that, consequently, a church which holds exclusively to adult baptism proceeds from a false principle, this individualistic position simply proves untenable. The same path also loses the Scriptural teaching that the church has significance for the world, for the development of human life, for civil society and its natural life potential.[12]

It is on the issues of the organic bond between the generations and covenant that we find the closest overlap between Calvinism and Judaism. Covenant and the organic relation between the generations are perhaps *the* defining features of the Jewish tradition. For example, we read in Deuteronomy 29:14–15: "Not with you alone who are standing here today in the presence of the Lord our God, am I making this covenant with its oath, but also with those who are not here today." Or, as the American Jewish theologian Michael Wyschogrod has put it:

The Jewish family is . . . the space in which the future membership of Knesses Israel [the congregation of Israel] is prepared. For Judaism, these future generations are not merely abstractions. In a capital case, according to the Mishnah, witnesses who are to testify against the defendant are warned that if they are not telling the truth, the blood of the accused and that of his potential descendants who will not be born because of the death of the accused will be on the witnesses' head. To cut off a Jew is to cut off a line and thereby to become guilty of the murder of future generations. That is how real unborn Jews are to Jewish consciousness.[13]

For Jews, the covenant between God and the people of Israel and the subsequent organic bond between generations stem from God's absolute sovereignty: "All is given from the one shepherd" (Ecclesiastes 12:11). God may make a covenant with whomever God chooses. So too, as wholly sovereign, God has no obligation to make a covenant with anyone. This means that God's covenant with the people of Israel can only be a gracious act on God's part: "The LORD did not set his love upon you, nor choose you, because you were more in number than any people; for you were the fewest of all people: *But because the LORD loved you,* and because he would keep the oath which he had sworn unto your fathers, hath the LORD brought you out with a mighty hand, and redeemed you out of the house of bondmen, from the hand of Pharaoh king of Egypt" (Deuteronomy 7:7–8).[14]

A belief in God's absolute sovereignty also forms the theological basis of Calvinism. Only a wholly sovereign God could choose to create a covenant with his chosen elect. Election, by definition, comes from God. The acceptance of God's covenant is then a choiceless choice or what Calvin calls "irresistible grace." Yet it is from this choiceless choice that true freedom will arise. In the Jewish tradition this dynamic is captured in the Israelites' response to Moses after he reads the book of the covenant: *na'aseh v'nishma,* "we will do and (then) we will hear" (Exodus 24:7). Similarly, for Calvin, true freedom arrives only by way of God's predestinational choice.

For both Judaism and Calvinism, the covenantal relation is political in two basic senses. First, God's covenant concerns a special, and indeed exclusive, relationship between God and God's elect. This special, everlasting relationship is expressed in Exodus 19:6: "You shall be for me a treasured people, a nation of kingly priests." Second, covenant, for both traditions, forms the basis of all political association. In the Hebrew Bible we find this secondary sense of covenant described in 1 Chronicles 11:3: "All of the elders of Israel came to the king at Hebron, and David made a covenant with them in Hebron before the Lord."

Calvin's and subsequently Kuyper's engagement with the political implications of covenant are well known, and the relation between Calvinism and modern politics is of course a topic of continuing interest. In the context of our consideration of parallels between Calvinism and Judaism, the seventeenth-century Calvinist thinker Johannes Althusius (1557–1638) is particularly significant. Althusius, in the words of one recent commentator, sought to show how

each new layer of political sovereignty is formed by covenants sworn before God by representatives of smaller units, and these covenants eventually become the written constitutions of the polity. . . . These constitutions define and divide the executive, legislative, and judicial offices within that polity, and govern the relations of its rulers and subjects, clerics and magistrates, associations and individuals. They determine the relations between and among nations, provinces, and cities, and between and among private and public associations—all of which Althusiaus called a form of "federalism" (from *foedus*, the Latin term for covenant).[15]

Historically speaking, Althusius's federalism is consistent with the basic framework of organized Jewish life in the medieval and early modern periods. Jewish communities were semiautonomous corporations that existed along with other corporate bodies loosely held together by the state.

More important, perhaps, Althusius's thought bears a deep affinity with normative Jewish political thought. The rabbis interpreted 1 Samuel 8 as delineating the proper conditions, powers, and limitations of kingship in relation to God's law. Medieval commentators developed this view further, asking and arguing about whether a king administers divine law, what kind of discretionary power a king might or might not have, whether a king is beholden to Noahide law, and, most basically, what the ultimate relation is between a king's law and the Torah's laws. Different medieval Jewish philosophers gave different answers to these questions, but they all agreed that the king's laws and the Torah's laws are of a piece with one another. That means, however, that the relationship is configured between the king's laws and the Torah's laws: both have political, moral, and theological status. Once again, this is because, for Jewish thought as a whole, God is the creator of all of creation, which encompasses the most mundane and the most exalted aspects of human life and experience. But human beings are also God's partners in creation. The relation between God and human beings mediates all law, divine as much as human. From a political perspective, neither a king's laws nor the Torah's laws are wholly sovereign. Instead, their sovereignties overlap and their relation must continually be negotiated. Alan Mittleman, following the lead of the late Israeli scholar Daniel Elazar (1934–1999), concisely summarizes the basic structure and vision of Jewish political thought:

Covenant is the essential, ongoing structural element of Jewish political existence. Indeed, covenant is the constitutive mode of Israel's being. Israel's covenant with God creates and recreates forms of political organization, all of which are federative (that is, covenantal) in nature. In federative forms of organization, power is diffused across competing

institutional centers. Since ultimate power is God's alone, human institutions are deabsolutized and conditional. Descriptively, federative or
covenantal organization is the typical form of Jewish polity. Normatively,
it is the optimal form of Jewish political order.[16]

Kuyper's delineation of what he calls "sphere sovereignty" has important affinities with the view of Jewish political thought that I have
just outlined. In Kuyper's words, "original, absolute sovereignty cannot
reside in any creature but must coincide with God's majesty." Yet "our
human life, with its visible material foreground and invisible spiritual
background, is neither simple nor uniform but constitutes an infinitely
complex organism. . . . Call the parts of this one great machine 'cog-
wheels,' spring-driven on their own axles, or 'spheres,' each animated
with its own spirit."

Let us sum up the important parallels between Calvinism and Judaism that we have discussed. First, as opposed to views informed by
readings of Luther, neither Calvinism nor Judaism affirms a dichotomy
between love and law (or between spirit and flesh). Second, both traditions understand justification not in terms of individual salvation but
rather in terms of membership in God's covenant. Third, neither tradition understands itself as a religion based upon individual belief. Instead,
both traditions emphasize what Kuyper calls the organic bond between
the generations. Fourth, a shared belief in God's absolute sovereignty
undergirds Judaism and Calvinism's respective conceptions of covenant.
Fifth, God's absolute sovereignty goes hand in hand with the doctrine
of election. Only a wholly sovereign God may choose his elect. Six, for
both Judaism and Calvinism the special covenant between God and
God's elect forms the basis not just for the relationships within the community of the elect but also for all human relations. And seventh, that
God is absolutely sovereign means that no human or human realm is
sovereign. This gives rise to overlapping spheres of sovereignties in
human life.

Let us turn now to consider Kupyer's "A Common Grace" and the
Jewish tradition's affirmation of what Rabbi Jonathan Sacks calls "The
Dignity of Difference."

A COMMON GRACE AND THE DIGNITY OF DIFFERENCE

Given the striking parallels between Judaism and Calvinism, it should not be surprising that Kuyper's "a common grace" and what Rabbi Sacks calls "the dignity of difference" bear important similarities to each other. After all, "a common grace" and "the dignity of difference" are both answers to the same question. This is a question that has always been put to the Jewish tradition and, because of its doctrine of election, Calvinism must answer the question as well: how can election be reconciled with universalism? How exactly does God's promise to Abraham—"I will make of you a great nation, and I will bless you, and make your name great, and you will be a blessing" (Genesis 12:2)—work?

Calvinism and Judaism answer this question in a similar way. For both traditions, God's special covenant with God's elect reveals not only God's sovereignty as elector but also God's sovereignty over all creation. God's revelation (for Calvinism, the death and resurrection of Jesus Christ and for Judaism God's giving the Jewish people the Torah at Sinai) cannot be understood apart from God's having created the world for all humanity. Franz Rosenzweig eloquently captures this dynamic when he writes:

> The past creation is demonstrated from out (of) the living, present revelation—demonstrated, that is, pointed out. In the glow of the experienced miracle of revelation, a past that prepares and foresees this miracle becomes visable. The creation which becomes visible in revelation is creation of the revelation. At this point the experiential and presentive character is immovably fixed, and only here can revelation receive a past. But it really must do so. God does not answer the soul's acknowledgment, its "I am thine," with an equally simple "Thou art mine." Rather he reaches back into the past and identifies himself as the one who originated and indicated this whole dialogue between himself and the soul: "I have called thee by name: thou art mine."[17]

For Kuyper, Calvinism expresses this same dynamic: "Christ . . . is connected with nature because he is the Creator, and at the same time connected to grace because, as Re-creator, he manifested the riches of grace in the midst of that nature."[18]

God the creator of all life lies at the heart of "a common grace" and "the dignity of difference." In terms of their respective understandings of God, Calvinism and Judaism are not so different. For both traditions, God is wholly sovereign and God's creation of the world is an act of divine grace. Let me stress that this is as much a Jewish view as it is a Calvinist one. Maimonides explains this well: "If we give a thing to someone to whom we are not obliged to give it, that action is called in our language grace or favor (*chaninah*). . . . God brings into existence and provides for, those towards whom He has no obligation to do so; for this reason He is called Gracious."[19]

As I emphasized at the beginning, Judaism, like Calvinism, affirms both love and law. Judaism's God is a compassionate and loving God who loves human beings even when they are not deserving of love. Despite caricatures that depict the Jewish God as a vengeful God and the Christian God as a God of mercy, the Jewish God is a compassionate God who shows mercy to his people. Claims that the Jewish tradition, and the so-called Old Testament, conceives of God as vengeful often refer to Exodus 20:6, which comes in the midst of the Ten Commandments: "He [God] does not remit all punishment, but visits the iniquity of parents upon children and children's children, upon the third and fourth generations." This verse does indeed describe from a biblical point of view what kind of God the Israelites' God is. But to conclude, based on this verse, that the Jewish God is a God of vengeance is wrong, for a number of reasons, the most simple of which is that the verse immediately prior to this one describes God in very different terms: "The Lord! The Lord! A God compassionate and gracious, slow to anger, abounding in kindness and faithfulness, extending kindness to the thousandth generation, forgiving iniquity, transgression, and sin." The description of a compassionate, gracious God, who is slow to anger, is found not only in the New Testament but also right in the "old" one. Commenting on these verses, the rabbis maintained that God's compassion was far greater than God's retribution: "The attribute of [God's] goodness exceeds that of retribution five hundred times. In the case of the attribute of retribution Scripture declares 'visiting the iniquity of the fathers upon the children . . .'; in the case of the attribute of good it is stated 'and showing mercy unto the thousandth generation.' It is thus seen that the attribute of good exceeds that of retribution."

Where Judaism and Calvinism part is not in their respective conceptions of God. Rather, they part in their respective conceptions of the human being. Kupyer's notion of common grace and its relation to creation are revealing here. Kuyper writes: "What we call nature is everything that has its origin and law in the original creation. Though all this suffered under the curse which began to work after the fall, common grace averted the lethal consequences of the curse and made possible and certain the continued, be it afflicted, existence all that came from the original creation."[20] Common grace, for Kuyper, comes in only after the fall. Without common grace, "the elect would not have been born, would not have seen the light of day. . . . On that basis alone all special grace assumes common grace. But there is more. Even if you assumed that their temporal death had been postponed so that the human race could have made a start, but that for the rest sin in all its horror had broken out unhindered, you would still be nowhere."[21]

Modern Jewish thinkers often claim that Judaism does not have a notion of sin. But this is a misconception. We need but recall Genesis 6:5 where we read about God's view of humanity before the flood: "And the LORD saw how great was man's wickedness on earth, and how every plan devised by his mind was nothing but evil all the time," and God's comment after the flood that "the devisings of man's mind are evil from his youth" (8:21). The Jewish tradition for the most part sees the human being as at the very least *tending toward* sin. However, sin, for much of the Jewish tradition, is understood as a deviation from God that results from human freedom to do so. Sin marks not human fallenness but the possibility (though not ease) of following God's law if one chooses to do so. As David Novak has noted, "the introduction of the term 'sin' (*het*) comes [only] after God's rejection of Cain and his offering in favor of Abel and his offering. . . . It is plausible to conclude from the scriptural text itself that Cain has done something wrong since God then tells him, 'Is it not so that if you do well, you will be uplifted, but if you do not do well sin (*hat'at*) crouches at the door, and unto you is its desire, but you shall master it" (Genesis 4:7). . . . The . . . point that emerges [here] is that Cain is responsible for his own actions. It is a matter of free choice, never one of inevitable fate."[22]

Rabbi Israel Salanter, the founder of the nineteenth-century Mussar (meaning chastisement) movement, was one modern Jewish thinker who, in keeping with earlier pietistic Jewish traditions, emphasized human sinfulness. However, Salanter, also in keeping with earlier Jewish traditions, emphasized equally that the human being, by following God's will, can change his nature. As Salanter put it: "Do not say that what God has made cannot be altered, and that because He, may He be blessed, has planted within me an evil force I cannot hope to uproot it. This is not so, for the powers of a human being may be subdued, and even transformed. Just as we see regarding [the nature of] animals, that man is able to tame them and bend their will to his will . . . and also to domesticate them . . . so has man the power to subdue his own evil nature . . . and to change . . . toward the good through exercise and practice."[23]

Let us return to love and law. For the Jewish tradition, God is a loving God and creation is an act of grace. God graciously offers a blessing and covenant to Noah after the flood, telling him, "And I will remember my covenant, which is between me and you and every living creature of all flesh" (Genesis 9:15). The special covenant between God and the people of Israel presupposes the covenant with Noah. If we translate the terms *common grace* and *special grace* to the Jewish tradition, God's covenant with Noah would represent the former and God's covenant with the people of Israel would represent the latter. In both cases, God's graciousness lies in the laws that God gives to people to instruct them on how they ought to live. Love and law are not antithetical here; God's love manifests itself in the gift of law.

For the Jewish tradition, the relationship between God and human beings is proclaimed by following God's laws. Let us recall God's description of Abraham in Genesis 18:19: "For I know him intimately and this is to lead to his commanding his children and his household after him, that they might keep the way of the Lord to practice righteousness and justice (*tsedaqah u-mishpat*)." For the Jewish tradition, it is difficult for us to walk in God's path, but we can choose to do so and we can succeed. We will, however, never be perfect, for this is what it means to be human. Put another way, the Jewish tradition suggests neither that human beings can overcome the limitations of their humanity nor that they should try to. This sentiment is captured well in the Jewish ethical treatise *Sayings of the Fathers*: "It is not for you to finish the work, but neither are you free to desist from it."

Kuyper's conception of a common grace suggests a different view of human nature. Once again, in Kuyper's words, "common grace averted the lethal consequences of the curse and made possible and certain the continued, be it afflicted, existence of all that came from the original creation." Before special grace, common grace transforms nature and, indeed, human nature. Kuyper's claim is that if common grace had not transformed our natures then there would be no goodness in the world whatsoever.

The implications of Kuyper's conception of common grace as transforming nature play out in his views of love. For Kuyper, to love is to love as God does—unconditionally and without concern for ourselves. Human love is at best a deformed, lower form of love. Kuyper gives an example of this lower form of love, which, he writes, "can be seen in girls of inferior moral development, who, when they become mothers, fall almost desperately in love with their babes; while in others, who stand much higher morally, maternal love is much more moderate."[24]

Judaism and Calvinism would seem to agree that a mother's love for her baby is a natural form of love. Where they would differ is on their evaluation of such love. For the Jewish tradition, we are all too human, for better and for worse. Judaism emphasizes that, in the well-known rabbinic dictum, "the Torah speaks in the language of men." God's special love of the people of Israel is a model for human love, not because God loves desperately as humans do but because we humans love desperately. Most fundamentally, the Jewish tradition suggests neither that human beings can overcome the limitations of their humanity nor that they should try to. By contrast, Kuyper suggests that grace allows human beings to be Godlike—when they love unconditionally and without concern for themselves, as we read in Matthew 5:48: "Be perfect, therefore, as your heavenly Father is perfect."

I HAVE ARGUED IN THIS CHAPTER that there are many striking parallels between Judaism and Calvinism. Both are traditions that value love and law and both are traditions based on a belief in God's absolute sovereignty. Where Judaism and Calvinism differ, I have argued, is not in terms of their accounts of the divine but rather in their accounts of the human. By way of conclusion, I will suggest one implication of this argument, which is an argument concerning love, for thinking about Kuyper's "A Common Grace."

As I have argued, "A Common Grace" is an answer to a question that has always been put to the Jewish tradition: how can election be reconciled with universalism? This question, though, is also a question about human difference. How can Calvinism (or Judaism) live in a world in which everyone is not a Calvinist (or Jewish)? The Jewish tradition, I believe, has an answer to this question that is rooted in its affirmation of our human nature. The answer is that all human beings love what is theirs. Just as mothers desperately love their own children, peoples desperately love their own. These loves are indeed perverted when we are unable to see them as rooted in God's gracious act of creation. But when we do properly understand our all too human loves as part of the majesty of God's creation, we can respect, though not always agree with, the loves of others not in spite of *but because of* our own particular loves. Put another way, I can understand why another mother desperately loves her baby because I desperately love mine. Rabbi Sacks describes this far more eloquently when he writes:

> Covenant tells me that my faith is a form of relationship with God—and that one relationship does not exclude others.... Nowhere is this more magnificently set out than in the vision of Isaiah in which the prophet sees a time in which the two great historical enemies of Israel's past— Egypt and Assyria—will one day become God's chosen alongside Israel itself:... "In that day Israel will be the third, along with Egypt and Assyria, a blessing on earth. The Lord Almighty will bless them, saying 'Blessed be Egypt my people, Assyria my handiwork, and Israel my inheritance.'"[25]

NOTES

An earlier version of this chapter was published in the *Kuyper Center Review* 2 (2011), 157–172.

1. Martin Luther, *Preface to Romans*, trans. J. Theodore Mueller (Grand Rapids, MI: Kregel Classics, 2003), xiv.

2. Martin Luther, *Commentary on Galatians*, ed. J. I. Packer and Edwin Sandys (Wheaton, IL: Crossway, 1998), 104.

3. John Calvin, *Sermons on Galatians*, trans. Arthur Golding (Audabon, NJ: Old Paths, 1995), 443.

4. Abraham Kuyper, *Lectures on Calvinism* (Mulberry, IN: Sovereign Grace, 2001), 44.

5. Moses Mendelssohn, *Jerusalem*, trans. Allan Arkush (Hanover, NH: University of New England Press, 1983), 102–3.

6. As quoted in Emmanuel Levinas, *Nine Talmudic Readings*, trans. Annette Aronowicz (Bloomington: Indiana University Press, 1994), xvii.

7. Krister Stendahl, "The Apostle Paul and the Introspective Conscience of the West," *Harvard Theological Review* 56, no. 3 (July 1963): 199–215, and *Final Account: Paul's Letter to the Romans* (Minneapolis: Fortress, 1993), 14.

8. N. T. Wright, *Paul in Fresh Perspective* (Minneapolis: Fortress, 2009): 122.

9. Friederich Schleiermacher, *On Religion* (New York: Cambridge University Press, 1996), 23.

10. Samson Raphael Hirsch, "Religion Allied to Progress," in *Judaism Eternal*, 2 vols., ed. I. Grunfeld (London: Socino, 1956), 2:243.

11. Kuyper, *Lectures on Calvinism*, 72.

12. Ibid., 191.

13. Michael Wyschogrod, *The Body of Faith* (Lanham: Jason Aronson, 1983), 253–54.

14. It is worth emphasizing here that these verses in Deuteronomy follow Deuteronomy 6, the basis of the Jewish creed Shema Yisrael, discussed earlier in the chapter.

15. John Witte, *The Reformation of Rights: Law, Religion and Human Rights in Early Modern Calvinism* (New York: Cambridge University Press, 2008), 10.

16. Alan Mittleman, *The Jewish Political Tradition and the Founding of Agudat Israel* (New York: State University of New York Press, 1996), 37.

17. Franz Rosenzweig, *The Star of Redemption*, trans. William W. Hallo (New York: University of Notre Dame Press, 1985), 182–83.

18. Abraham Kuyper, *A Centennial Reader* (Grand Rapids, MI: Eerdmans, 1998), 173.

19. Moses Maimonides, *Guide of the Perplexed*, ed. and trans. Shlomo Pines, intro. Leo Strauss (Chicago: University of Chicago Press, 1963), 1:54.

20. Kuyper, *A Centennial Reader*, 174.

21. Ibid.

22. David Novak, *Natural Law in Judaism* (New York: Cambridge University Press, 1998), 32.

23. As cited and translated in Immanuel Etkes, *Rabbi Israel Salanter and the Mussar Movement*, trans. Jonathan Chipman (Philadelphia: Jewish Publication Society, 1993), 289–90.

24. Abraham Kuyper, *The Work of the Holy Spirit* (New York: Funk and Wagnalls, 1900), 510.

25. Isaiah 19:24–25. Jonathan Sacks, *The Dignity of Difference: How to Avoid the Clash of Civilizations*, 2d ed. (London: Bloomsbury Academic, 2003), 203.

6

"A MOTHER TO ALL"

Love and the Institution of Community in Augustine

Nils F. Schott

And since the same medicine is not to be applied to all, although to all the same love is due, so also love itself is in travail with some, becomes weak with others; is at pains to edify some, dreads to be cause of offense to others; stoops to some, before others stands with head erect; is gentle to some, and stern to others; and enemy to none, a mother to all.

—Augustinus Aurelius, Bishop of Hippo, *The First Catechetical Instruction* XV.23:50

AUGUSTINUS AURELIUS, BISHOP OF HIPPO, develops a theory and a practice of love that combines a classificatory account of types of love, its interaction with fear, the consequences of its presence and absence, with a deeply felt acknowledgment of its fundamental ungraspability. Love, for Augustine, is independent of the individual soul, but in an important sense it is also channeled, so to speak, even produced by the soul. The soul receives and returns love or is at least capable of doing so. Central to this account is that love unfolds in a community. Accordingly, Augustine's *De catechizandis rudibus* reflects his involvement in everyday pastoral care and yet betrays the theologian's systematic impulse. It is an occasional work, written in response to a request by a deacon named Deogratias, who, despite his reputation as a well-learned and skilled teacher, worries that his ignorance of the mechanics of instruction may be the cause of boredom on the part of his audience and of dissatisfaction on his part. In response, Augustine sets out, first, to outline the precepts of a "full and perfect" delivery,[1] based largely on the idea that the oration has to be adapted to its audience or, more generally, to each particular situation; second, to make suggestions for the catechist's self-motivation; and, finally, to provide two exemplary catecheses. These goals are separable only in theory; they are unified by love in its many variations. The following discussion seeks to disentangle the strands of

Augustine's argument and, at the same time, to reconstruct their unity under the headings of a psychological economy of love and fear; the withdrawal of narrative in favor of its meaning, love; and the employment of questions for the confirmation of a shared understanding at the basis of a community.

THE PROBLEMATIC LOVE OF GOD

Life eternal, the immensity of God's love—these are incommunicable in everyday speech. Deogratias's failure is part and parcel of his effort at complete communication; his dissatisfaction may be understandable, yet it is inevitable. That is his problem, but it is also why, according to Augustine, he is to understand his frustration as relative to an impossible effort. The benefit others derive from his instruction outweighs his own apprehensions and is to spur him on. Aware of both the usefulness of his endeavor and of the limits imposed on all humans, following a set of rules will lead the catechist to a "full and perfect" delivery, provided God grants an understanding of the requisite "cheerful giving" and "furnishes" us with the right ideas.[2] Deogratias's task, therefore, is to make the best of his situation. Within the confines of a particular place, a particular allotment of time, a particular audience, the instantaneous idea of the eternal (of God), according to Augustine, can be conveyed appropriately, such that it can be built upon, if the catechist is able to pitch his injunctions and exhortations at the correct level and to convey the joy of preaching the truth.

Of the elements of the presentation, the choice of content is of particular importance, for the catechist's *narratio* has to relate nothing short of the truth. Such a choice as to what counts as truth has to be a double one, qualitative as well as quantitative—what to talk about and how much to say about it. Yet in Augustine's conception of narration, the term *narratio* does not refer exclusively to content but becomes the name of a methodology as well. Narrative does not merely unfold the general truths contained in exemplary events; it is the precondition for the success of the didactic effort. A coherent narrative keeps exemplary facts clear and distinct and, by providing a context, renders them comprehensible. Narrative, in operating a choice and limiting the extent of the delivery, makes it possible for the listener to focus his attention on what is most important and does not unduly tax his memory.[3] This view of teaching as a psychological and narrative economy is reinforced by the two roles Augustine assigns to Scripture: as a preparation for the coming of the Messiah, on the one hand, and as an example for us after his coming, on the other; this intervention of Christ we may understand as the coming or intervention of love. Accordingly, Augustine, in reference to 1 Timothy 1, defines the overall goal of catechesis as sincere charity or love. This goal is set for the speaker and the listener, both of whom face a twofold obstacle. On the one hand, we must be granted God's love to be capable of love; the fulfillment of the commandment of love is not entirely up to us. On the other, love as the New Law is the fulfillment of the Old. This raises the question of what role Scripture and traditions may have left to play. Since God took human form, addressed us and redeemed us, why would we need anything else? Augustine holds that Scripture is given to us as a guide to fulfilling the demands articulated by Jesus and as admonitions for our failure to live up to them. In this they are expressions of the same love that is manifest in God's giving his only son for our sins.[4] The authority of Scripture and the church, the "body of Christ," therefore step in to reveal—catechistically—the transformative power of love. Beyond the argument that we need the law in order to become aware of our sinful state and that, therefore, the law "is made not for the righteous" but precisely for those who are not righteous, Augustine insists on the doctrinal and hierarchical elements of the first letter to Timothy attributed to Paul. There the rejection of myths is intimately tied to a soundness of doctrine personified by the apostle-author figure, who is said to have written

> I urge you, as I did when I was on my way to Macedonia, to remain in Ephesus so that you may instruct certain people not to teach any different doctrine, and not to occupy themselves with myths and endless genealogies that promote speculations rather than the divine training that is known by faith. But the aim of such instruction is love that comes from a pure heart, a good conscience, and sincere faith. Some people have deviated from these and turned to meaningless talk, desiring to be teachers of the law, without understanding either what they are saying or the things about which they make assertions.[5]

Out of love, the church, in the succession of Christ and the apostles, enforces doctrine so as to preclude the nefarious consequences of misguided narratives. In promoting ignorance under the guise of knowledge, "myths and endless genealogies" separate us from God. As disciples of a God who humbled himself by becoming human, we must counter the haughty pride of false knowledge with trust in God. And this, in a second step, is to lead to obedience to the guardians of God's legacy, obedience to the Catholic Church. If indeed all of Scripture is a preparation for the coming of Christ, then the successors of Christ alone have the authority to determine how it is to serve in the preparation of the individual's encounter with Christ in the catechumen's integration into the church as body of Christ. Augustine—the catechist—intervenes in this process of integration with a reading of the Old Testament as a "veiling" of the New, and of the New Testament as an "unveiling" (*revelatio*) of the Old. This reading, taken directly from Paul,[6] allows him to juxtapose uncharitable love of self to generous giving. While the new law of love is superior to the older law, the latter is still needed to overcome the self-righteousness exhibited by those with a pharisaical conception of knowledge and the law. Only if the New Law, the double commandment of love toward God and toward one's neighbor, is shown to be the true content of the Old Law can the pride of those who, to fulfill the law, rely on their own ability and not on God's mercy be shown to be insufficient and to constitute an obstacle to their actually living up to the law.[7] "In the Old Testament, the New is concealed, and in the New the Old is revealed. In keeping with that concealment, carnal men, understanding only carnally, both then were and now are, made subject to the fear of punishment. But in keeping with this revelation spiritual men, understanding spiritually . . . are made free by the bestowal of love."[8]

While it remains true that Jesus came to show how much God loves us, this only underscores the fact that God's love is a gift, not an acquisition on our part. The constant threat to our spiritual life that consists in trusting our (supposed) knowledge or in doubting revealed doctrine is to be countered both by a fear of God and, in the tradition of Jesus and the apostles, by the humility of his servants. Drawing on his experience with those who consider converting to Christianity on the basis that it may procure them some kind of advantage, who hope for social or political influence, for example, or think that, for a chance at eternal life, a conversion can't hurt, Augustine stresses that the precondition for becoming a Christian is fear of God, for an absence of fear indicates indifference toward, if not pride and disdain for, the gift that is God's love. The believer fears God, but because he is loved by God he can love God and is worthy of doing so.

Most of the time, however, we love only ourselves. We would simply like to enjoy the advantages of being true Christians (eternal life, for example), and that kind of indulgent self-love and insincerity are punished. This punishment is then to induce in us a salutary fear of God. Faith, for Augustine, is trust in God's love, yet as long as we do not fear God but consider ourselves self-sufficient we have no desire for this love and feel no need to entrust ourselves to it. It is therefore the task of the catechist to instill this desire. This is not to be done by taking the position of a superior who points out failures in the purely exterior observance of the law; such was the position of the Pharisees. Instead, those who teach are to follow Jesus's example: the humility of those who follow the law and still consider themselves in need of God's mercy will do more to incite faith than will the merely external threat of sanctions.[9] The humility of God is the remedy for the pride of man. Love as God loves you and you will instill love is the suggestion to the instructor.[10]

Vivid examples of "that very severity of God, by which the hearts of mortals are agitated with a most wholesome terror" may serve as external incitements to an inner conversion, the point at which the fear of being unworthy of God's love turns into the acceptance of this love. Their didactic interest lies in that they help the catechist discern whether the desire for God's love expressed in the wish to convert to Christianity is genuine. For, if it is, then it is the duty of the Christian, following the double commandment of love, to help his neighbor love and honor God:

> For faith consists not in a body bending but in a mind believing. But undoubtedly the mercy of God is often present through the ministry of the catechist, so that a man impressed by the discourse now wishes to become in reality what he had decided to feign. And when he does begin to desire this let us assume that now at least he has come in earnest. True, it is hidden from us when it is that one whom we now see present in the body does really come in spirit; nevertheless, we should deal with him in such manner that he may conceive this desire even though it does not as yet exist. For none of our labor is wasted, since if the desire is there, it is in any case strengthened by such dealing on our

part, although we may be ignorant of the time or of the hour at which it began.[11]

Faith is not a matter of the outside, of the body observing, in words and actions, some external law. It is a matter of the soul. Yet the desire for God's love, at least, can be instilled. As long as there is the slightest effort discernible on the part of the catechumen, the catechist's task is to find out as much as possible about him in order to tailor his catechistic effort to him, in order to fulfill the commandment of love by adapting the narration. And indeed Augustine's exhortation to Deogratias insists on the centrality of love as the precondition and end, as the sum of Christian virtue: "With this love, then, set before you as an end to which you may refer all that you say, so give all your instructions that he to whom you speak by hearing may believe, and by believing may hope, and by hoping may love."[12]

On the basis of this extraordinarily clear connection between narrating, believing, hoping, and loving,[13] Augustine proceeds to give specific advice to Deogratias, advice that is carefully attuned to the particularity of each catechetical situation. He lays out a general sequence: discerning the interlocutor's motivation, followed by insisting on the goodness of the world at creation, retelling the history of salvation, instilling horror at the penalties for impiety, proclaiming the joys of the rewards reserved for the righteous, and urging the catechumenate to follow the example of righteous men. And, although he also provides an exemplary catechesis, he insists time and again on two central points. First, any catechetical effort must be tailored to the particular audience to be instructed; hence his detailed discussions of particular groups and possible objections they may raise. The second point Augustine stresses follows directly from the theological reflections we have discussed so far: it is love. It figures in Augustine's discourse in a variety of guises—*caritas*, *spes*, *fides* as trust in God, *hilaritas* as gift from God, etc.[14]—yet the fundamental point to be made remains the same in all instances: in the absence of love all rules are futile, and neither salvation after death nor community in this life is possible.

LOVE AND FEAR

This section rehearses Augustine's arguments in light of these two points: the importance of adaptation and the overruling importance of love. Let me begin with Augustine's conception of the relation of love and fear.

Both the most reliable marker of the right disposition toward God and the most effective means for inducing such a disposition in the catechumen, fear is intricately tied to love. Indeed, fear intervenes in an economy of love—an economy that is eventually destabilized by the greatness of God's love. How does such an economy work?

> For there is nothing that invites love more than to be beforehand in loving: and that heart [*animus*] is overhard which, even though it were unwilling to bestow love, would be unwilling to return it. But if we see that even in the case of sinful and base attachments those who desire to be loved in return make it their one concern to disclose and display by all the tokens in their power how much they love; if they also strive to counterfeit genuine affection in order that they may, in some measure, claim a return of love from the heart which they are designing to ensnare; if, again, their own passions are the more inflamed when they perceive that the hearts which they are eager to win are also moved now by the same fire; if then, I say, both the hitherto callous heart is aroused when it is sensible of being loved, and the heart which was already aflame is the more inflamed the moment it learns that it is loved in return, it is obvious that there is no greater reason either for the birth or growth of love than when one, who as yet does not love, perceives that he is loved, or when he loves already hopes either that he may yet be loved in return, or actually has proof that he is loved. And if this holds good even in the case of base passions, how much more so in friendship? For what else do we have to be on our guard against in an offense against friendship than that our friend should think either that we do not love him, or that we love him less than he loves us? And if he believes this, he will be cooler in that love which men enjoy by the exchange of intimacy; and if he is not so weak that this offense causes him to grow cold in his affection altogether, he yet restricts himself to that form of affection which has as its object not enjoyment but utility.[15]

The complexity of the problem Augustine addresses is apparent in the strains put on the translation: "love" must translate not only *amor* but *dilectio* as well (and, just a few sentences earlier, *caritas*); these are related both to *amicitia*—friendship—and to *familiaritas*—intimacy; and complicated relationships of agency, described by verbs such as *impendere, rependere, adficere, movere, appetere, excitare,* and *accendere*—expend or impend, compensate, affect, move, long for, arouse, and inflame—in both their active and passive meanings hint at the complexity of the human soul as Augustine sees it.[16] Love, in an important sense, is independent of the soul, but in an equally important sense it is channeled, so to speak, even produced by the soul, which receives and returns love or is at least capable of doing so. Every soul, Augustine holds, even the basest, craves love and will go to any length of effort, even deception, to attain it. Such desire—and this is crucial to Augustine's conception—is amplified by the mere perception of love (the verb used is *sentire*), be it in others or in oneself. This is true whether one is loved yet or not, even true whether one loves or not.[17] There is always a yearning for more, and love will breed love—more than that: *hoping* for love will breed love, for how can we truly hate someone we truly want to love us? If, Augustine asks, this is true for shameful kinds of attachments (*in turpibus amoribus*), how much more must it be true for friendship (*amicitia*)? Augustine's example subtly prepares the discussion of fear in that he does not simply transpose the mechanism just described to the higher level, as it were, of friendship but introduces negatives: first, he notes that we have to be careful not to offend friendship (instead of keeping in line with the argument presented thus far and simply stating that we have to enrich it); second, he describes this precaution as motivated by apprehension, if not lack of (self-) confidence, on our part about a friend's disposition toward us. Given that feeling or perception can foster love, the simple possibility that our friend *think*, or judge, that we do not love him at all, or that we do not love him as much as he loves us, is cause for concern. For, either way, and depending on the strength of our friend, the fire of love may cool from the intimacy of *familiaritas* to the politeness requisite for mutually beneficial social interaction or even "freeze over" altogether. The vividness of the imagery of heat and cold conveys not just differences in degree but an implicit hierarchy.[18] And Augustine indeed switches to using the terms *superior* and *inferior*. This switch marks a generalization that consists in providing the categories for every interaction thinkable. For Augustine, there will always be a superior and an inferior involved.[19] If this generalization holds, though, love is *always* at stake as well, and not only among friends, say, or lovers. Augustine leaves no doubt about where he is taking his argument; the entire passage traces a movement that culminates in (its mention of) God, or rather does not, *cannot* culminate in (its mention of) God because God will always be greater, and thus the line of thought has to end . . . in a question:

> But again, it is worth while to observe how, although even those that are superior desire to be loved by those that are inferior and are pleased by the eager deference these give them—and the more they become sensible of this affection the more they love them—yet, with how much love is one who is inferior fired when he discovers that he is loved by him who is superior. For love is more welcome when it is not burnt up with the drought of want, but issues forth from the overflowing stream of beneficence. For the former springs from misery, the latter from commiseration. And, furthermore, if the inferior person has been despairing that even he could be loved by the superior one, he will now be unspeakably moved to love if the superior one deigns of his own accord to show him how much he loves one who could by no means venture to promise himself so great a blessing. But what could be higher than God when he judges, and what more hopeless than man when he sins?—than man who had so much the more submitted himself to the custody and dominion of insolent powers which cannot make him blessed, as he had the more despaired of the possibility of becoming the care of that power which wills not to be exalted in wickedness but is exalted in goodness?[20]

Since the previous passage ended on a negative note, the cooling of affection caused by doubt and fear, Augustine has to begin anew, as it were, at the top after having slid down the scale to the point of affection freezing over; the "but" (*autem*) marks this jump back up. In order to make his general point, however, Augustine has to downplay this jump, for the giving of love must never stop, even for the worst of sinners. He therefore sidelines the superior's desire to be loved and immediately reinterprets it as a means to prompt the giving of all the more love on the superior's part. It is this love of the superior for the inferior that counts, as it is allegedly free of interest or utility and spurs on the inferior's desire to be loved. Augustine, in fact, distinguishes two kinds of love. These he defines relatively to superiors and inferiors. The inferior's love for the superior is as if triggered by the superior's love; it receives its fervor from elsewhere. In this secondary agency, as it were, the inferior's love is always insufficient, it tries to make up for a *lack*. The inferior stands in need of, craves, *desires* love and is thus marked by *misery*. The superior's kind of love, however, flows from *commiseration*, that is, it is characterized by plenitude and "issues forth from the overflowing stream of beneficence." In other words, the love of the superior for the inferior is a superior kind of love because it does not lack, does not *want* anything. The less love is given as a response; the less it is deserved or to be expected; the less, that is, it is a complement and the more it is a supplement, and the greater the difference between the superior and the inferior: the more superior that love will be, and—this is the decisive step—the "more" *unspeakably* (*ineffabiliter*) will the inferior be moved to love in return. In distinguishing between superior and inferior, between a love born of commiseration and a love born of misery, Augustine establishes a generally applicable criterion.

The introduction of the couple *superior–inferior* makes it possible to articulate love in its purest form, a task whose difficulty, as we saw, the vocabulary indicates. In its *purest* form because it comes from the most superior, from God who does not want or lack anything but simply *is*, from the creator who could not be more different from his creatures precisely because he is wholly self-sufficient, deriving from no one but himself and lacking nothing.[21] "But what could be higher than God when he judges, and what more hopeless than man when he sins?" The stakes raised by this opposition of *Deus iudicans* and *homo peccans* are considerable, for it pushes the relation of superior and inferior to the extreme. There is nothing greater than God, nor anything less deserving of his love than the sinner. This pushes both God and the sinner off the scale, as it were: There can be nothing and no one superior to God, nor can there be anything inferior to the sinner, nothing hotter than God's love and nothing colder than the sinner's punishment. In sinning, the sinner has in the most literal sense absolved himself—loosened himself, set himself apart, to his detriment, from the absolute, unrestrained love of God. Cut off from this love, the sinner is desperate and hopeless *and cannot help but be so.* Always already destabilized, as creature and as off-spring of Adam and Eve's, the sinner who manages to distance himself from his sins and to realize his fundamental insufficiency is thrown into a state of deep uncertainty and fears for his soul should God not grant him love. The reasons for God's granting us this love must remain obscure to us; what we know is that it is there for us through Jesus Christ. But we would not have this knowledge if it were not for fear, which is literally constitutive: "Love must be built up out of that very sternness of God, which makes man's heart quail with a most salutary fear, so that man, rejoicing to find himself loved by Him whom he fears, may make bold to love Him in return, and at the same time may shrink from offending His love towards him, even if he could do so with impunity."[22]

Augustine does not elaborate on God's severity here, yet the term suggests a link to his position as a superior without equal. His severity is the impression his absolute unapproachability conveys; the salutary fear or "wholesome terror" Augustine speaks of is the despair of the sinner, the realization of the hopelessness of any attempt to bridge the unbridgeable gap between creator and creature, superior and inferior. This fear marks the realization on the part of the sinner of his inferiority; it is in this sense that fear is what love is built upon. It testifies to the enormity of the distance between the sinner and his God and prepares the sinner for the acceptance of—and the ability to return—God's love. It also prevents him from abusing God's love as a means to an end, the way one might do with the benevolence of an equal. Faith, in this passage as in 1 Corinthians, goes along with love (*caritas*), to be built up from fear (and, much more implicitly, hope),[23] and anything detracting from it—false motives in wishing to become a Christian, for example—is swept away by God's mercy.[24] Faith in Christ is an acknowledgment of the unbridgeable gap between sinner and God; this acknowledgment of misery is characterized by fear and leads to a love of God, who—wholly unprompted, completely of his own accord—has not only granted his mercy but also the very fear of losing this grace. More than that: God gives love and the ability to love, and he also gives the ability both to fear not being loved and to fear not being able to love. Above all, he gives himself in Jesus Christ, who came to and died for us in order to manifest God's love. Augustine returns to this point, which introduced the discussion of the couple *inferior–superior*, after the (strictly speaking unanswered and unanswerable) question of God's superiority and the sinner's inferiority.

Christ, *deus homo*, is the mediator whose intervention in the economy of love bridges the unbridgeable gap between the sinner and his god. The reason for Christ's coming is to show God's love for us and to enable us to show ourselves worthy of it; his coming is *the* central event in human history. It is not simply an intervention or correction. It marks a reconfiguration, that is, it reveals love to be the true content of the law, the prophets, and all other "inspired books." Love is what sets us free from a (albeit necessary) bondage that is the fear of punishment caused by the law. The Old Testament is thus read as a testament to God's severity, and the New Testament as a testament to love. Yet love is to be built from fear, and neither the revelation that the Old Testament is a preparation for love nor the advent of Christ itself discards fear. Instead, the good news of Christ's coming gives rise to a new fear. The old fear of punishment was the fear of a future *loss* (of well-being, for example, be it one's own or that of one's descendants). The new fear is the fear of not being able to make up for a present and future insufficiency or *lack*. It is the fear of being not just undeserving, by lack of deeds, but unworthy, by lack of trust or faith, of God's love, and the uncertainty of remaining in his love. This uncertainty can be overcome only by faith, by trust in God, not by human reason. It takes a leap, there can be no bridge other than Christ. The intervention of love opens us up for perfection, yet most of us remain caught up in the imperfections of the flesh and remain ever so much more in need of grace.[25]

TEACHING (THROUGH) LOVE AND FEAR

Central to the teacher's effort, therefore, is a concern to discern and instill a desire for God's love on the part of the student. In keeping with the economy of love just outlined, Augustine holds that an individual's desire—real or pretended—to become a Christian in all cases demands an empathetic engagement on the part of the instructor, for if we do not sow love, we will reap none: if we are not examples in the faith, who will be? The desire to be a Christian, as Augustine sees it, implies the awareness of a lack, and is thus linked to what I've called the new fear. And indeed, fear serves as an important indication of whether someone's wish to become a Christian is properly motivated.[26] The fear Augustine is concerned with, the fear from which love is to be built up, is an inner, spiritual fear, not an external, bodily fear of punishment or of other disadvantages; such an external fear, if unaccompanied by an inner one, only leads one to wish to *fake* Christianity. Even a bodily fear, however, can be a starting point. Through the catechist's effort—though unbeknownst to him—God's mercy might convert the bodily fear of some disadvantage into a spiritual awareness of lack and thus give rise to a positive *desire*. *Might* convert—it surely has the power, but the catechist cannot know.[27] This ignorance is to be remedied by an inquiry into the motives of the would-be convert, preferably thanks to information from trustworthy others, but his own statements will do. It must be remedied, for the catechist needs a starting point for his instruction, *even if that starting point be a lie*. Should the catechist be told a lie, that lie nonetheless is a start: a praiseworthy intention, after all, remains praiseworthy, no matter if it is a particular individual's actual intention or not. The catechist's response must be a sincere praise of the intention, for, if such approval is sincere, it will make the interlocutor, an inferior in the faith, feel loved, with the consequences described earlier.[28]

But even an admonition aims at attuning the listener to the spirit of Scripture, at which point the narration can begin. The unfolding of the narrative must carefully preclude any dwelling on the extraneous: no event must stand out too much and allow the listener's mind to wander off. Yet the truth of what is narrated is a spiritual truth and defies a simple emplotment; a mere retelling will not do, for that too may lead the listener's imagination astray. The sense of the "facts and events" chosen as exemplary is entirely determined by "that end of love from which in all our actions and words our eyes should never be turned away,"[29] and hence the "causes and reasons" of what is narrated have to be conveyed in order to keep the listener's mind focused on the spiritual meaning of the narrative. Thus the narrative is to point toward a meaning that lies beyond it; narrative is to withdraw from the listener's attention "like the gold which holds together in harmonious arrangement the jewels of an ornament without becoming itself unduly conspicuous."[30] The goal is to keep the listener's attention in focus, yet focused on something that is neither visible nor audible nor intelligible.

A "well-ordered statement of the causes" combines the teleology of love with a realization that any narrative, especially a well-constructed and delivered one, will spark the imagination; yet the listener's mind must not be allowed to stray. Staying on the right path is not an exercise in following general rules,[31] like the Old Law; it is a task that has to contend with all sorts of individual contestations or, in Augustine's vocabulary, temptations. The hortatory conclusion to the catechetical narration, as Augustine outlines it "with due regard for the capacity and powers of our hearer and the time at our disposal,"[32] supplements the teleology of love with a teleology of fear. He adds "the stick" to love and thereby adapts the narrative strategy to the psychological economy of love and fear in order to reconfigure each individual's life in the here and now. And although not each and every temptation or scandal can be addressed in a roundabout way,[33] this does not imply that the catechumen is practically offered up to the manipulations of an adverse outside world.[34] For Scripture itself offers the blueprint for a God-pleasing life: "Let also the precepts of a Christian, upright manner of live be at the same time briefly and appropriately presented, that he may not be so easily led away. . . . [W]e must instruct him fully by the evidences from the sacred books."[35]

Straightened out by the rules of an "upright manner of life," an externally conditioned behavior will help prevent the interior from being led astray—but only in the same way as exterior love may or may not spark interior love. This marks a decisive extension, for love is now seen as what establishes the *inner* bonds of a community. If even the name *Christian* is such an external mark, and there is, despite all efforts at "driv[ing] out the wicked,"[36] nothing we can do except believe that everything will play itself out as it is foretold, faith in the love of God is at the basis of our individual and communal lives. For, in the end, it is vain to think that that we could be justified by our own actions, no matter whose righteous example we follow; the "examples of good men" are there for us to orient our manner of life, such that "if we imitate them, we also shall be justified by him who justified them."[37] Augustine combines this understanding of justification with an understanding of his own vocation as catechist such that we may learn to love from being loved, learn from Christ's example and embark on the *via Christi*, which is the *via excellentior* of love. The crucial step has been taken: through (*per*)—*not* "because of" or "thanks to"—the ministry of the catechist, the catechumen understands that he has received a gift. This is only an implicit understanding, the acknowledgment of a transformation he *dare* not assign to himself or the catechist, dare not assign to another human being. Jesus's love for the sinner, an enemy whose affection had cooled to icy hatred, has made the enemy a friend. This justification makes the sinner a friend—*ut iustificans faceret amicum*—not just of Jesus, but "in him and for his sake" makes him a friend to himself and to others. This fulfillment of the double commandment of love thanks to justification by Christ reveals the gift that is Christ's coming to be love: *justification is an economy of love*. The acceptance of Christ's involvement in our lives constitutes *the* decisive event from which everything else flows, including the mechanics of instruction. Justification and our inner acknowledgment of it are spiritual; any account of them, catechetical, pastoral, theoretical, or otherwise, is necessarily external and needs to adapt itself.[38]

THE QUESTION OF LOVE/LOVE IS THE ANSWER

Augustine translates this insight into catechetical practice. The bond of love is, for example, the remedy for the tedium of repetition:

> If it be distasteful to us to be repeating over and over things that are familiar and suitable for little children, let us suit ourselves to them with a brother's, a father's, and a mother's love, and when once we are linked to them thus in heart these things will seem new even to us. For so great is the power of sympathy, that when people are affected by us as we speak and we by them as they learn, we dwell each in the other and thus both they, as it were, speak in us what they hear, while we, after a fashion, learn in them what we teach.[39]

Love breeds love, and the free giving of the gift entails a renewal of the gift; it institutes a community. (We may call this *one* direction of the action of love through the catechist, *per nos.*) Yet, through the action of the catechist, the catechumenate comes to see how creation, by virtue of its mere existence, testifies to the skill and design of the its creator.[40] If catechesis leads the candidates "to study God, on whose account all things that should be learned are to be learned," those catechizing participate in their renewal,[41] in their opening up to the spiritual, in their transition from the "death of error to the life of faith."[42] The opening up of the catechist is strictly analogous to the opening up of the

catechumenate and the formation of a spiritual community, a communion with God.[43] This clarifies the idea that the joy of good works lies
in performing them, not in the reward they may yield. Since the performance consists in keeping oneself open to the spirit, the performance is
the reward, which reward cannot be isolated. The more we love our
listeners, the more we want them to benefit from what we offer them.
If it appears they do not benefit, and especially if we do not know if
they understand that they stand to benefit, the feeling of futility is devastating to us and debilitates our effort. What seems to concern Augustine the most, once again, is the detrimental effect of the tension between
a certainty—we know where we are going with our preaching—and
the uncertainty of whether we are taking our listeners along. *We simply
do not know* whether their silence is due to awe or shyness, whether they
fail to understand or, simply, out of disdain, choose not to understand.
In order to do our work, we must understand the causes of their apathy
such that we may adapt our teaching. The remedy consists in unsettling
the listener so as to "dislodg[e] him from his hiding-place." By gently
prodding him, we must break the external shell, as it were, to make him
feel comfortable enough to speak up. The main tool for breaking the apathy of the listener is questioning: "We must by questioning him find out
whether he understands; and must give him confidence so that if he
thinks there is an objection to make he may freely lay it before us. We
must at the same time enquire of him whether he has ever heard these
things before, and so perhaps they, as being things well-known and
commonplace, fail to move him."[44]

The task of questions is to pierce complacency and prod the candidate to furnish the information necessary for the completion of an appropriate (that is, adequately adapted) narrative and for avoiding an over-
emphasis on what is already known. They are to elicit answers according
to which the catechist can adapt his teaching for the sake of conveying
essentials.[45] To fill in perceived gaps in knowledge and understanding,
Augustine recommends concentrating on exemplary problems.

If all else fails, Augustine suggests a procedure reminiscent of Paul's
tools, love and the "stick," a procedure that once again places the catechist in a central mediating position. The catechist is bound in love to
his student and *for that reason* bound to do anything in his power to open
up the student to the love of God. He has to put up with the student—
the student in Augustine's phrase "is to be suffered mercifully"—but he

must not put up with ignorance. If need be, the candidate must be scared into accepting the most *necessary* truths. In Augustine's words, these are "to be impressed terrifyingly." Yet that does not make them any less true nor the catechist's love any less genuine, especially if this first direction of the catechist's agency (the *per nos*) toward the catechumen is supplemented by a second direction toward God. The catechist's prayer, advocating for the catechumen through the teacher, *per nos*, may even be more important than any instruction he could provide: "But if he is exceedingly slow-witted, and out of accord with and averse to every such inducement, we should bear with him in a compassionate spirit, and after briefly running through the other points, impress upon him in a way to inspire awe the truths that are most necessary concerning the unity of the Catholic Church, temptations, and the Christian manner of living in view of the future judgment; and we should rather say much on his behalf to God, than say much to him about God."[46]

Such straightforward imposition is certainly an extreme case, yet the general point that complacency or apathy must be overcome with any suitable means at our disposal still holds.[47] In the second (and much shorter) of two exemplary catecheses addressed to an urban, uneducated, male audience, Augustine goes so far as to reprimand his fictional interlocutor: "Suppose again that some one is present who wishes to be a Christian, and that when questioned, he makes the same answer as did the former candidate [i.e., that he is interested in "rest hereafter"]; for even if he does not so answer *we may say that he ought to have so answered*."[48]

Augustine does not let himself be sidetracked. The answer he has to hear is that the candidate seeks eternal rest, not immediate advantage. The purpose of the question is to confirm a disposition. This sleight of hand combines question and admonishment and thus sums up the thrust of catechesis: the overall goal is love, but for the catechist this means that the need for this love must become clear to the candidate, whatever the means necessary to bring about this realization.

The exhortation to have love as one's goal places the catechist in this economy of love and fear. All love comes from God, and the instructor in the faith is a mediator in the succession of the apostles. He intervenes not only, so to speak, on behalf of God in the life of the candidate but also with prayer on behalf of the sinner.

The ministry of the catechist is part of a process of integration in the community. In Augustine's example this process reaches a first milestone, the acceptance of the candidate who can now prepare for baptism. The preceding instruction has ended with a hortatory flourish that has destabilized the candidate or at least shown the stakes of the transition ahead. This transition toward acceptance by the community is marked by a question, but a question that merely confirms the only possible answer. For Augustine, here as elsewhere, it is not a question of *if* but of *when* the right answer is given. The task of the question is thus to confirm a change of heart, of accepting faith and willing obedience to the traditions of the church as precondition for acceptance by the church. "After the instruction you should ask him whether he believes these things and desires to observe them. And when he answers that he does, you should of course sign him, with due ceremony, and deal with him in accordance with the custom of the Church."[49]

Importantly, the process of integration does not stop here, nor does it come to an end after baptism. Everyone, including the catechist, has to make a continuing effort to remain within God's good graces. The catechist's intervention is only a first step, a preparation for a spiritual journey toward knowledge of God, a journey whose only true guide is the word of God summarized in the catechism and the double commandment of love:

> Next you should make use of this opportunity to admonish him that if he hears anything even in the Scriptures that has a carnal ring, he should believe, *even if he does not understand*, that something spiritual is therein signified that has reference to holy living and the life to come. Now this he learns *in brief*, so that whatsoever he hears from the canonical books that he cannot refer to the love of eternity, and truth, and holiness, and to the love of his neighbor, he may believe to have been said or done with a figurative meaning, and endeavor so to understand as to refer it to that two-fold love.[50]

In the interest of facilitating our turn to God, the catechist elaborates a narrative economy in which fear and love act through threats and promises. Yet just as the catechist removes obstacles that keep us from accepting God's love, so the narrative must not distract from what it narrates, the eternal truth of God's word. But, because we are embodied and temporal, our words are unable to capture even the instantaneity of our own thoughts, even less what is absolutely superior to us. Rather than try to do the work itself, narrative therefore points away from itself at that which reveals itself to us. Narrative withdraws, blends in, points beyond the words to the meaning they enwrap.

The successful catechist creates an awareness of lack and an understanding that this very realization is a *gift* of God's love. His goal is to facilitate what we may call an "experience of meaning"—of love—*beyond* words and narrative. The destabilization brought about by fear is but one step in opening the listener up to this meaning. More generally, the interrogative elements of Augustine's discourse serve as interpellations: even though they are questions, they "call us out on" our complacency, ignorance, or lapse of attention.

In short, the goal of catechesis is to pry us away from our attachment to the world and to attach ourselves to God. Augustine's questions seek to find out whether we are in a position to hear the call. This hearing—and heeding—of the call is a continuing challenge, and it is a challenge we can live up to only within a community. It is in loving others and being loved by them within the concrete community that we, as it were, catch a glimpse of the immensity of the love of God.

NOTES

Throughout this chapter I will be referring to Augustinus Aurelius, Bishop of Hippo, *The First Catechetical Instruction*, trans. and annot. Joseph P. Christopher, rev. ed. (Westminster: Newman, 1946 [1926]), abbreviated as *CR*; occasional quotations in Latin are taken from the *Corpus Augustinianum Gissense*, ed. Cornelius Mayer (Basel: Schwabe, 1995), abbreviated as *CAG*. References are given by chapter and section numbers, followed by page numbers.

1. *CR* II.4:17 (translation modified), *CAG* 4:124.
2. *CR* II.4:17–18, *CAG* 4:123–24; the term *cheerful giving* is adopted from 2 Corinthians 9:7.
3. *CR* III.5:18–19, *CAG* 4:125, quote ibid.
4. *CR* III.6:19, *CAG* 4:125–26. Two relevant passages from Paul are Romans 15:4 and 1 Corinthians 10:11.
5. 1 Timothy 1:3–11.
6. Specifically from Romans 10:4.
7. *CR* IV.7–8:21–24, *CAG* 4:126–29. Significantly, the passage from the Gospel explicitly speaks of Jesus *silencing* the Sadducees with his knowledge of Scripture,

which silencing is said to incite a Pharisee "expert in the law" to ask Jesus what, in his view, is the greatest commandment. This is supposed to trip Jesus up, yet his answer, the double commandment of love toward God and toward one's neighbor, the New Law, is taken from the old law (Deuteronomy 6:5 and Leviticus 19:18) and thus as unassailable as any teacher's response. What might be considered unorthodox is his observation that "all the Law and the Prophets hang on these two commandments," a point that both Paul and Augustine stress. The idea does not, however, originate with Jesus; compare, for example, Hillel's interpretation of the Torah as a commentary on the Golden Rule (Shabbat 30b–31a, Babylonian Talmud, in Lawrence H. Schiffman, ed., *Texts and Traditions* [Hoboken: Ktav, 1998], 514). With a further proof of his profound familiarity with the Judaic tradition, Jesus manages to completely silence the Pharisees: "from that day on no one dared to ask him any more questions" and what is new about his teaching—the supreme importance of love—remains unchallenged. In other words, knowledge of the Old Testament establishes the teaching of the New Testament as unassailable truth; knowledge of the old law brings about understanding of the new; see Matthew 22:23–46, especially 34–40 and 46.

8. *CR* IV.8:23, *CAG* 4:128.

9. *CR* IV.7:22, *CAG* 4:127.

10. *CR* IV.7:21–22, *CAG* 4:126–27, and V.9:24–26, *CAG* 4:129–30.

11. *CR* V.9:24–25, *CAG* 4:129, quote ibid.

12. *CR* IV.8:24, *CAG* 4:129.

13. Extraordinary not only for its clarity but for the theological rearticulation of what later would be called the three cardinal virtues (faith, love, hope) in terms of a catechetical, that is also narrative, strategy.

14. Augustine employs other terms in this semantic field, for example, *voluntas, fiducia, iustitia, misericordia, gratia*; opposites also play an important role, for example *cupiditas* as opposed to *caritas*, or *superbia* as opposed to *humilitas*; a special role is assigned to fear (*timor, terror*).

15. *CR* IV.7:21–22, *CAG* 4:127.

16. An excellent overview of the difficulty of translating *dilectio, caritas, agapē*, etc., can be found in the *OED*'s discussion of *charity*.

17. An amplification of love perceived in others but not in or for oneself can lead to the worst excesses of jealousy and craving for affection; take Richard of Gloucester in Shakespeare's *Richard III* as an example of the spurned soul's false affection of love and friendship and its promises and enticements (many other villains in Shakespeare display similar behavior). On the independence of loving, see chapter 2.

18. It must nonetheless be said that Augustine's metaphors sometimes get ahead of themselves, for example when, a few lines down, the metaphors of cold and heat, thus of fire and its absence, and of water, are mixed and supplemented with wordplay. *CR* IV.7:22, *CAG* 4:127.

19. Augustine does not allow for any kind of genuine equality or partnership; this seems to be related to the idea that attachment to anything outside the soul (except God) leads to an imbalance.

20. *CR* IV.7:22–23, *CAG* 4:128.

21. The "wickedness" and "goodness" Augustine speaks of, "non malitia sublimis esse vult, sed bonitate sublimis est," reinforce this contrast between, on the one

hand, lack and wanting and, on the other, overflowing benevolence. Compare the definition of evil as lack of good that Augustine gives in *The City of God*, book 11, chapter 9: "Mali enim nulla natura est: sed amissio boni, mali nomen accepit" (*CAG* 6:330).

22. *CR* V.9:24, *CAG* 4:129.

23. Hope here is assimilated to fear in that it builds up faith from a negative: hoping for a benefit that we are not entitled to.

24. "Mercy," like "commiseration," translates *misericordia*; I retain it here to distinguish God's mercy from any other superior's commiseration, for the latter term suggests a suffering and lack that cannot be attributed to God's absolute superiority, the suffering of Christ notwithstanding.

25. *CR* IV.8:23–24, *CAG* 4:129.

26. *CR* V.9:24, *CAG* 4:129.

27. *CR* V.9:25, *CAG* 4:316.

28. Should this approval make him feel bad about cheating, that may not be too bad a thing either, for it may just entice him to try sincerely to make up for his deception. Augustine does not discuss the possibility of this approval being faked in turn. He does, however, provide a very forceful attack in the first exemplary catechesis that conceals the reproach for the sin in an attack on the sinner; see *CR* XVI.25:53–55, *CAG* 4:149–51.

29. *CR* VI.10:27, *CAG* 4:131.

30. Ibid.

31. "General" in the sense of binding for generally defined groups of people.

32. *CR* VI.11:27–28, *CAG* 4:131.

33. Cf. 1 Corinthians 4:21, along with my essay, "Love and the Stick—the Worldly Aspects of the Call in the First Letter to the Corinthians," in Ward Blanton and Hent de Vries, eds., *Paul and the Philosophers* (New York: Fordham University Press, 2013), 310–26.

34. *CR* VI.11:28, *CAG* 4:132.

35. *CR* VI.11:28–29, *CAG* 4:132.

36. 1 Corinthians 5:13.

37. *CR* VI.11:29, *CAG* 4:132.

38. *CR* VI.11:29, *CAG* 4:133 (my emphasis).

39. *CR* XII.17:41, *CAG* 4:141.

40. Cf. *Confessions* XI.8.

41. Augustine here returns to the vocabulary used earlier of heat and cold. The renewal is described as "warming" (*fervescat*) the catechist, especially if the preceding exhortation has been "cool" (*frigidior*).

42. *CR* XII.17:41–42, *CAG* 4:141.

43. This links up with the Paulinian definition of the church as the body of Christ; compare also Matthew 18:20: "For where two or three are gathered in my name, I am there among them."

44. *CR* XIII.18:42–43 (quote 43), *CAG* 4:142 (quote ibid).

45. Questions thus play a propaedeutic role, they assist in the interpretation of candidates' behavior. Their employment here does not mark a shift from the acroamatic (lecture-based) to the erotematic (interrogatory) method, for the answers are not known.

46. *CR* XIII.18:43, *CAG* 4:142.

47. Augustine still works within the framework of the psychological economy he has laid out: the truths stick because they are impressed with fear and therefore prepare the ground for love. This undertaking is facilitated by the catechist's (and any other member of the community's) prayers, which solicit God's love.

48. *CR* XXVI.51:83, *CAG* 4:174 (my emphasis).

49. *CR* XXVI.50:82, *CAG* 4:173, quote ibid.

50. *CR* XXVI.50:82, quote ibid., *CAG* 4:173–74, quote ibid. (my emphasis).

7

LOOKING EVIL IN THE EYE/I

The Interminable Work of Forgiveness

Orna Ophir

From a psychoanalytic point of view, specifically the one offered by Austrian-born British psychoanalyst Melanie Klein and the English school of psychoanalysis that followed in her footsteps, forgiveness can be seen as a lifelong process of an interminable working through, which takes place only if one is ready, as the title of this chapter suggests, to look evil in the eye/I. In the face of trauma, but also of lesser pains, if one is to forgive, one has to move beyond collusion with aggression and transcend the horror; overcome disbelief with regard to human brutality and malice and its denial; and shift from a position of mere condemnation, revenge, and retaliation to a courageous, sober working through of the evil done or imagined, first and foremost, by oneself. Looking in the "eye of evil" implies, precisely, not evading the full bleakness and terror of one's own impulses of life and death, Eros and Thanatos, libido and aggression. Looking evil in the eye thus demands, first and foremost, looking evil in the *I,* that is to say, continuously observing and confronting the violence and harm at the heart of one's self.

Although forgiveness is closely related to topics that since the very foundation of the discipline were of much interest to psychoanalysts—such as trauma, mourning, guilt, and the need for punishment—

psychoanalysis has had remarkably little to say about the phenomenon in question, at least until the 1990s. According to the psychoanalyst Salman Akhtar,[1] who was trying to fill this lacuna, the main reason for this neglect was that Sigmund Freud himself did not consider forgiveness to be worthy of his scientific attention. He and his pupils believed it to be a phenomenon that touched more upon the interpersonal or social level and less on the intrapsychic one; it was regarded as a positive rather than a pathological aspect of human experience. For them, the concept of forgiveness carried too many religious overtones ("to err is human, to forgive divine") and hence belonged to a terrain from which analysts, respecting Freud's own profound ambivalence toward the subject, were trying to distance themselves. But by the end of the year 2000 psychoanalysis was the exception in avoiding the subject. A profusion of publications on forgiveness (four hundred thousand books listed on Amazon.com), together with a host of workshops on the topic, and even institutes for forgiveness offering to "heal the heart," led Henry Smith, a New England psychoanalyst, to warn psychoanalysts that forgiveness was a "morally seductive term" that had no place in psychoanalytic theoretical or clinical work. Indeed, he claimed, "there are some hazards to giving it one."[2]

While keeping these reservations in mind, there is every reason to paint a fuller and more nuanced picture as to psychoanalysis's willingness and ability to shed more light on the concept and practice of forgiveness in all its aspects. As I will argue, in particular Melanie Klein's "genealogy of morals," as Jacques Derrida once called her contribution to psychoanalysis,[3] can offer a profound insight into the complexity of the intrapsychic dynamic that is relevant to what I suggest we should see as a lifelong process of forgiveness, which alone in turn enables the experiencing of love.

LET ME BEGIN with a "case study" of precisely this type of forgiveness, drawing on a 2012 cover story in the *International Herald Tribune* by Robert F. Worth entitled "The Torturers Now Captive."[4] Although this is an article about recent events in Libya, it exemplifies a much more common universal intrapsychic dynamic that underlies the phenomenon of forgiveness. Trying to look beyond the specifics of the place and the time, I would like to draw attention to the working-through process the main protagonist of the story, a man named Nasser Salhoba,

undergoes, which, I want to suggest, is necessary for the kind of forgiveness that could short-circuit the vicious cycle of violence, the recy-
cling of aggression, and, finally, the all too predictable transformation
of victims into aggressors.

Describing the role reversal that turned former captives into current guards, Worth reports that some of the Libyan militias simply rep-
licated the worst tortures carried out under the old regime, but also that
many more have tended to exercise restraint in the use of physical and
psychological violence. In Worth's own words: "Almost all of them have
offered victims a chance to confront their former torturers face-to-face,
to test their instincts, to balance the desire for revenge against the will
to make Libya into something more than a madman's playground."

The restraint the new guards were able to exercise, Worth goes on
to suggest, has to do *not only* with the fact that they were willing and
able to look at the torturers and their evil face-to-face, as it were. Yet,
basing oneself on a Kleinian understanding of the working through of
aggression and employing a terminology that Worth himself does not
use directly, one is tempted to extrapolate and conclude that it is, *precisely*, the guards' looking at the evil "in the I," namely "testing their own
instincts" and their very own "desire for revenge," that made all the difference in their attitude toward their victims (and, often, their own former guards) as the tables and roles were suddenly reversed. Experiencing the intrapsychic struggle between their own instincts of life and
death, libido and aggression, love and hate, these former captives now
turned guards must find a proper balance in which the wish for revenge
and the infliction of more pain would be overcome by the will to repair,
to do good, and restore lost sanity. In other words, the restraint shown
by these individuals was an indication that, in this struggle of intimate
no less than external forces, life and love had gotten the upper hand.

The difficult task for former victims, then, is not merely facing their
worst enemies, that is to say, looking at the evil "out there," and being
reminded of their own victimhood, the intense, often unthinkable, physical and psychic pain they endured at the hands of their guards now
themselves captives. The more challenging work is that of finding extreme aggression and violent wishes for life's destruction, of finding madness "in there," that is to say, within one's own proper mind. The former
victims had to experience their own murderous wishes, to witness their
very own sadistic desire to inflict pain, and to acknowledge their incli-

nation to cause severe damage to other human beings, aspects that are usually split off from consciousness and are thus distanced from the one's awareness. It seems that, facing their brutal fantasies in their full intensity, these victims/guards were required to undergo two stages of a painful mourning process. First, they had to see the other in themselves, the murderous demons inside their very own intrapsychic world. Second, they had to differentiate themselves from these evildoers and give up their will for destruction.

With this acknowledgment that both victim and perpetrator share violent fantasies, although they remain genuinely separate and different, and thus responsible for each other, begins the very process that Klein calls reparation.[5] This process, which can only be initiated with the recognition of the damage one has done (in phantasy even before undergoing an externally inflicted pain) and the loss one must suffer, is conceptually, if not always practically, grounded in respect and love for the separate other, the other who is one's proximate exteriority, so to speak. Reparation promotes a virtuous rather than a vicious cycle by furnishing an escape from the repetitive onslaught of evil and harm that alone allows one to regain the very peacefulness and sanity that seemed out of reach.

The moving story of Nasser Salhoba, a victim turned guard, and Marwan Gdoura, a torturer now captive, begins with the painful reality that Nasser's brother Omar Salhoba, a forty-two-year-old doctor, was shot and killed. Two days after the fall of Tripoli, in Yarmouk where he was imprisoned for his insistence on treating injured fellow prisoners, Omar was executed by Marwan Gdoura, one of Quaddafi's soldiers, who in a curious turn of events became a captive in the hands of Omar's older brother, Nasser. Indeed, Nasser soon became the resistance brigade's chief interrogator, with direct responsibility for his brother's executioner's fate.

Worth tells us that Nasser's outrage against Quaddafi did not begin with the merciless killing of his brother Omar, but went back a long way to another, similarly traumatic, event. In 1996, while Nasser was in training to become a police investigator, his other brother, Adel Salhoba, was gunned down in a Tripoli soccer stadium. The fans had dared to boo Saadi el-Qaddafi, the dictator's son and the sponsor of a local team, and Saadi's guards opened fire, killing at least twenty people. When the Salhoba family was told they could not receive Adel's body unless they signed a form stating that he was a hooligan, Nasser went straight to interior ministry headquarters and there, in an unthinkable act of defiance, confronted officials. Guards quickly subdued him, and on his family's advice he fled to Malta, where he stayed for seven years, earning a meager living by smuggling cigarettes and falling into drinking and drugs. Even after he returned to Libya his rampage at the interior ministry kept him blacklisted and he could not find steady work. It was his younger brother, Omar, a successful pediatrician with two young daughters, who kept him going, lending him money and urging him to clean up his act.

During the 2011 revolution, while Nasser waited it out, "cynical as ever," Omar—the "family's frail idealist"—risked his life by providing thousands of dollars' worth of medical supplies to the rebels. On June 7 of that year, while he was operating on a child at his clinic in Tripoli, two intelligence agents arrived and bundled Omar into a car. No one knew where he was taken. More than two months later, on August 24, Nasser received a call telling him Omar had been shot in the Yarmouk prison.

The three men responsible for Omar's death were all now living one floor below the office in which Worth interviewed Nasser, Omar's older brother. Marwan Gdoura, twenty-eight years old, shot Omar and the other five victims first; the other two guards fired only after Marwan had emptied two clips from his AK-47. When Worth asked Nasser what it felt like to interrogate the man who murdered his brother, he got up from his office chair, walked out of the room and immediately reappeared with Marwan. Worth, who observed the two men in the same room, looked first for signs of evil in Marwan's face or demeanor. Yet he found none. The rebels told him that Marwan was very devout, that he spent most of his time praying or reading the Qur'an. When Worth asked him about the execution, Marwan spoke softly but without hesitation. "One thing is very clear," he said. "You're a soldier, you must obey orders. At that moment, if you say no, you will be considered a traitor and added to the victims. And if you don't do the execution, others will." While he was speaking, Worth was also observing Nasser. He was listening to Marwan, smoking quietly, now and then glancing at him with "a look of professional detachment." Knowing full well that his brother had pleaded with Marwan just before the latter executed him, Nasser's "professional detachment" seemed hardly a denial or disavowal of the evil committed. He also knew that, as a matter of principle and fact,

Marwan could have chosen differently, and now it seemed that Nasser's own potential murderousness in whatever violent response he felt would be justified was put to the test. But, Worth reported, Nasser remained thoughtful instead. He confronted Marwan with his all too humane wish to deny his very own aggression, to project it onto the abstract role of a soldier who must always obey, and demanded that he engage in thinking more seriously about the damage and loss that he should not disown: "During all the months after Tripoli fell, did you think about the six people you executed?" he asked him. Marwan answered: "I did think about them and also about the prisoners who were killed and burned in the hangar." "But this was different," Nasser insisted in the conversation Worth reported. "You executed these six people yourself. Did you talk about it with the other soldiers?" Nasser went on, stressing Marwan's direct responsibility, confronting him as the evildoer, and demanding that he process, in thought and conversation, what he would wish he could simply forget. "No," Marwan replied quietly.

Then, there was a long pause. Nasser looked away, as if he felt he ought to stop, but then turned back toward Marwan. "You say you followed orders," he went on. "Suppose I get an order to do the same thing to you. Should I do it?" Nasser thus presented his insight that evil is not only out there, in Marwan, in the world, but also within, in himself, and hence that it could be acted out any moment, this time just as well by him as a potential executioner.

Later, after Marwan had been taken back downstairs, Nasser told Worth that he still wanted to kill him. But, more than that, he wanted to understand why. As I suggested earlier, part of being able to engage in the ongoing process and task of forgiving has to do with acceptance of one's own, intrapsychic, sadistic aspects. Thus, paradoxically, fantasies of revenge can actually facilitate the process of forgiveness, and some analysts see them as necessary stepping-stones rather than as stumbling blocks in this process. And whereas Akthar, for example, indicates that these fantasies turn the victim's hitherto passive ego into an active agent, eliciting a sense of mastery and enhancing self-esteem,[6] I would claim that fantasies of hurting the evildoer, of effectively killing him, are not only allowing one to feel in control, but rather bring one to contact with one's own potential sadism and aggression. Exploring them imaginatively and unreservedly, thinking them through, instead of acting them out, makes one's own sadistic fantasies potentially *curative*. The process that is needed, as Wilfred Bion,[7] one of Klein's most influential follow-ers, has rightly suggested, is that of transforming unthinkable murder-ous affects into elements of thoughts, dreams, and myth.

Nasser is thus engaged, and demands that Marwan, too, take active part, in the same process that occurs in any psychoanalytic treatment worthy of its name. It is a demanding task, but Nasser does not give up. Speaking of Marwan, he noted: "I've asked him repeatedly why and how . . . I've talked to him alone and in groups."

While one could question whether Worth's article presents Nasser as an almost superior being or, on the contrary, as a masochistic charac-ter, a genuine martyr, of sorts, he makes sure to give a full and balanced picture, telling us also that Nasser, indeed, once beat Marwan with the *falga*, that is to say, with a wooden stick used to raise prisoners' legs in order to subsequently hit them painfully on the soles of the feet. Yet, paradoxically, this release of one's own aggression, especially when it is limited, could well serve to reduce the hatred felt toward the perpetra-tor whose violence one suffered, as it, precisely, challenges the all too common split between the "torturous beast," who is so far removed from anything that would count as humane, and the "saintly forgiver," who seems to lack humanity for the opposite reasons. As we are neither beasts nor angels, as Blaise Pascal once aptly observed, our sadism is human, all too human.

In his relentless study of both the murderer of his brother and his own various reactions to him, over the course of several months talking to Marwan, Nasser arrived at a painful point from which, onward, he could only see the person in front of him as a nonhuman part-object, as "the head of the snake." Living in a world made of these kinds of ob-jects makes one's surroundings, internal and external, fragmentary and persecutory. Not willing to let this be the conclusion of this process, Nasser decided to observe his prisoner in the presence of Marwan's family.

He called Marwan's father and invited him to come see his son. When members of his family arrived in the prison, Nasser greeted them at the door and led them downstairs. "It was a very emotional moment," he said to Worth. "You can imagine how I felt when I saw my brother's killer embracing his brother." The two brothers hugged each other for a long time, sobbing, until finally Nasser pushed them apart, because he could not bear it anymore. Again, it was apparent that Nasser's invitation to Marwan's family was not about inflicting more pain upon himself, inducing unhelpful masochistic pleasure, but was rather a matter of engaging in a process of exploration that would allow him to metabolize the conflict, digest the pain, balance the impulse to harm with the drive to make reparation. Resisting the urge to take the easier way of disbelief and denial while face to face with a fellow human being's calculated and demonstrated cruelty, Nasser seemed to be seeking not only the truth to be known, but to demand that it would be experienced and felt in its full and painful psychic reality, too. When he told Marwan's cousin what Marwan had done, the cousin listened carefully and then hugged Nasser before the family left the prison.

For Nasser, the family meeting was a revelation, Worth reports. "He was very emotional," he said of Marwan. "His sister loves him; his brother loves him. You see him with them, and it's such a contrast with this cold killer." The realization that even in the cruelest killer, in the person who came to signify the embodiment of evil for him, there was a good object that was loved by others was yet another truth Nasser had to face, but, in a paradoxical way, this new complexity was also comforting. He seemed less burdened, and, although he could not say exactly why, I want to suggest that learning that even Marwan was not completely without love, and thus did have some at least residual access to guilt and remorse, was the proof Nasser needed that Marwan must be experiencing some pain for his irreparable harm to sentient life. He told Worth that after this encounter he felt he understood Marwan a little better, even if his crime remained a mystery. Here Nasser faced the challenge evil presents to our rationality, a scandal that rattles us even more than evil itself, namely the complementary, if hidden, relationship that evil entertains with good.

As Worth continues to follow Nasser's mental movements, he tells readers that the following Friday Marwan's father returned, this time with two relatives. Nasser helped them carry crates of food—yogurt, fruit, and homemade biscuits—down to Marwan's cell. When Nasser came back upstairs, Marwan's father was standing by the door. He went straight up to Nasser and, full of sorrow, looked him in the eye. "He embraced me and kissed me on the forehead," Nasser said. "So he must know."

Nasser's attitude and gesture toward Marwan's father shows that when the response to evil is not more evil, aggression or violence, but, rather, an insistence on the acceptance of the dual nature of the human animal (which, again, is neither a beast nor an angel), the reciprocal reaction may well turn out to be mourning and the eventual assumption of full responsibility for acts committed. The accompanying feelings of remorse, sorrow, and sadness, for the damage that will sadly never be repaired as well, lead to an experience of genuine love and deep gratitude. It allows sad to replace mad, or, in Klein's terms (to which I will now turn in more detail), it facilitates a shift from the paranoid-schizoid position to its depressive counterpart.

MELANIE KLEIN'S UNDERSTANDING of our ability to move from envy, greed, and aggression to love, guilt, and reparation (when these moves are not mere "shortcuts," so to speak) is fundamentally related to her insights into the mental process of the digestion of physical and psychic pain of aggression. These insights can be utilized not only on the level of the single individual person but also, as Klein claims in her 1933 paper, "The Early Development of Conscience in the Child,"[8] within the larger project of "improving humanity," of making humanity more peaceful. That attempts to do so have often failed so far, Klein contends, is due, first of all, to our fateful misunderstanding of the "full depth and vigor of the instincts of aggression innate in each individual."[9] For Klein, we cannot overcome the deleterious effect of these instincts simply by encouraging our positive, well-wishing impulses while denying or suppressing our negative and aggressive ones. On the contrary, overcoming aggression can only be accomplished by knowing it intimately and thereby diminishing the anxiety that accentuates this instinct. It requires us to break up—or break through—the mutual reinforcement of hatred and anxiety, whose resonance knows neither beginning nor end.

The anxieties Klein is interested in originate in early infantile states. Hostile attitudes, desperation, and suspicion spring from these anxieties, which in turn intensify aggression. However, when these anxieties are alleviated, they modify the destructive instinct and give way to "kindlier and more trustful feelings towards one's fellow-men," Klein writes. And, when and where this happens, "people may inhabit the world together in greater peace and good-will than they do now."[10] Yet, although she never neglected this understanding of the interpersonal/social domain, Klein's main contribution to psychoanalytic theory and praxis lies in her exploration of *intrapsychic* conflicts, and especially the conflict between love and hate. In "The Emotional Life of Civilized Men and Women," a series of public lectures she and Joan Riviere gave in 1936 that were subsequently published in the 1937 volume *Love, Hate, and Reparation*, Klein writes:

> The two parts of this book discuss very different aspects of human emotions. The first, "Hate, Greed, and Aggression, "deals with the powerful impulses of hate, which are a fundamental part of human nature. The second, in which I am attempting to give a picture of the equally powerful force of love and the drive to reparation, is complementary to the first, for the apparent division implied in this mode of presentation does not actually exist in the human mind. In separating our topic in this way we cannot perhaps clearly convey the constant *interaction* of love and hate; but the division of this vast subject was necessary, for only when consideration has been given to the part that destructive impulses play in the interaction of hate and love, is it possible to show the ways in which feelings of love and tendencies to reparation develop in connection with aggressive impulses and in spite of them.[11]

For Klein, then, love, the most complex of all human emotions, cannot be considered without first exploring the destructive impulses. To do so, Klein goes back to the psychic life of infants, where the level of anxiety is at its highest, and where mental life begins through the transformation of sensations and affects into meaningful elements of thoughts. Exploring childhood and infanthood in order to understand the adult's mental life was a central teaching of Freud's, who, after all, found that the "child was father to the man." Klein, in his footsteps, is considered the one to have added that it was the infant who gave birth to the child, and thus to the adult.[12]

Investigating the emotional situation of infants in order to understand the unconscious of human adults, she finds that the first object that the completely dependant infant relates to is its mother, or more specifically her breasts.[13] When the mother satisfies the infant's needs for nourishment, alleviating its feeling of hunger and giving it the sensual pleasure that it experiences when its mouth is stimulated by sucking at her breasts, the infant, evidently, loves its mother. But when it is hungry and its desires are not gratified, or when it is feeling bodily pain or discomfort, the whole situation suddenly changes. Hatred and aggressive feelings are aroused and give rise to the most painful psychic-somatic states (choking, breathlessness, and the like). This vicious cycle, in which internal distress gives rise to an aggressive phantasy and, in turn, creates a feeling of despair, can be short-circuited only when the need-creating pain is first being addressed. Immediate and primary relief of the infant's painful states of hunger, hate, tension, and fear by the immediate satisfaction of its desires and needs gives rise to a feeling of security, which greatly enhances the gratification itself. As a consequence, a virtuous cycle, replacing the vicious one, is set in motion. Later in life, too, whenever a person receives love, she will, first of all, feel secure. This applies to the infant and to the adult and pertains to the simple forms of love as well as to its more elaborate expressions and articulations.

Klein's theory of the basic human conflict between love and hate is bound up with her concept of *unconscious phantasy*.[14] Although Freud described it first, it was in Klein's theory that it came to play a central role. In her view, as elaborated by the British psychoanalyst, Susan Isaacs,[15] unconscious phantasies are the mental representation of those events in the body that comprise the instincts. In other terms, they are physical sensations that are interpreted as relationships with the objects that cause them. They underlie every mental process and accompany all mental activity; they are the mental expressions of *both* libidinal/loving *and* aggressive/hating impulses, including the simultaneously operating defense mechanisms against each one of these contrasting impulses.

Some have characterized the psychoanalytic process as the attempt to convert unconscious phantasy into conscious thought. Unlike Freud, who was more interested in the quantities of the drives and the structure of the mind, Klein saw instincts in purely psychological terms and focused on the qualitative features and actual content of children's phantasies (and the later function these have in the mental life of adults as well). She found that children were preoccupied with phantasies—both conscious and unconscious—about birth, death, the primal scene, bodily processes in themselves and in their parents, the external and the internal world of good and bad objects, and so on and so forth. Eventually, Klein conceptualized the various phantasies she discovered in both children and adults in terms of so-called coalescences in organization of the mind, whose two extremes she described as the *paranoid-schizoid* position and the *depressive* position, respectively. These positions, or states of mind, Klein went on to claim, remain unconsciously active within the adult psyche. Each position includes a specific anxiety, a set of unique defense mechanisms against this very same anxiety, just as it is characterized by specific sorts of object relations.

Although Klein designates the precise age at which these positions develop in the infant (the paranoid-schizoid position from birth to three months, the depressive position from three to six months), she also clearly states that in later, adult life one constantly shifts between them. While she mentions these positions in many of her writings, two of her papers are considered to be most important in the development of her thought on this subject: first, her 1935 paper, "A Contribution to the Psychogenesis of Manic-Depressive States," in which she first described the depressive position, second, her 1946 paper, "Notes on Some Schizoid Mechanisms," in which she describes the paranoid-schizoid position.[16]

In contrast to Freud, who sees the development and maturation of the personality as occurring in stages, Klein writes that "a 'position' is an always available state, not something one passes through." Since I want to claim (a) that the lifelong process—or, as I would rather say, lifelong work—of forgiveness can be understood as a shift from the paranoid-schizoid position to the depressive one, and (b) that this shift is a constant occurrence, not a unique event someone passes through in a single instant, once and for all, let me briefly describe these two positions and the underlying and ongoing transformations that enable the always possible shift, back and forth, between them.

The main characteristic of the paranoid-schizoid position is the high intensity of annihilation anxiety that the ego seeks to defend itself against by splitting of both self and object into good and bad, with, at first, little or no integration between them. In early development the death instinct, the trauma of birth, and the experience of hunger and frustration are the main sources of the extreme anxiety experienced by the very young infant. Although the infant's ego is rudimentary, it is able to alleviate the sense of anxiety by operating primitive defense mechanisms. Again, the first stage in this defense process is the splitting of the self and objects into good and bad, loved and hated, invested in life instincts (in the first case) or cathected with death impulses (in the second). The second defense is that of projection. The split-off parts of the infant's mind are imagined to be projected out and into the split object. In the third defensive maneuver, the good object (the one invested with the infant's life instincts) and the bad object (the one cathected with the death drive) are introjected back into the self. Yet the cycle of projection and introjection extends even further. Due to the intense anxiety and the denial of bad experiences out of a sense of omnipotence, alongside the idealization of the good experiences, a binary experience of the objects is created. Good objects are felt as ideal objects while bad objects are experienced as dangerous, hostile, and persecutory. During early infancy, this split is essential in enabling the infant to hold on to "purely" good experiences that provide a core of the ego around which the good and bad aspects of both self and object can be integrated and emotional development may take place. The formation of this "good" core is also a prerequisite for the later working through of the depressive position.

As I mentioned earlier, Klein observed the operation of these infantile anxiety situations in older children and adults as well, and these situations could therefore be understood as states of minds, forever oscillating in the life of the mind. Although for the adult in the paranoid-schizoid position the anxiety is not as devastating as it once was for the helpless infant, the content of the anxiety is very similar to that of the infant in its early development, and the defense mechanisms that are operated in order to alleviate it are roughly the same. An adult who experiences the world through the paranoid-schizoid position feels persecuted and fears annihilation. He splits his self and his objects into idealized ones and persecuting ones. Because of the attack on the integration of his ego, his ability to have a sense of history and continuity in time is compromised and hence his thought processes are characterized by the inability to symbolize in a mature way, as the latter requires precisely the ability to separate between the thing-in-itself and its symbol. These limitations add to an overall feeling of fragmentation, which creates further anxiety. Consequently, the vicious cycle of severe anxiety that calls for extreme defensive measures leads to feelings of increasing persecution and fragmentation.

If, during infancy, the infant has enough good experiences, due, no doubt, both to constitutional factors (such as the innate intensity of the drives and thereby of the anxiety) and to the nurturing environment (i.e., the ability of the maternal figure to alleviate its frustrations and anxieties), then the paranoid-schizoid position is successfully worked through. The "good" and the "bad" are no longer felt in their extremity and a rudimentary integration, now leading to the depressive position, is made possible.

The growing integration between the bad aspects of the self and the object and their good ones leads to the painful recognition that, since the loved object is also the hated one, the attacks that (in the infant's phantasy, in the previous phase) were lashed out at it could have damaged it. The persecutory anxiety of the paranoid-schizoid position gives way to a depressive anxiety in which the greatest danger becomes the loss of the loved object due to the infant's own aggressive attacks on it. This depressive anxiety calls for different defense mechanisms. First, the infant may revert to an even more paranoid-schizoid state. When the guilt that is the result of the imagined damage done to the loved one cannot be borne, the person resorts to a split that keeps the previous clear order in which the good is idealized and the bad is demonized intact. As a consequence, the confusing confluence of love and hate is prevented. Second, manic defenses are set into motion. A sense of omnipotence, that is to say, denial of psychic reality, disparagement and devaluation of the object, and, finally, an unrelenting attempt to master and control other objects characterize these defenses. As a result of manic defenses, the damage done to the object is denied so that no serious guilt or dependence on the object is needed or felt.

Alternatively, if and when guilt can be tolerated, the ego is driven to seek methods of reparation for the damage done in phantasy—or, worse, in reality—to the object (loved or not). In this case the harshness of the guilt, together with the superego-like quality of the internal object, is softened, and elements of forgiveness can slowly develop. The coming together of good and bad objects, and hence also of the impulses of love and hate, marks the onset of a new respect for the reality of external objects. Crucially, absence can begin to be tolerated without it being marked as the presence of a "bad object." Indeed, Klein makes it very clear that there is no final solution to the depressive position and that the attempt to deal with aggression against objects one also loves and depends on is a gradually evolving thread of the human psyche throughout life.

Although criticized for seeing all too complex emotional states in very young infants, Klein, in her famous 1937 paper "Love, Guilt, and Reparation," states fiercely that "even in the small child, one can observe a concern for the loved one which is not, as one might think, merely a sign of dependence upon a friendly and helpful person. Side by side with the destructive impulses in the unconscious mind both of the child and of the adult, there exists a profound urge to make sacrifices, in order to help and to put right loved people who in phantasy have been harmed or destroyed."[17] In the same article she further claims that generosity toward others arises from identification with the kindness of one's parents, but also from a desire to undo the injuries one has done to them in phantasy when they were frustrating one's desires. She terms this dually determined attitude one of "making reparation."[18] By this she means the recognition of one's own hostility, a recognition that facilitates the wish to repair the (imagined or factual) damage done to others. The child forgives the parents for their having frustrated it while simultaneously seeking their forgiveness for its own sadistic attacks on them. The urge to make reparation alleviates the despair that arises from guilt and foster hope and love. Thus Klein ties forgiveness to love: "If we have become able, deep in our unconscious minds, to clear our feelings to some extent towards our parents of grievances, and have forgiven them for the frustrations we had to bear, then we can be at peace with ourselves and are able to love others in the true sense of the word."[19]

Echoing Klein, Donald Winnicott, the British child analyst who greatly contributed to our understanding of the importance of aggression for the development of a love that is not narcissistic but acknowledges, accepts, and originates from an acute sense of difference, imagined a psychic process in which aggression, paradoxically, enables love. In this process the infant phantasizes that it aggressively attacks the frustrating mother. If she loves the infant and survives, and does not retaliate, the child thus learns that its aggression is not necessarily destructive. In a lecture at the New York Psychoanalytic Institute and Society, under the heading "The Use of the Object and Relating Through Identification,"[20] Winnicott describes the positive aspect of aggression as he explains how love makes aggression creative and how aggression makes love real.

The love of the "good enough mother" (to use Winnicott's term),[21] who survives the rage and destruction of her infant and remains available to be discovered again and again, makes her infant's aggression creative. For her survival means that she was constituted as a separate subject that belongs to the external reality and does not operate under the sway of the infant's phantasies. The mother's love allows her child's aggressive phantsies to discover, indeed, create her as a separate human being. This is precisely why the infant's aggression is creative.

By the same token, the infant's aggression "makes love real," since it now becomes affection toward a real, that is, external object and not toward a phantasized extension of its own self. One can add that the infant's love is real in yet another sense, namely it is now tested and proven, no mere whim; it was fought for and gained.

THE SHIFT FROM THE PARANOID-SCHIZOID position to the depressive one, from experiencing the self and objects as either good or bad, idealized or persecutory, loved or hated, to embracing their complexity—and nothing else could diminish resentment and the wish for revenge—is continuously occurring during the whole lifespan of a person. Both positions are viewed by Klein and her followers as forever alternating states of mind, always oscillating and allowing, as Bion suggests,[22] a fluctuation between disintegration (paranoid-schizoid) and integration (depressive). Even when individuals become well-integrated, under sufficient stress they will be prone to feel persecutory anxiety and to split the world and themselves in evil beings, on the one hand, and saints, on the other. As Klein explains in her essay "Envy and Gratitude": "Complete and permanent integration is . . . never possible. For under strain from external and internal sources, even well-integrated people maybe driven to stronger splitting processes, even though this maybe a passing phase."[23]

If forgiveness is enabled by the shift from the paranoid-schizoid position to that of the depressive position, and if these positions are in constant fluctuation, that is, if they are indeed forever alternating states of mind, then surely we can conclude that forgiveness, too, is a continuous process, always in the making.

When Henry Smith, in the paper I cited at the very beginning of this chapter, is concerned with the seductiveness of the concept of forgiveness and with the danger of losing sight of the "enormously varied set of conflictual processes that we lump together under the heading of forgiveness and that themselves need to be analyzed as efforts to deal with profound aggressive and erotic wishes, self-punitive reactions to those wishes, and the terrors they awaken,"[24] he seems to severely underestimate the real possibility that forgiveness is not an achievable end but, on the contrary, a lifelong process. That rather naive way of seeing forgiveness, as a one-time and unique event, an interpersonal, feel-good encounter, instead of seeing it as a lifelong, intrapsychic process, is apparent when Akhtar, tellingly, brings up the famous-infamous handshake between Yitzhak Rabin and Yasser Arafat, in 1995 at the White House, as emblematic of mutual forgiveness between two fierce opponents. What is obviously missing in his depiction of that moment is that, at this very event, when Shimon Peres, then foreign minister of Israel, wanted to shake Arafat's hand, Rabin—publicly and explicitly, one could say quite aggressively—stopped Peres from completing the gesture. But then again, it was, perhaps, also the very imperfection of this moment— Rabin's discourteous and ill-disposed act—that made this potentially mutually forgiving event somewhat authentic and real. "You know, we have a lot of work to do," Mr. Rabin said somberly, according to a Clinton aide. "I know and I am prepared to do my part," Mr. Arafat answered.[25] Clearly, a single handshake was not going to do it.

Forgiveness, then, is a demand and a responsibility that consists in the lifelong working through of the depressive position. Not unlike Freud's key concept and practice of analytic working through, of *Durcharbeiten*,[26] as the terminology goes, to forgive is a process, that is, nothing short of an interminable—and, I have argued, first of all, intrapsychic—commitment and task.

NOTES

1. Salman Akhtar, "Forgiveness: Origins, Dynamics, Psychopathology, and Technical Relevance," *Psychoanalytic Quarterly* 71 (2002): 175–212.

2. Henry F. Smith, "Leaps of Faith: Is Forgiveness a Useful Concept?" *International Journal of Psychoanalysis* 89 (2008): 919–36, here 922.

3. Jacques Derrida, "Freud and the Scene of Writing," in *Writing and Difference* (New York: Routledge, 2002), 290.

4. Robert F. Worth, "In Libya, the Captors Have Become the Captive," *New York Times Magazine Herald Tribune*, May 9, 2012.

5. Melanie Klein, "Mourning and its Relation to Manic-Depressive States" (1940), in *Love, Guilt, and Reparation and Other Works, 1921–1945* (New York: Free Press, 1975), 344–69.

6. Akhtar, "Forgiveness," 180.

7. Wilfred R. Bion, *Learning from Experience* (Northvale: Jason Aronson, 1994).

8. Melanie Klein, "The Early Development of Conscience in the Child" (1933), in *Love, Guilt, and Reparation*, 248–58.

9. Ibid., 257.

10. Ibid.

11. Melanie Klein, "Love, Guilt, and Reparation" (1937), in *Love, Guilt, and Reparation*, 306–44, here 306.

12. Juliet Mitchell, *Selected Melanie Klein* (London: Hogarth, 1986), 27.

13. The father likewise plays an important role in the child's emotional life, but the infant's early relations to him are modeled on the one it entertains with the mother whom it gradually comes to know, while still in the uterus, by hearing her voice and being an integral part of her bodily rhythms.

14. Klein distinguishes between *fantasy* with an *f* and *phantasy* with *ph* to differentiate between the more conscious reveries, daydreams, fantasies and the unconscious phantasies that stem from genetic needs, drives, and instincts and are their mental representations.

15. Susan Isaacs, "The Nature and Function of Phantasy," *International Journal of Psychoanalysis* 29 (1948): 73–97.

16. Melanie Klein, "A Contribution to the Psychogenesis of Manic-Depressive States" (1935), in *Love, Guilt, and Reparation*, 262–90, and "Notes on Some Schizoid Mechanisms" (1946), in *Envy and Gratitude and Other Works, 1946–1963* (New York: Free Press, 1975), 1–25.

17. Melanie Klein, "Love, Guilt, and Reparation," 311.

18. Ibid., 313.

19. Ibid., 343.

20. Donald W. Winnicott, "The Use of an Object and Relating Through Identification" (1968), in Donald W. Winnicott, Claire Winnicott, Ray Shepherd, and Madeleine Davis, eds., *Psycho-Analytic Explorations* (Cambridge: Harvard University Press, 1989), 217–28.

21. Donald W. Winnicott, "Transitional Objects and Transitional Phenomena—a Study of the First Not-Me Possession," *International Journal of Psychoanalysis* 34 (1953): 89–97.

22. Wilfred Bion, *Elements of Psychoanalysis* (London: Heineman, 1963).

23. Klein, "Envy and Gratitude" (1957), in *Envy and Gratitude*, 176–235, here 233.

24. Smith, "Leaps of Faith," 932.

25. Akhtar, "Forgiveness," 179.

26. Sigmund Freud, "Remembering, Repeating and Working-Through (Further Recommendations on the Technique of Psycho-Analysis II)" (1914), in *The Standard Edition of the Complete Psychological Works of Sigmund Freud, 1911–1913: The Case of Schreber, Papers on Technique and Other Works* (Hogarth: London, 1956–1974), 12:145–56.

8

BEYOND RIGHT AND WRONG

An Exploration of Justice and Forgiveness

Albert Mason

FORGIVENESS IS A SUBJECT OF great importance and is rarely addressed directly in film, literature, or psychoanalysis. Yet every day millions of people ask to be forgiven for their trespasses and state automatically, and without too much thought, "as we forgive those who trespass against us." Forgiveness is clearly something we hope we can receive and hope we can give, and yet the painful truth seems to be that vengeance is common and forgiveness is rare.

It is strange that psychoanalysts, therapists, and psychiatrists have written so little about this subject. One unpublished paper I read that did address the topic was composed in 1987 by Dr. Tom Grant, a deceased member of the Psychoanalytic Center California in Los Angeles. Theoretically, Grant linked forgiveness to a state of mind that Melanie Klein called the depressive position. Perhaps, while we Kleinians don't explicitly call it forgiveness, we do understand that forgiveness is implicit in the concept of the depressive position. We realize that both the capacity for forgiveness and the attainment of the depressive position are psychological goals we strive for in ourselves and our patients.

One of Klein's important discoveries was that, for development to take place beyond the initial confused stage of the infant, a splitting of the object into all good and all bad needed to occur first. At this stage there are ogres and fairy godmothers, blacks and whites, Jews and

Muslims or Muslims and Christians, God and the Devil—all in opposition to each other. We have also split ourselves into good and bad, projected the bad onto others, and now experience paranoia. Aptly, Klein called this state of mind the paranoid-schizoid position. It is also the stage of wanting vengeance for wrongs or imagined wrongs.

A more advanced developmental stage or state of mind is the stage of integration of good and bad and the understanding that all human beings contain both aspects. At this stage, through integration, we have hopefully modified our extreme states of mind and our extreme points of view. This is the stage when our intense emotions of love and hate merge to produce that precious human quality called understanding. It is the stage at which concern for those other than ourselves begins—a stage or state of mind that Klein termed the depressive position. Winnicott has called Klein's discovery and description of the depressive position her greatest contribution, one that ranks with Freud's discovery of the Oedipus complex.[1]

The depressive position is also the stage in which we can recognize and value others of a different age, color, culture, or religion from ourselves because we see them as essentially similar to ourselves, that is, as thinking and feeling beings. This understanding should lead to a new acceptance of the bad or destructive aspects of others, provided that *we* have admitted to having *both* good and bad qualities and have integrated the bad aspects of ourselves with the good. Then, hopefully, forgiveness of the bad in others can occur because identification with the other has taken place. In addition to being able to identify with the bad—and hopefully good—aspects of the perpetrator, we would need to see in him or her genuine regret, remorse, and some attempt to repair the wrongs that have been committed. Feelings of guilt normally follow the awareness of having damaged what one loves, be it a brother or a neighbor or a valued quality of oneself—like loyalty or kindness—that is the basis of self-esteem. Any repair would depend upon and follow the perpetrator feeling and accepting guilt and conveying a direct *verbal* apology to the victim of his crime.

It is interesting to note here that a central tenet of Alcoholics Anonymous and other twelve-step programs is the importance of making amends. This is accomplished by taking a systematic inventory of the wrongs one has committed and making an equally systematic attempt to ameliorate these wrongs by a verbal apology to the victims of one's destructiveness. One is reminded of a phrase in Romans: "For one who believes with the heart and so is justified, and one who confesses with the mouth and so is saved" (Romans 10:10).

The Torah tells us that anyone who rejects three separate pleas for forgiveness from another will be regarded as cruel. Jews find the concept of forgiveness so important that they are supposed to say nightly: "Master of the Universe, I hereby forgive anyone who angered or antagonized me or who sinned against me—whether against my body, my property, my honor, or against anything of mine; whether he did so accidentally, willfully, carelessly, or purposely; whether through speech, deed, thought, or notion. . . . May no man be punished because of me."[2] In addition, Jewish law requires that a person who has injured another physically, monetarily, or through words ask him or her for forgiveness. If the injurer does not do so, then, so the tradition teaches, even God cannot forgive him.

In his 2012 Yom Kippur sermon, Los Angeles Rabbi Beau Shapiro tells us that Jewish law is very clear: if we refuse to grant forgiveness after being sincerely apologized to three times, the sin is on us. He goes on to say, "We often think forgiveness is for the perpetrator of the sin, but it's really for the victims of the sin. Harboring anger and resentment doesn't hurt the other, it hurts us. It's about the possibility of a different future. Forgiveness doesn't change the past, it changes the future." He adds that we have all hurt those closest to us and wonders how we can expect forgiveness if we refuse to grant it. Shapiro further states that lack of forgiveness is related to the expectation of perfection in others and ourselves and that, presumably, the acceptance of imperfection is part of the act of forgiving.[3]

The Qur'an mentions the concept of forgiveness sixty-four times. The references tell us that the perpetrator must be a believer, must ask Allah for forgiveness, and must not knowingly persist in what he or she has done. Then, surely, Allah will be forgiving and merciful (2:199), even ample-giving (2:268). It is also made clear that one cannot ask for forgiveness for anyone else; even if one asks seventy times. All perpetrators must ask for forgiveness for themselves. Buddhism calls for ceaseless empathy and compassion toward all beings, especially one's enemies. The Bhagavad Gita, the classic Hindu text, reminds us that it is only the brave who can forgive (11:41–42).

In contrast, it is clear that attacking the attacker will occur when one feels nothing but hatred and the wish to put back into the attacker the pain that one has suffered at his or her hands. Such action will produce a hopeless state of escalation of violence in which pain and injury is forever passed back and forth. In fact, the perpetrator can unconsciously welcome a counterattack, as it can be felt to exculpate his own guilt and prove to him that violence is the only solution to conflict. The victim then actually becomes as cruel and violent as the original perpetrator.

It is not difficult to understand psychoanalytically the perpetrator of genocide and the horrific violence his act demonstrates, for the perpetrator has in some way succeeded in dehumanizing his victim. This is accomplished with the help of propaganda, internal or external, that splits the victim and makes him all evil, like a scourge, a plague, or a monster. In Kleinian terms, the perpetrator regresses to the paranoid-schizoid state. He has split himself (in phantasy) and projected those aspects of himself that he hates and wishes to disown into his victim, who then becomes an inhuman and cruel monster fit only for extermination. As such, the victim can now be annihilated without remorse. It is far easier and quicker to split off our own badness and project it into others than to own our own faults and go through the slow, painful, and difficult process of correcting them.

This splitting process was first described in 1946 by Melanie Klein, who called it *projective identification*.[4] It is a common human defense and classically consists of believing that one possesses all the good aspects of one's victim and that the victim possesses all the bad aspects of oneself. When the victim is seen to be all bad, one's violence against him can actually be felt to be justified and of great service to the world, as Hitler claimed in his campaign to cleanse Europe of the scourge of the Jews, gypsies, homosexuals, mentally ill persons, and other so-called deviants. His rationalized destructiveness struck a chord in a whole nation who blindly followed him. Hitler, who thought of himself as superman, maintained that he was purifying the Aryan race to produce a super-race free of all ills. In biblical terms, this is the principle of *scapegoating*, in which the villagers projected all their collective sins into two innocent goats. One was killed and the other banished into the wilderness (Leviticus 16:7–10). Thus the villagers were purified by slaying and disowning their own badness at a safe distance from themselves.

THE PROBLEM OF FORGIVENESS

It is important for the victim of abuse to differentiate between forgiveness and weakness. It may be felt that granting forgiveness is a sign of weakness and thus to be rejected. But forgiving, on the contrary, is a sign of real moral strength. It is certainly essential to defend oneself against real attacks, for one cannot forgive if one does not survive. When one does survive an attack, however unjust, it may be that punishing the attacker achieves the unwanted aim of relieving and exculpating the attacker's guilt. If he is attacked back, the perpetrator's fantasy is that now he or she has paid the price for his crime, his guilt is washed away, and she now feels free to repeat the attack. Punishment, in fact, can be welcomed as an absolution of one's crimes—as a cleansing.

Only the mobilization and acceptance of genuine guilt that stems from love and concern will bring real and substantial change, the mark of which is true remorse and the desire to repair the damage done as best one can. The American soldiers who massacred villagers at Mỹ Lai in Vietnam later banded together and rebuilt the village for the survivors and paid to educate the children who remained, just as some of the perpetrators in the Rwandan genocide have rebuilt the homes they destroyed. If we do not forgive the truly remorseful perpetrator, we will carry inside of ourselves a damaged and reproachful object that produces unconscious guilt and its consequences. Failure to forgive appropriately occurs in persons who harbor the wound—real or imagined—as a grudge and who cannot let it go.

This is particularly true when the wound inflicted is undeserved. The victim repeats internally the price he wishes to exact and fantasizes over and over again the suffering and pain he or she wishes to inflict. It is not just an eye for an eye he wants, but revenge with interest: a nose, an ear, and a tongue for an eye—and even then there is no satisfaction. The nursed grudge is not only felt toward the perpetrator, but augments any subsequent injury—real or imagined—and produces a state of mind that resembles paranoia. This state of mind can color one's life with a low-grade suspicion, cynicism, and lack of trust, souring even the sweetest drink. In *The Merchant of Venice*, Shylock is offered twice what he is owed in restitution, ten times what he is owed, but he will not budge. It is not money Shylock wants, but Antonio's life for the pain he has inflicted on Shylock. He wants the total annihilation of the perpetrator; only wiping him off the earth will do. Like the goat, Antonio must be sent to perish in the wilderness.

Forgiveness essentially consists in a reversal of the process of dehumanization. We must first see our perpetrator as human by integrating the split view of him as a monster and seeing the whole person with his bad and good qualities, just like ourselves. When perpetrators come to us expressing heartfelt regret for their destructive acts, we may actually begin to see some goodness in them. Secondly, we must see and accept that we also are whole—not ideal—and contain many attributes, both kind and cruel, both good and bad. The failure to forgive impoverishes us because of the grudge we harbor, whereas the capacity to forgive deepens and enriches us internally.

One often hears the phrase "forgive and forget," but it is important to differentiate between these two dynamics. To forget is basically to suppress. To forget is to clear from one's mind the wound one has suffered at the hands of someone else. From this perspective, one may feel one has dealt with the trauma because it is no longer experienced, but the trauma is still festering in the unconscious. In fact, one of the most important features of psychoanalysis is the recovery of traumas and painful experiences that have been "forgotten," which means that they were suppressed, a suppression initially acted as a defense. While consciously the trauma is not present, it continues to have an effect—like depression—until it is made conscious and worked through. Whereas forgiving allows us to forget (in some sense), at the same time we remember in a modified form. Forgetting is not remembering consciously, but the effects of the trauma are still experienced in the symptoms produced by the suppressed anger and hate.

It is easier to forgive if the perpetrator comes seeking forgiveness, for this implies that the perpetrator has accepted that he committed wrongdoing and is feeling guilt and remorse. If the perpetrator never admits his wrong, he adds a sense of injustice to the victim's pain and makes the possibility of forgiving more difficult and less likely.

When Jesus asked God to forgive his crucifiers, he pleaded, "Father, forgive them; for they do not know what they are doing" (Luke 23:34). Christ meant that his perpetrators were ignorant of their crime—similar to the insanity defense of criminals. Perhaps God can forgive such crimes, but it is beyond the capacity of most mere humans, who require the perpetrator's direct acknowledgment of his crimes and verbal expression of regret and guilt to his victim. We cannot ask for forgiveness on be-half of anyone else; only the perpetrator can do this, and only the victim has the right to grant the pardon.

Forgetting is only blotting out the conscious awareness of the pain one has suffered, while forgiving represents the modification of the hate and the wish for revenge both consciously and unconsciously. Holding in a grudge and phantasies of revenge through torture, humiliation, and complete control of the object imprison it and represent a rigid, consti-pated state of mind. I believe that we do not actually let go of our hos-tile, revengeful wishes, but modify them by the mobilization—through identification and compassion—of our loving, constructive feelings. This amalgam of hate, love, and compassion results in that precious quality called forgiveness. It contains the memory of our pain but is devoid of the wish to reinflict our suffering on others.

ANALYTIC FORGIVENESS

During my training as an analyst, I had the good fortune to be forgiven by many extraordinary teachers. Throughout my exposure to these orig-inal thinkers, I do not believe I ever heard the word *forgiveness*. How-ever, I felt forgiven by all of them many times for qualities I didn't have enough of—like restraint, ignorance, or humility—and for qualities I had too much of—like impatience, omnipotence, knowing, and cer-tainty. Above all, at that time I wanted to teach patients rather than learn from them. I now believe that each of my mentors was talking about and demonstrating forgiveness in slightly different terms.

Melanie Klein writes repeatedly that the infant seeks the breast not only for nourishment but for the relief of persecutory anxiety.[5] Psycho-analytically, the patient seeks relief from persecutory anxiety and ob-tains this in analysis through his or her negative transference being first accepted, tolerated, and later understood. Understanding is then con-veyed through interpretation. The patient's positive transference is felt toward the nourishing function the analyst provides and is easy for any analyst to accept, while tolerating the patient's negative transference—the patient's projected pain and attacks—is clearly much more difficult.

I believe that this aspect of the analytic process is linked to forgive-ness, as any practitioner who has been subjected to the abuse of the borderline or psychotic patient will understand. They will have felt the withering contempt leveled with unnerving accuracy at our age, appearance, our poor taste in furniture and clothing, our failure to understand, our misattunement. And then there is the matter of our vacations (too long or too short); the "monstrous" size of our bills or our egos; or the patient's scathing comparison of our own "inept" treatment to medication, behavioral modification, biofeedback, massage, or whatever the latest cure is thought to be. One patient, after some years of not much change, told me when he *did* improve that it was the effort of getting to his sessions that helped him and nothing I had ever said or done.

When, in the middle of a session, a patient attached a radio to her ear and muttered, "Shut up—the BBC—you can depend on them!" there was no mistaking what she felt. And when she later complained about the lack of cooking facilities while devouring a raw steak in my office, I wondered what had made me give up the peaceful world of anesthesia. Our toleration of whatever patients say or do—short of real physical assault—and our realization that they are demonstrating their pain and reinflicting on us their past trauma or communicating their distress in the only way they can—does call for sacrifice and forgiveness on the part of the analyst, who is trained and able to stand back and not take the attacks personally.

Meltzer taught us that the breast—the maternal function of the analyst—is at times felt to be like a toilet needed by patients to flush away their pain, anxiety, hostility, and frustration.[6] This is much like a mother cleaning up her children's incontinence and lack of control, delusional hatred, and paranoid view of her. It is often difficult *not* to take the patient's assaults personally and *not* to tell him or her that you agree that biofeedback sounds like a better approach. Containing the assaults of pain the patient cannot tolerate is a necessary sacrifice a clinician makes in order to convey to the patient that his or her state of mind is not overwhelming and intolerable.

Bion talked about the need to contain the patient, which implies the acceptance of their pain and anger—their hostile projections—so that they could identify with us, as containers and not reinflicters of pain and hostility.[7] Eventually, by this identification, the patient should come to be able to contain his own overwhelming distress. While it is easy to *say* that we analysts detoxify beta elements and restore alpha function, actually doing so requires inordinate patience, tolerance, understanding, and something akin to forgiveness.

So, while forgiveness was not mentioned directly by any of my mentors, I believe that Klein's idea of the *toleration of the attacks of the persecuted patient*, Meltzer's concept of the *toilet breast*, and Bion's theory of the *container* all include forgiveness as a part of the relationship of the analyst to the patient, just as a good parent accepts its child's hatred as well as its love. Clinicians need to keep in mind that initially patients "know not what they do" and forgive and tolerate being "done to" in the service of their patients' treatment.

Psychoanalysts are familiar with the mechanism of idealization, that necessary phantasy we (as infants) attach to parents in order to feel safe. The ideal parent is supposed to give us all we need, even before we feel the need. He or she should be always available—allowed no vacations or weekends—and must never get ill, impatient, or die. However, since human beings can never live up to these unrealistic expectations, we must eventually forgive them and ourselves; otherwise we live a sour, crabbed, Scrooge-like existence. Where idealization was, the acknowledgment of reality shall be. Reality itself needs to be forgiven, because it cannot possibly live up to our delusional expectations.

In essence, Klein, Winnicott, and Metzler all seem to have suggested that the *metabolism* of aggression in the crucible of the mother-infant dyad lies at the root of forgiveness versus vengeance. This process could be described in Bion's terms as beta elements metabolized and transformed into alpha elements. If the aggression is well metabolized and love predominates in the relationship, forgiveness can be experienced and identified with. If not, then seeds of revenge-seeking tendencies are sowed.

FALSE FORGIVENESS

In his 1999 book *No Future Without Forgiveness*, Anglican Archbishop Desmond Tutu stated that forgiving and being reconciled are not about pretending things are other than they are. It is not about patting one another on the back and turning a blind eye to the wrong. True reconciliation exposes the awfulness, the abuse, the pain, and the degradation of the truth. This exposure might even make things worse. It is a risky undertaking, but in the end it is worthwhile because seeing and dealing with the real situation helps to bring real healing. Spurious reconciliation can bring only spurious healing. Tutu's book provides a consideration of the profound difficulties and complexities involved in the act of forgiving.

In psychoanalytic terms, Tutu is talking about manic rather than true reparation and really speaks to a process akin to placating the perpetrator and helping him evade guilt and true reparation. The verbal request for forgiveness must occur when the words are a heartfelt expression of remorse and not a rapid and glib request. An analyst recently described a young patient he treated hitting a younger boy repeatedly and after each blow pleading, "I'm sorry, I'm sorry," as he continued hitting. The boy's sorrow was clearly confined to his words alone.

Anita Epstein quotes Elie Wiesel as having said, "I cannot and I do not want to forgive the killers of children; I ask God not to forgive."[8] Epstein elaborates that she cannot forgive Germany—that only the victims can do that, and they are all dead. She makes the point that only the victim of the crime is in a position to forgive his perpetrator—much like Dennis Prager in his *Wall Street Journal* article "The Sin of Forgiveness."[9] We cannot seek forgiveness on behalf of someone else.

THE WHY OF FORGIVENESS

Having discussed the universal need for forgiveness amongst various religions and, indeed, amongst all of us, the question now arises: why is forgiveness such a vital need?

There are, of course, conscious, unconscious, and semiconscious reasons. A boy asking consciously for forgiveness for hitting his brother, stealing cookies, or breaking his toys fears that he will lose his parents' love. He also fears punishment, but, as discussed before, punishment can also be welcomed because it is felt to exculpate the guilt and the damage done by wiping the slate clean. It is basically the loss of love that is terrifying because it threatens us with many consequences that are not too difficult to understand consciously. If the child is not loved, he believes he will be rejected and thrown out. Since he is helpless and has no resources, he will die. Even worse than death, the unloved outcast will be reviled, humiliated, and mocked. His safety, security, and survival will all be lost, since the child depends on his parents and believes that they will withdraw their support. To be unloved means not only that the child's essential supplies will be cut off but also that the child will conclude he is bad and therefore will lose self-esteem and hope.

It is basically the same for the adult; wishing for forgiveness is not only the wish to be loved, accepted, and secure, but is linked to something even more primitive: that is, the wish not to be hated. Unforgiving hatred is feared by that primitive part of us that believes another person's hatred can actually harm us. We find ourselves wearing apotropaic amulets and necklaces; we touch wood, carry lucky charms, mutter *keina hora*, and use all sorts of protective devices to turn away the evil eye, bad luck, and other omnipotent destructive forces that can strike us down if we are cursed and hated—that is, unforgiven. Forgiveness relieves us of persecutory anxiety, shame, the terror of being cast out, and the unbearable pain of guilt.

In addition, the child feels that if he is hated because he is bad he will lose what belongs to him and it will possessed by someone else. Added to the pain of loss is the pain of jealousy toward the person who now has what he lost—the mother herself, his siblings, or his other parent—and overwhelming guilt is added to his plight. He reproaches himself for his neglect or destructiveness, which, he believes, has produced this catastrophic state.

To be unloved and bad in the present echoes back to the earliest misdeeds—real and imagined—that have been perpetrated. Regression to a state of persecutory anxiety now occurs. The early anxieties are related to envious phantasies like devouring the breast and mother to take over all her possessions and then the devoured first object is felt to pursue the child, wishing to kill or consume. The child's ideas of marrying Mommy or Daddy produce terrifying phantasies of the displaced parent pursuing him; externally to kill or castrate, internally as an introjected superego that tortures and withholds peace from the child or adult forevermore. So forgiveness by the victim is forgiveness of envy, jealousy, and greed—in fact, of all the underlying phantasies that produce hostility and hatred and are present in all of us. All too often these phantasies lead to murderousness, as in Cain toward his brother Abel, Laius toward his son Oedipus, and children toward their parents.

The heaven of parental love and acceptance will become hell on earth to the unforgiven child. Yet it is precisely the same when we are unforgiven as adults who believe in God or Fate, which take us in when we are forgiven and cast us out when we are not. Whether we are Catholics at confessional or Jews, Protestants, or Muslims at prayer, we are praying for forgiveness in order to be loved and to enter the heaven of peace and security, to escape the hell and loneliness of being unaccepted, unforgiven, unloved, and cast out. Those of us who do not consciously pray still believe, in our depths, in Luck or a Fate that smiles on us when we are good or forgiven and deserts us when we are not. Logic and intelligence are no match for our primitive superegos. If they were, there would be no need for psychoanalysis!

In *The Merchant of Venice* a speech by Portia shows how close mercy comes to forgiveness:

The quality of Mercy is not strained
It droppeth as the gentle rain from heaven
Upon the place beneath: it is twice blest.
It blesseth him that gives and him that receives.
(4.1.173–176)

Like mercy, forgiveness enriches both the forgiver and the forgiven. It is clear that in an hour, a day, or even a year one cannot discuss all the ramifications of such a vast and important subject, so I will end now and ask your forgiveness for the many things I am sure I have omitted.

NOTES

This chapter takes up a lecture delivered at the University of California, Los Angeles, on November 17, 2012.

1. Donald Winnicott, "A Personal View of the Kleinian Contribution," in *The Maturational Processes and the Facilitating Environment* (London: Hogarth, 1962), 171–78.

2. *The Complete ArtScroll Siddur: Weekday/Sabbath/Festival*, ed. and trans. Nosson Scherman and Meir Zlotowitz (Brooklyn: Mesorah, 1985), 288–89.

3. M. Beaumont Shapiro, Sermon Yom Kippur 5773, September 26, 2012, http://www.wbtla.org/document.doc?id=194.

4. Melanie Klein "Notes on Some Schizoid Mechanisms" (1946), in *Envy and Gratitude and Other Works, 1946–1963* (New York: Free Press, 1975), 1–25.

5. See especially Melanie Klein's book *The Psycho-Analysis of Children* (London: Hogarth, 1932).

6. See, for example, Donald Meltzer, *The Psycho-Analytical Process* (London: Heinemann Medical, 1967).

7. Wilfred Bion, *Attention and Interpretation* (New York: Jason Aronson, 1970), especially the chapters "Container and Contained" (pp. 72–86) and "Container and Contained Transformed" (pp. 106–24).

8. Anita Epstein, "Why I Cannot Forgive Germany," June 9, 2010, http://forward.com/articles/128652/why-i-cannot-forgive-germany/.

9. Dennis Prager, "The Sin of Forgiveness," *Wall Street Journal*, December 15, 1997.

9

REMARKS ON LOVE

Jacques Derrida

AMY ZIERING KOFMAN: Just whatever you want to say about love . . .

DERRIDA: About what?

AZK: Love.

DERRIDA: Love or death?

AZK: Love, not death. We've heard enough about death.

DERRIDA: Love?

AZK: Love.

DERRIDA: I have nothing to say about love. At least pose a question. I can't examine "love" just like that. You need to pose a question. I'm not capable of talking in generalities about love. I'm not capable . . . Maybe that's what you want me to say in front of the camera, that I have nothing to say about love in general.

AZK: Could you explain why this topic has concerned philosophers for centuries? It's an important philosophical subject, isn't it?

DERRIDA: You can't ask this of me, Amy. Why have philosophers always spoken of love? That's how philosophy started—No, no. It's not possible. I have an empty head on love in general. And, as for the reason philosophy has spoken of love, I either have nothing to say or I'd just be reciting clichés.

AZK: Plato often spoke about this, maybe you could just talk about that.

DERRIDA: One of the first questions one could pose . . . I'm just searching a bit . . . is the question of the difference between the who and the what. Is love the love of someone or the love of some thing? OK, supposing I loved someone. Do I love someone for the absolute singularity of who they are? I love you because you are you. Or do I love your qualities, your beauty, your intelligence? Does one love someone or does one love something about someone? The difference between the who and the what at the heart of love separates the heart. It is often said that love is the movement of the heart. Does my heart move because I love someone who is an absolute singularity or because I love the way that someone is? Often love starts with some type of seduction. One is attracted because the other is like this or that. Inversely, love is disappointed and dies when one comes to realize the other person doesn't merit our love. The other person isn't like this or that. So, at the death of love, it appears one stops loving another not because of who they are, but because they are such and such. That is to say, the history of love, the heart of love, is divided between the who and the what. The question of Being, to return to philosophy—because the first question of philosophy is What is it "to Be"? What is Being? The question of being is itself always already divided between the who and the what. Is "Being" someone or some thing? I speak of it abstractly, but I think that whoever starts to love, is in love, or stops loving is caught between this division of the who and the what. One wants to be true to someone—singularly, irreplaceably—and one perceives that this someone isn't x or y. They didn't have the qualities, properties, images that I thought I'd loved. So fidelity is threatened by this difference between the who and the what.

NOTE

These remarks are taken from the transcript of the interview film *Derrida*, directed by Kirby Dick and Amy Ziering Kofman, published as *Derrida: Screenplay and Essays on the Film* (New York: Routledge, 2005), pp. 79, 81. Reproduced with permission of Routledge Publishing Inc. in the format Republish in a book via Copyright Clearance Center.

TO FORGIVE

The Unforgivable and the Imprescriptible

Jacques Derrida

Pardon, yes, pardon.

I have just said "pardon," in English.

You don't understand anything by this for the moment, no doubt.

"Pardon."

It is a word, "pardon," this word is a *noun*: one says "*un pardon*," "*le pardon*." In the French language it is a noun. One finds its homonymic equivalent, more or less in the same state, with more or less the same meaning and with uses that are at least analogous in other languages; in English, for example ("pardon," in certain contexts that will become clearer later on), although the word is, if not Latin, at least, in its tortuous filiation, of Latin origin (*perdon* in Spanish, *perdâo* in Portuguese, *perdono* in Italian). In the Latin origin of this word, and in too complex a way for us to tackle it head-on today, one finds a reference to the "*don*," [the "gift"], to "*donation*," [to "gift-giving"]. And more than once we would have to carry over the problems and aporias of the "gift" (such as I have tried to formalize them, for example, in *Given Time* and in particular in the last chapter of this book, entitled "The Excuse and the Pardon"),[1] to transfer them, so to speak, to the problems and non-problems that are the aporias of forgiveness, aporias that are analogous and, what is more, linked. But one must neither yield to these analogies between the gift and forgiveness nor, of course, neglect their necessity; rather, one must attempt to articulate the two, to follow them to the point where, suddenly, they cease to be pertinent. Between giving and forgiving there is at least this affinity or this alliance that, beside their unconditionality on principle—one and the other, giving and forgiving, giving for giving [*don par don*]—have an essential relation to time, to the movement of temporalization; even though what seems to bind forgiveness to a past, which in a certain way does not pass, makes forgiveness an experience irreducible to that of the gift, to a gift one grants more commonly in the present, in the present, in the presentation or presence of the present.

I have just said "experience" of forgiveness or the gift, but the word "experience" may already seem abusive or precipitous here, where forgiveness and gift have perhaps this in common, that they never *present themselves as such* to what is commonly called an experience, a presentation to consciousness or to existence, precisely because of the aporias that we must take into account; and for example—to limit myself to this for the time being—the aporia that renders me incapable of giving enough, or of being hospitable enough, of being present enough to the present that I give, and to the welcome that I offer, such that I think, I am even certain of this, I always have to be forgiven, to ask forgiveness for not giving, for never giving enough, for never offering or welcoming enough. One is always guilty, one must always be forgiven the gift. And the aporia becomes more extreme when one becomes conscious of the fact that if one must ask forgiveness for not giving, for never giving enough, one may also feel guilty and thus to have to ask forgiveness on the contrary, for giving, forgiveness for what one gives, which can become a poison, a weapon, an affirmation of sovereignty, or even omnipotence or an appeal for recognition. One always takes by giving: I have, in the past, insisted at length on this logic of giving-taking. One must a priori, thus, ask forgiveness for the gift itself, one has to be forgiven the gift, the sovereignty or the desire for sovereignty of the gift. And, pushing it farther, irresistibly, to the second degree, one would even have to be forgiven forgiveness, which may itself also include [*comporter*] the irreducible equivocation of an affirmation of sovereignty, indeed of mastery.

These are the abysses that await us and that will always lie in wait for us—not as accidents to avoid but as the ground [*fond*] itself, the ground without ground or groundless ground [*fond sans fond*] of the thing itself called gift or forgiveness; but the two are, above all, not the same thing. The verbal link of *don* to *pardon*, which is marked in Latin languages but not in Greek, for example, as far as I know (and we will have to ask ourselves about the apparent presence or absence of forgiveness in the strict sense in ancient Greek culture; an enormous and delicate question), this verbal link of *don* and *pardon* is also present in English and German: in English, *to forgive, forgiveness, asking for forgiveness*, and one will oppose *to give* and *to get* (this extraordinary word in the English language to which one would have to devote years of seminar) in *to forgive* versus *to forget*, forgiving is not forgetting (another enormous problem); in German, although *verzeihen* is more common—*Verzeihung, jemanden um Verzeihung bitten*: to ask someone for forgiveness—and this is the word Hegel uses in the *Phenomenology of Spirit* (we should return to this), one often uses *Entschuldigung* (more in the sense of an excuse) and *entschuldbar* in the equivocal sense of the forgivable-excusable, literally deculpabilizable, relieved of, exonerated from a debt remitted. There is nonetheless a word in German, a lexical family that maintains this link between the gift and forgiveness; *vergeben* means "to forgive," "*ich bitte um Vergebung*" [I ask for forgiveness], but its usage is usually reserved for solemn occasions less common than those that elicit *verzeihen* or *entschuldigen*. This link between the uses of the word "pardon," those uses said to be common and everyday and light (for example when I say "pardon," "sorry" at the moment I must pass in front of someone as I get out of an elevator) and the serious uses, reflective, intense uses, this link between all types of uses in very different situations, this link should be one of our problems, both a semantic problem of the concept of forgiveness and a pragmatic problem of the acts of language or pre- or ultra-linguistic practice. *Vergebung* is used more frequently—but this frequency and this probability are precisely a question of practice, of context and social gesture—more foreseeably; thus, a religious sense (Biblical-Koranic here) of the remission of sins, although the use of the lexical family (*vergeben, Vergebung, Vergabe*) is both flexible and perverse: *Vergeben* can mean the misdeal [*maldonne*], the corruption of the gift, *sich etwas vergeben*: to compromise oneself; and *Vergabe* is an invitation to tender [*marché attribué*], an auctioning . . .

"Pardon": "pardon" is a noun. It can sometimes be preceded (in French) by a definite or indefinite article (*le pardon, un pardon*) and inscribed, for example as subject, in a constative sentence: forgiveness [*le pardon*] is this or that, forgiveness [*le pardon*] has been asked by some-

one or by an institution, a pardon [*un pardon*] has been granted or refused, and so forth. . . . Forgiveness asked by the Episcopate, by the police, by doctors, forgiveness that the university or the Vatican has not yet
asked for, and so forth. This is the noun as reference of the constative—
or theoretical—type. One could devote a lecture to the question, the
subject, the theme of forgiveness, and this is basically what we are pre-
paring to do (forgiveness thus becomes, to this extent, the name of a
theme or of a theoretical problem, to be treated in a horizon of knowledge), unless the actors of the lecture ask or grant forgiveness in theoretically treating forgiveness. And when I opened this lecture by saying
"pardon," you did not know, you still do not know, what I was doing, if
I was begging your pardon or if, instead of using it, I was mentioning
the noun "pardon" as the title of the lecture. For in the single word "pardon," with or without an exclamation point, one can, although nothing
forces one to do so if a context does not require it, already here an entire
sentence implicit in it, a performative sentence: Pardon! I am begging
your pardon, I am begging you [*vous*] to pardon me, I am begging you
[*te*] to pardon me, pardon me, I beg you [*pardonnez-moi, je vous prie*],
pardon me, I am begging you [*pardonnez-moi, je t'en prie*].

(I am already marking, as I have just marked it as if in passing, beginning with a long digression in parentheses, this distinction between
the *tu* and the *vous* in order to situate or announce a question that will
long remain suspended but on which no doubt everything will also hang;
if the "you" is not a "*vous*" of respect or distance, as this "*Vous*" that Levinas says is preferable to Buber's "*Tu*," which signifies too much proxim-
ity or familiarity, or even fusion, and risks canceling out the infinite transcendence of the other; if thus the "you" of "I beg your pardon," "pardon
me" is a collective and plural "you," the question then becomes one of a
collective pardon—collective either because it involves a group of subjects, others, citizens, individuals, and so forth, or because it already involves, and this is even more complicated, but this complication is at
the heart of "pardon," a multiplicity of agencies [*instances*] or moments,
instances [*instances*] or instants, of "I"s inside the "I." Who forgives or
who asks whom for forgiveness, at what moment? Who has the right or
the power to do this, "who [to] whom?" And what does the "who" signify here? This will always be the almost ultimate form of the question,
most often of the question insoluble by definition. However formidable
it may be, this question is perhaps not the ultimate question. More than

once we will be faced with the effect of a preliminary question, prior to this one, which is the question "who" or "what"? Does one forgive someone for a wrong committed, for example a perjury (but, as I would argue, a fault, an offense, a harm, a wrong committed is in a certain sense always a perjury), or does one forgive someone something, someone who, in whatever way, can never totally be confused with the wrongdoing and the moment of the past wrongdoing, nor with the past in general. This question—"who" or "what"—will not cease, in its many forms, to return and to haunt, to obsess the language of forgiveness, and this not only by multiplying aporetic difficulties but also by forcing us finally to suspect or suspend the meaning of this opposition between "who" and "what," a little as if the experience of forgiveness (of a forgiveness asked for, hoped for, whether granted or not), as if, perhaps, the impossibility of a true, appropriate, appropriable experience of "forgiveness" signified the dismissal of this opposition between "who" and "what," its dismissal and thus its history, its passed historicity.

But between the "pardon" of the "pardon me" ["*pardonne-moi*"] and the "pardon" of the "pardon me" ["*pardonnez-moi*"] or the "pardon us" ["*pardonnez-nous*"] or the "pardon us" ["*pardonne-nous*"] (four essentially different possibilities, four different hands [*donnes*] of forgiveness between the singular and the plural that must be multiplied by all the alternatives of "who" and "what"—this makes a lot), the form that is the most massive, the most easily identifiable today of this formidable question, and we will begin with it, would be the one of a singular plural: can one, does one, have the right, is it in accordance with the meaning of "forgiveness" to ask more than one, to ask a group, a collectivity, a community for forgiveness? Is it possible to ask or to grant forgiveness to someone other than the singular other, for a harm or a singular crime? This is one of the first aporias in which we will constantly be entangled.

In a certain way, it seems to us that forgiveness can only be asked or granted "one to one," face-to-face, so to speak, between the one who has committed the irreparable or irreversible wrong and he or she who has suffered it and who is alone in being able to hear the request for forgiveness, to grant or refuse it. This solitude of two, in the scene of forgiveness, would seem to deprive any forgiveness of sense or authenticity that was asked for collectively, in the name of a community, a church, an institution, a profession, a group of anonymous victims, sometimes dead, or their representatives, descendants, or survivors. In the same way, this singular, even quasi-secret solitude of forgiveness would turn forgiveness into an experience outside or heterogeneous [*étrangère*] to the rule of law, of punishment or penalty, of the public institution, of judiciary calculations, and so forth. As Vladimir Jankélévitch pointedly reminds us in *Le pardon*,[2] forgiveness of a sin defies penal logic. Where forgiveness exceeds penal logic, it lies outside, it is foreign to [*étranger*] any juridical space, even the juridical space in which the concept of a crime against humanity after the war, and, in 1964, in France, the law of the imprescriptibility of crimes against humanity appeared. The imprescriptible—namely, what is beyond any "statute of limitations"— is not the un-forgivable, and I am indicating here very quickly, too quickly, a critical and problematic space toward which we would have to return again and again. All of the public declarations of repentance that are multiplying in France today (*Eglise de France*, the police and the medical profession—still not the Vatican as such, nor the university in spite of its accomplishments [*records*] in the area in question), declarations that were preceded, at a certain rate and in various forms in other countries, through similar gestures—the Japanese prime minister or V. Havel presenting excuses to certain victims of the past, the episcopacy in Poland and Germany proceeding to an examination of conscience at the fiftieth anniversary of the liberation of Auschwitz, the attempt at reconciliation in South Africa, and so forth. All of these public manifestations of repentance (whether state sponsored or not), and most often of "forgiveness asked," very new manifestations in the history of politics, are determined by the background of the historical-juridical resources [*s'enlèvent sur ce fonds historico-juridique*] that carried the institution, the invention, the foundation of the juridical concept of Nuremberg in 1945, a concept still unknown then, of "crime against humanity." Be this as it may, the concept of forgiveness—or the unforgivable—which is often put forward in all of these discourses, and in their commentary, remains heterogeneous to the judiciary or penal dimension that determines both the time of prescription or the imprescriptibility of the crimes. That is, unless the non-juridical dimension of forgiveness, and of the unforgivable— there where it suspends and interrupts the usual order of law—has not in fact come to inscribe itself, inscribe its interruption in the law itself. This is one of the difficulties that awaits us.

The little book of Jankélévitch that follows *Le pardon* and is entitled *L'imprescriptible* bears in epigraph several lines of Eluard, whose interest is paradoxical, and to my eyes usefully provocative, insofar as the lines oppose salvation, but salvation on earth, to forgiveness. Eluard says:

> There is no salvation on earth
> for as long as executioners can be forgiven.

> *Il n'y a pas de salut sur la terre*
> *tant qu'on peut pardonner aux bourreaux.*

Insofar as it almost always happens, and in a non-fortuitous way, that one associates—we will often return to this—expiation, salvation, redemption, and reconciliation with forgiveness, these remarks have at least the merit of breaking with common sense, which is also that of the greatest religious and spiritual traditions of forgiveness—the Judaic or Christian traditions, for example, that never remove forgiveness from a horizon of reconciliation, hope for redemption and salvation, through confession, remorse or regret, sacrifice, and expiation. In *L'imprescriptible*, from the very foreword of the text entitled "Should We Pardon Them?" a foreword that dates from 1971, Jankélévitch yields, without saying it in these terms, to a kind of repentance, since he admits that this text seems to contradict what he had written four years earlier in the book *Le Pardon* of 1967. In addition, the short polemical essay "Should We Pardon Them?" was written in the context of the French debates of 1964 about the imprescriptibility of Hitler's crimes and the crimes against humanity. As Jankélévitch makes clear: "In *Le pardon*, a purely philosophical work that I have published elsewhere, the answer to the question Must we pardon? seems to contradict the one given here. Between the absolute of the law of love and the absolute of wicked (*méchante*) freedom there is a tear that cannot be entirely unsewn [*décousu*]. I have not attempted to reconcile the irrationality of evil with the omnipotence of love. Forgiveness is as strong as evil, but evil is as strong as forgiveness."[3]

Naturally, what we have here are statements and a logic that we have barely begun to debate, with which we are just beginning to struggle. Nonetheless, the texts of *L'imprescriptible*, participating as they do in the debate I have just evoked and to which we will return concerning imprescriptibility, firmly conclude with the impossibility and inopportuneness, indeed with the immorality, of forgiveness. And in order to do this, in this polemical and impassioned debate, they form a continuity of meanings that we must rigorously dissociate, and which, moreover, Jankélévitch himself dissociates in what he calls his "purely philosophical study," namely, for example, forgiveness, prescription, and forgetting. "Should We Pardon Them?" begins with this question: "Is it time to forgive, or at least to forget?"[4] Jankélévitch knows perfectly well that forgiveness is not forgetting, but in the spirit of a generous polemical demonstration, and in horrified fear before the risk of a forgiveness that might end up engendering a forgetting, Jankélévitch says "no" to forgiveness, alleging that one must not forget. He speaks to us, in short, of a duty of non-forgiveness, in the name of the victims. Forgiveness is impossible. Forgiveness should not be. One should not forgive. We will have to ask ourselves, again and again, what this "impossible" might mean, and if the possibility of forgiveness, if there is such a thing, is not to be measured against the ordeal [épreuve] of the impossible. Impossible, Jankélévitch tells us: This is what forgiveness is for what happened in the death camps. "Forgiveness," says Jankélévitch, "died in the death camps."

Among all of Jankélévitch's arguments to which we would have to return constantly, there are two I would like to bring to your attention. They are also two axioms that are far from self-evident.

A. The *first* is that forgiveness cannot be granted, or at least one cannot imagine the possibility of granting it, of forgiving thus, unless forgiveness is *asked* for, explicitly or implicitly asked for, and this difference is not nothing. Which would then mean that one will never forgive someone who does not admit his wrong, who does not repent and does not ask, explicitly or not, for forgiveness. This link between forgiveness granted and forgiveness asked for does not seem to me to be a given, even if here again it seems required by an entire religious and spiritual tradition of forgiveness. I wonder if a rupture of this reciprocity or this symmetry, if the very dissociation between forgiveness asked for and forgiveness granted, were not de rigueur for all forgiveness worthy of this name.

B. *The second axiom* is that when the crime is too serious, when it crosses the line of radical evil, or of the human, when it becomes monstrous, it can no longer be a question of forgiveness; forgiveness must remain, so to speak, between men, on a human scale—which seems to me as problematic, although very powerful and very classical.

Two quotations in support of these two axioms.

1. *The first* presupposes a *history of forgiveness*; it begins at the end of this history and it dates the end of the history of forgiveness (we might later say, with Hegel, of history as forgiveness) by the project of the extermination of the Jews by the Nazis; Jankélévitch emphasizes what in his eyes is the absolute singularity of this project, a project without precedent or analogy, an absolutely exceptional singularity which would allow one to think, retrospectively, a history of forgiveness. This history would have deployed itself and since exposed itself, precisely, since or starting from its final limit. The "final solution" would be in sum, so to speak, the final solution of a history and of a historical possibility of forgiveness—all the more so, and the two arguments are intertwined in the same reasoning, that the Germans, the German people, if such a thing exists, have never asked for forgiveness: How could we forgive someone who does not ask to be forgiven? Jankélévitch inquires more than once. And here I would repeat my question, a question that should never stop echoing in our ears: Is forgiveness only possible, with its meaning as forgiveness, on condition that it be asked for?

Here then, before discussing them, are some of the strongest lines in Jankélévitch's argument: *"Forgiveness! But have they ever asked us for forgiveness?* [the "they" and the "us" would obviously have to be determined and legitimated]. *It is only the distress and the dereliction of the guilty that would give forgiveness a meaning and a reason for being."* Thus, it is clear for Jankélévitch—as it is clear for more than one tradition, those traditions from which an idea of forgiveness comes to us in effect, but an idea of forgiveness the very legacy of which conveys a force of implosion whose deflagrations we will constantly be registering, a legacy that contradicts itself and gets carried away, fired up, I would say more coldly "deconstructs itself"—it is thus clear that for Jankélévitch forgiveness can be granted only if the guilty party mortifies himself, confesses himself, repents, accuses himself by asking for forgiveness, if consequently he expiates and thus identifies, in view of redemption and reconciliation, with the one of whom he asks forgiveness. It is this traditional axiom, which has great force, certainly, and great constancy, which I will be constantly tempted to contest, in the very name of the same legacy, of the semantics of one and the same legacy, namely that there is in forgiveness, in the very meaning of forgiveness a force, a desire, an impetus, a movement, an appeal (call it what you will) that demands that forgiveness be granted, if it can be, even to someone who does not ask for it, who does not repent or confess or improve or redeem himself, beyond, consequently, an entire identificatory, spiritual, whether sublime or not, economy, beyond all expiation even. But I will leave this suggestion in a virtual state, we would have to come back to it incessantly, in a way that is incessant; I return now to my quotation of this very violent text, as if carried away by an anger that is felt to be legitimate, righteous anger.

> Forgiveness! But have they ever asked us for forgiveness? It is only the distress and the dereliction of the guilty that would give forgiveness a meaning and a reason for being. When the guilty are fat, well nourished, prosperous, enriched by the "economic miracle," forgiveness is a sinister joke. No, forgiveness is not for swine and their sows. Forgiveness died in the death camps. Our horror before that which understanding cannot, properly speaking, conceive of would stifle pity at its birth . . . if the accused "could inspire pity in us."[5]

What follow are remarks of such polemical violence and such anger against the Germans that I do not even want to have to read them or cite them. That this violence is unjust and unworthy of what Jankélévitch has elsewhere written on forgiveness it is only just to recognize that Jankélévitch himself knew. He knew he was letting himself get carried away, in a guilty way, by anger and indignation, even if this anger gave itself airs of righteous anger. That he should have been conscious of it comes through for example in an interview he gave several years later in 1977, in which Jankélévitch writes the following. I quote this *on the one hand* in order to note an expression that might well serve as the title of what I am trying to do here (namely a "hyperbolical ethics," or an ethics beyond ethics) and *on the other hand* in order to underline the more or less guilty tension that, along with Jankélévitch, we must admit to and try to be forgiven, a tension or a contradiction between the hyperbolical ethics that tends to push the exigency to the limit and beyond the limit of the possible *and* this everyday economy of forgiveness that dominates the religious, juridical, even political and psychological semantics of forgiveness, a forgiveness held within the human or anthropo-theological limits of repentance, confession, expiation, reconciliation, or redemption. Jankélévitch says this; he admits this:

I have written two books on forgiveness: one of them, simple, very aggressive, very polemical [*pamphlétaire*] whose title is: *Pardonner?* [this is the one from which I have just quoted] and the other, *Le pardon*, which is a philosophy book in which I study forgiveness in itself, from the point of view of Christian and Jewish ethics. I draw out an ethics that could be qualified as *hyperbolical* [my emphasis], for which forgiveness is the highest commandment; and, on the other hand, evil always appears beyond. Forgiveness is stronger than evil and evil is stronger than forgiveness. I cannot get out of this. It is a species of oscillation that in philosophy one would describe as dialectical and which seems infinite to me. I believe in the immensity of forgiveness, in its supernaturality, I think I have repeated this enough, perhaps dangerously, and on the other hand, I believe in wickedness (*mechanité*).[6]

It is obvious that the passage I read before on the finite history of forgiveness, on the death of forgiveness in the death camps, on forgiveness not being for animals or for those who do not ask for forgiveness, that this passage obeys the so-called polemical [*pamphlétaire*] logic, which the logic of a hyperbolical ethics resists, and resists infinitely, a hyperbolical ethics that would command precisely, on the contrary, that forgiveness be granted where it is neither asked for nor deserved, and even for the worst radical evil, forgiveness only acquiring its meaning and its possibility of forgiveness where it is called on to do the impossible and to forgive the un-forgivable. But the polemical [*pamphlétaire*] logic is not only a logic of circumstance; we must take it very seriously and pay it careful attention because it picks up on the strongest, the most strongly traditional, logic of the religious and spiritualist semantics of forgiveness, which grants it when there is repentance, confession, a request for forgiveness, a capacity to expiate, to redeem oneself, and so forth. One of the great difficulties that awaits us, in effect, stems from the fact that the hyperbolical ethics, which will also guide me, *both* lies in the wake of this tradition *and* is incompatible with it, as if this tradition itself carried in its heart an inconsistency, a virtual power of implosion or auto-deconstruction, a power of the impossible—that will require of us once again the force to re-think the meaning of the possibility of the impossible or the im-possibility of the possible. Where, in effect, we find the un-forgivable as inexpiable, where, as Jankélévitch in effect concludes, forgiveness becomes impossible, and the history of forgiveness comes to an end, we will ask ourselves whether, paradoxically, the possibility of forgiveness as such, if there is such a thing, does not find its origin: We will ask ourselves if forgiveness does not begin in the place where it appears to end, where it appears im-possible, precisely at the end of the history of forgiveness, of history as the history of forgiveness. More than once we would have to put this formally empty and dry but implacably exigent aporia to the test, the aporia according to which forgiveness, if there is such a thing, must and can forgive only the un-forgivable, the inexpiable, and thus do the impossible. To forgive the forgivable (*pardonable*), the venial, the excusable, what one can always forgive, is not to forgive. Yet the nerve of Jankélévitch's argument in *L'imprescriptible*, and in the section of *L'imprescriptible* entitled "Should We Pardon Them?" is that the singularity of the Shoah reaches the dimensions of the inexpiable; and that for the inexpiable there is no possible forgiveness, or even a forgiveness that would have a sense, that would make sense (because the common axiom of tradition, finally, and that of Jankélévitch, the axiom we will perhaps have to call into question, is that forgiveness must still have a sense, and this sense must be determined on the basis of [*sur fond de*] salvation, reconciliation, redemption, expiation, I would even say sacrifice).

Jankélévitch had in fact previously declared that in the case of the Shoah: "One cannot punish the criminal with a punishment proportionate to his crime . . . for next to the infinite all finite magnitudes tend to be equal; in such a way that the penalty becomes almost indifferent; what happened is literally *inexpiable*. One no longer even knows whom to put the blame on or whom to accuse."[7] Jankélévitch seems to assume, like so many others, like Hannah Arendt, for example,[8] that forgiveness is a human thing. I insist that this anthropological feature that determines everything (for it will always be a matter of knowing whether forgiveness is a human thing or not) is always a correlate of the possibility of punishing—not of taking revenge, of course, which is something else, to which forgiveness is alien, she says, but of punishing and that, I quote: "The alternative to forgiveness, but by no means its opposite, is punishment, and both have in common that they attempt to put an end to something that without interference could go on endlessly. It is therefore quite significant, a structural element in the realm of human affairs [my emphasis] that men are unable to forgive what they cannot punish and that they are unable to punish what has turned out to be unforgivable."

Thus Jankélévitch, in *L'imprescriptible*, and not in *Le pardon*, establishes this correlation, this proportionality, this symmetry, this common measure between the possibilities of punishing and forgiving, when he declares that forgiveness no longer has a sense where the crime has become, as has the Shoah, "inexpiable," disproportionate, out of proportion with any human measure. He writes, in effect: "Properly speaking, the grandiose massacre [the Shoah, the "final solution"] is not a crime on a human scale any more than are astronomical magnitudes and light years. Also the reactions that it inspires are above all despair and a feeling of powerlessness before the *irreparable*" [the irreparable:[9] Interrupting the quote, I underline this word for three reasons:

1. *First reason.* "Irreparable" will be Chirac's word to describe, in a text to which we will return, the crime against the Jews under Vichy ("France, that day," he declared, "accomplished the irreparable") ["*La France, ce jour-là accomplissait l'irréparable*"].

2. *Second reason* to underline "irreparable." We will have to ask ourselves if the irreparable means the unforgivable; I think "No," no more than the "imprescriptible," a juridical notion, belongs to the order of forgiveness and means the un-forgivable. Thus everything must be done to discern as subtly and as rigorously as possible between the unforgivable on the one hand and the imprescriptible on the other, but also all the related and different notions which are *the irreparable, the ineffaceable, the irremediable, the irreversible, the unforgettable, the irrevocable, the inexpiable.* All of these notions, in spite of the decisive differences that separate them, have in common a negativity, a "[do] not," the "[do] not" of an impossible which sometimes, or at the same time, signifies "im-possible because one cannot," "impossible because one should not." But in all cases, one should not and/or cannot go back over a past. The past is past, the event took place, the wrong took place, and this past, the memory of this past, remains irreducible, uncompromising. This is one way in which forgiveness is different from the gift, which in principle does not concern the past. One will never have treated forgiveness if one does not take account of this being-past, a being-past that never lets itself be reduced, modified, modalized in a present past or a presentable or re-presentable past. It is a being past that does not pass, so to speak. It is this im-passableness, this im-passivity of the past as well, and of the past event that

takes on different forms, which we would have to analyze relentlessly and which are those of the irreversible, the unforgettable, the ineffaceable, the irreparable, the irremediable, the irrevocable, the inexpiable, and so forth. Without this stubborn privileging of the past in the constitution of temporalization, there is no original problematic of forgiveness. Unless the desire and the promise of forgiveness, indeed of reconciliation and redemption, do not secretly signify this revolt or this revolution against a temporalization, or even a historicization that only makes sense if one takes into account this essence of the past, this being of the being-past, this *Gewesenheit*, this essence of the having been as the very essence of being. But also this eventness of being, the "it has been" ["*ça a été*"], the "it happened" ["*c'est arrivé*"]. It is in this horizon that we would have to reread all the thinking, which, like that of Hegel or, otherwise, Levinas (and in Levinas differently at different moments in his trajectory), makes the experience of forgiveness, of the being-forgiven, of the forgiving-each-other, of the becoming-reconciled, so to speak, an essential and onto-logical (not only ethical or religious) structure of temporal constitution, the very movement of subjective and intersubjective experience, the relation to self as a relation to the other as temporal experience. Forgiveness, forgivenness [*la pardonnéité*], is time, the being of time insofar as it involves [*comporte*] the indisputable and the unmodifiable past. But this pastness of an eventness [*passéité d'une événementialité*], the being past of something that happened is not enough to ground the concept of "forgiveness" (whether asked for or granted). What else is needed? Suppose we were to refer to this being-past of what happened by the seemingly simple term of "fact." Something has happened, a *fact* or a *deed* [*Il y a eu là un fait*] (past participle, which says that something took place, something that remains indisputable; something done, a deed). For there to be a scene of forgiveness, such a fact or deed (*fait*), such an event as done, must be not only an event, something that happens, a neuter/neutral and impersonal fact, this fact will have had to have been a *misdeed* or *wrong-doing* [*méfait*] and a *wrong done* [*méfait fait*] by someone to someone, a harm, a fault, implicating an author who is responsible and a victim. In other words, it is not enough for there to be a past event, a fact or even an irreversible misfortune for one to have to ask for forgiveness or to forgive. If, a century ago, an earthquake devastated a people or engulfed a community, if this past is a past harm, a terribly unfortunate and indisputable fact, no one will think, however, of forgiving or asking for forgiveness for this past event, for this "fact"—unless, that is, one still suspects some malevolent design or some malicious intent.

One would also have to discern, for you know, here as elsewhere, one must never give up distinguishing, dissociating as well, I will say relentlessly and without mercy—and the analysis of "forgiveness," of "pardon," is interminable—one must also discern between not only vengeance and punishment but also between punishing or punishment and the right to punish, then between the right to punish in general and the juridical right to punish, penal legality. Arendt could still say that forgiveness is a correlative of punishment without concluding thereby that there is, necessarily, a juridical dimension to it; the example par excellence of an incarnation, I am indeed saying an incarnation, of absolute and sovereign forgiveness as the right to forgive, as the right to punish, is the king's right to grant clemency [right of reprieve]. Of course, between forgiveness and clemency (just as between gift and "thank you [*merci*]," "to have at one's mercy [*merci*]"), there is this affinity that comes to us from an abyssal history, a religious, spiritual, political, theological-political history that should be at the center of our reflection. The only inscription of forgiveness in the law, in juridical legislation, is no doubt the right to grant clemency, the kingly right of theological-political origin that survives in modern democracies, in secular republics such as France or in semi-secular democracies such as the United States, where the governors and the president (who in the United States swears an oath of office on the Bible) have, if I am not mistaken, a sovereign right to "pardon" (moreover, one also says "pardon" in English in this case).

The king's right to grant clemency, this all-powerful sovereignty (most often of divine right) that places the right to forgive above the law, is no doubt the most political or juridical feature of the right to forgive as the right to punish, but it is also what interrupts, in the juridical-political itself, the order of the juridical-political. It is the exception to the juridical-political *within* the juridical-political, but a sovereign exception and a sovereign interruption that found the very thing from which they exclude or exempt themselves. As often, the foundation is excluded or exempted from the very structure that it founds. It is this logic of the exception, of forgiveness as absolute exception, as the logic of the infinite exception, that we would have to ponder over and over again. One should not be able to say "pardon," ask for or grant forgiveness, except in an infinitely exceptional way. If, furthermore, we listen to Kant (as we would often have to do, especially on the subject of "radical evil"), if we listen to him on the subject of the right to grant clemency, precisely in his *Doctrine of Right* (the first part of the *Metaphysics of Morals*) when he discusses Public Right, and in this the right to punish and to grant clemency (Introduction to §50 and following), what he tells us still has considerable scope if one transfers it onto forgiveness. The gist of what he says is this: that the right to grant clemency (*ius aggratiandi, Begnadigungsrecht*), the right to lessen or remit the penalty of a criminal, is, of all sovereign rights, the most delicate, the slipperiest, the most equivocal (*das schlüpfrigste*). It gives the most splendor to greatness, to the highness of the sovereign, to sovereignty (and we will have to ask ourselves whether forgiveness should or should not be "sovereign"), but the sovereign thereby runs the risk of being unjust, of acting unjustly (*unrecht zu tun*) in the highest degree. Nothing can be more unjust than clemency. And Kant adds a fundamental caveat here, he marks an inner limit to the sovereign's right to grant clemency: the latter does not, *should not under any circumstances*, have the right to grant clemency for a crime committed where he is not the one intended; he should not have the right to grant clemency for crimes committed by subjects against subjects—thus for crimes between those who for him are also third parties. Because this impunity (*impunitas criminis*) would be the greatest injustice toward the subjects. The right to grant clemency—and thus to pardon—should only be exercised where the crime is against the sovereign himself, a crime of *lèse majesté* (*crimen laesae maiestatis*). And even in this case, the sovereign should not exercise his right to grant clemency except on condition that this clemency not constitute any danger for his subjects. Thus limited, severely limited, this right is the only one that deserves the name of majesty, the right of majesty (*Majestätsrecht*).

At the very least, what one gathers from this fundamental remark, by extending it to forgiveness, is that forgiveness in general should only be permitted on the part of the victim. The question of forgiveness as such should only arise in the head-to-head or the face-to-face between the victim and the guilty party, never by a third for a third. Is this possible? Is such a head-to-head, such a face-to-face possible? We would have to return to this more than once. Forgiveness perhaps implies, from the outset, as if by hypothesis, the appearance on the scene of a third party whom it nonetheless must, should, exclude. In any case, according to common sense itself, no one seems to have the right to forgive an offense, a crime, a fault committed against someone else. One should never forgive in the name of a victim, especially if the latter is radically absent from the scene of forgiveness, for example, if this victim is dead. One cannot ask forgiveness of living beings, of survivors for the crimes whose victims are dead. As are sometimes its authors. This would be one of the angles from which to approach all the scenes and all the declarations of repentance and requests for forgiveness that have been multiplying for some time on the public scene (in France, the Catholic Church, the police, doctors, and perhaps one day, who knows, the university or the Vatican) and that we will have to analyze closely.

3. *Third reason* to underline "irreparable": As I will not cease to repeat, it is only against the unforgivable, and thus on the scale *without scale* of a certain inhumanity of the inexpiable, against the monstrosity of radical evil that forgiveness, if there is such a thing, measures itself.

I return now to my quotation of Jankélévitch:

> Also, the reactions it inspires are above all despair and a feeling of powerlessness before the irreparable. One can do nothing [A very strong sentence: everything becomes impossible, including forgiveness]. One cannot give life back to the immense mountain of miserable ashes. One cannot punish the criminal with a punishment proportionate to his crime: for next to the infinite all finite magnitudes tend to be equal [What Jankélévitch seems to exclude, with the full sense and common sense of a tradition, is the infinity of human forgiveness and thus the very hyperbolicity of the ethics by which he seemed to be and said he was inspired in his book on *Le pardon*], for next to the infinite all finite magnitudes tend to be equal, in such a way that the penalty becomes almost indifferent; what happened is literally *inexpiable*. One no longer even knows whom to attack or whom to accuse.[10]

Jankélévitch himself underlines the word "inexpiable"; and what he means to show is that where there is the inexpiable, there is the unforgivable, and where the unforgivable arises, forgiveness becomes impossible. It is the end of forgiveness and of the history of forgiveness: Forgiveness died in the death camps. We would have to ask ourselves, as far as we are concerned, if, on the contrary, forgiveness (both *in* and *against* the concept of forgiveness, in and beyond, or against the idea of forgiveness that we inherit—and whose legacy we must question, perhaps contest the legacy while inheriting from it—and this is a reflection on inheritance that we are beginning here), if forgiveness must not free itself from its correlate of expiation and if its possibility is not called forth precisely and only where it seems to be impossible before the un-forgivable, and possible only when grappling with the im-possible.

Since I have been quoting this page of *L'imprescriptible: "Pardonner?"* about a forgiveness that must be asked for and about a forgiveness that would have died in the death camps, I think we would also be interested in what follows, and that concerns the *waiting [attente]* to be asked for forgiveness. Jankélévitch will tell us that he was waiting for the word "pardon," this word with which we began ("Pardon!") and which can have the value of a performative sentence (Pardon!, I ask your pardon, pardon me [*pardonnez-moi*], pardon me [*pardonne-moi*]), this word that asks for forgiveness. Jankélévitch will tell us that he was waiting, as were others, to be asked for forgiveness, implying thereby that forgiveness must be asked for, that it asks to be asked for. And in a certain way, by saying that he was waiting, as others were, and in vain, for a word of pardon, a request for forgiveness, Jankélévitch admits in short that he was asking for forgiveness to be asked for (this would be a problem for us, of course, but I would like to emphasize here a feature of this scene: It is asked, it is expected that the word pardon be uttered or implied, signified, in any case, as pardon beseeched). What is essential is not that the word be said but that it be signified, that a pardon-beseeched be signified, such as a plea for mercy [*grâce demandée*], a plea for "thank you" [*"merci" demandé*], and with this pardon-beseeched, before it, expiation, remorse, regret, confession, a way of accusing oneself, of pointing an accusatory and self-referential, auto-deictic finger at oneself, something that, as one says, rather quickly, the animal would be incapable of, the mea culpa of the one who can beat his breast and, by recognizing his crime, dissociate himself from the guilty subject, from the subject having been guilty. We should return to this structure of temporality and of temporal specularity. For the moment, I will quote this request for a forgiveness requested in order to associate *two references* to it.

Jankélévitch writes thus: "To ask for forgiveness! We have long been waiting for a word, a single word, a word of understanding and sympathy . . . we have hoped for it, this *fraternal* word!"[11] I italicize the word "fraternal"; this word "fraternal" to describe a "fraternal word" must be given a very strong and very precise meaning; it does not only mean sympathy or effusion, compassion; it bespeaks the sharing of humanity, the fraternity of men, of sons recognizing their belonging to the human race, as will become clearer still; and it is hard to erase the profoundly Christian tradition of this humanist, familialist, and fraternalist universalism, in keeping with Jesus's message, among others, for example in Matthew 23: "Yes, you have one rabbi and you are all brothers, *unus est enim magister vester, omnes autem vos fratres estis, pantes de umeis adelphoi este.*" "We have hoped for it, this fraternal word! Certainly, we were not expecting our forgiveness to be implored. . . . But we would have received words of understanding with gratitude, with tears in our eyes. Alas, in the way of repentance, the Austrians have made us a present of the shameful acquittal of the executioners." And a little further on, as often elsewhere, Jankélévitch violently attacks Heidegger.[12] I would be tempted—this is the first of the two references that I mentioned—to relate this remark to what many interpreters of Celan's poem ("Todtnauberg")—that he wrote in memory and in testimony to his visit to Heidegger—have read as the trace of a disappointed expectation [*attente*], of Celan's anticipation [*attente*] of a *word* from Heidegger that would have signified a *pardon* beseeched. I myself will not venture to confirm or invalidate, I will not, out of respect for the letter and the ellipsis of Celan's poem, rush into an interpretation so transparent and univocal; I abstain from this not only out of hermeneutic prudence or out of respect for the letter of the poem, but also because I would like to suggest that forgiveness (granted or asked for), the address of forgiveness, must forever remain, if there is such a thing, undecidably equivocal, by which I do not mean ambiguous, shady, twilit, but heterogeneous to any determination in the order of knowledge, of determinate theoretical judgment, of the self- presentation of an appropriable sense [*de la présentation de soi d'un sens appropriable?*] (it is an aporetic logic that, at least from this point of view, forgiveness would have [in common] with the gift, but I will leave this analogy in progress or undeveloped here). What "Todtnauberg" says, Celan's poem that bears this title, what it says and on the basis of which the interpreters who rush to transform it into a clear narration find their authority (a narration of the type: "Celan-came,-H.-did-not-ask-the-Jews-for-forgiveness-in-the-name-of-the-Germans,-Celan-who-was-waiting-for-a-word-of-forgiveness,-a-"pardon!,"-a-request-for-forgiveness-left-disappointed-and-he-made-a-poem-of-it-he-recorded-it-in-one-of-his-poems), no, what the poem says, is at least this:[13]

> Arnika, Augentrost, der
> Trunk aus dem Brunnen mit dem Sternwürfel drauf
>   in der
> Hütte
> die in das Buch
> —wessen Namen nahms auf
> vor dem meinen?—,
> die in dies Buch
> geschriebene Zeile von
> einer Hoffnung, heute,
> auf eines Denkenden kommendes
> Wort
> im Herzen, [. . .]

Arnica, eyebright, the / draft from the well with the starred die above it, / in the / hut, / the line / —whose name did the book / register before mine?—, / the line inscribed / in that book about / a hope, today, / of a thinking man's / coming / word / in the heart, [. . .]

Arnica, Casse-Lunettes (euphrasia, euphraise), la / gorgée à la fontaine surmontée du / dé étoilé, / dans la / hutte / la ligne dans le livre / le nom de qui a-t-il / accueilli avant le mien?— / la ligne écrite dans ce / livre d'un / espoir, aujourd'hui, en la / parole / à venir / au cur / d'un penseur; [. . .]

However one interprets the meaning and testimonial reference of such a poem, it links its signature as poem (and of a poem that signs itself by naming a signature in a book, a name left in a book [. . .] to, I quote, one must quote, the hope for words [*parole*], for a word (*Wort*) that comes in the heart, that comes from the heart, of a thinking being; and because it is a question of a past, of the signature and the trace of names left in the book of another, as that which is named, it is the hope for a word to come—or not—thus of a gift and a gift of thought, of a gift to come or not from a place or from a thinking being (*kommendes, eines Denkenden*—and you know how Heidegger is known for having often associated *Denken* and *Danken*: to thank, to acknowledge, to express one's gratitude, the thank you of acknowledgment, and think further of the relation between thanks and mercy [*grâce*], "to grace [*faire grâce*]" or "to beg for mercy, an act of grace [*demander grâce*]"), for all of these reasons, the motifs of the gift and acknowledgment belong as much to its thematics as they do to the act or essence of the poem, to the gift of the poem; and this poem says all of these things, the gift, and the gift of the poem and the gift of the poem which it itself is. As much because it gives as because it receives, from the past that it recalls and from the hope it calls forth [*appelle*], through its recall [*rappel*] and its calling forth [*appel*], it belongs to the element of the gift—and thus to the element of forgiveness, of a forgiveness asked for or a forgiveness granted, both at the same time no doubt, the moment it says the poetic experience both as appeal for acknowledgment (in the sense of consciousness, of the acknowledgment that recognizes and admits or the acknowledgment that gives thanks, acknowledgment as gratitude), the poetic experience as gift and forgiveness hoped for, asked for, granted, for the other, in the name of the other; as if there were no poetic experience, no experience of language as such without the experience of the gift and forgiveness—whether or not they are asked for, granted, given—the question mark around the name that comes before my own in the book (*wessen Namen nahms auf vor dem meinen?*—whose name was received before mine, with this untranslatable alliteration, *Namen nahms auf*, that evokes hospitality [*aufnehmen*]), the reception offered to the other, this question mark around the identity of the other, around the name of the other who will have preceded me and with whom I am, whether I want it or know it, bound, bound up in the strange community, the strange genealogy of this book: This question mark indeed marks this anguish or this anxiety as to the name of the other, as to this other to whom I am given over with my eyes blindfolded, passively, although I sign, the other having signed before me and marking, sur-marking in advance, my signature, appropriating my signature in advance, as if I always signed in the name of the other who also signs thus, in my place, the other whom I countersign or who countersigns me, who countersigns my own signature, the gift and forgiveness having taken place, or not, having taken place and having been nullified, carried away, without my ever even having to make a decision. This abyssal countersignature forms one body with the poem, with the experience of language itself, always as the language of the other, something that Celan knew and acknowledged so singularly, but which is also a universal experience of language (I must say that I myself signed this book in the hut, at the request of Heidegger's son, with as much anxiety, an anxiety that extended as much to all those in whose following, without knowing it, I signed, as to what I myself scribbled in haste, both things likely to be equally at fault, perhaps even judged unforgivable). Naturally, in order to begin doing justice to *Todtnauberg*, one would have to read as attentively what precedes and what follows each of the words, and the break after each word, for example "*Der Mensch*," the man, to designate the driver, *deutlich* to designate, so close to *deutsch* (a classical and quasi- proverbial association), to designate, thus, the univocal distinction between the words that were then uttered, once the words *Namen* and *Wort*, proper noun and words, had already found their echo in the poem, and especially the word "*viel*," many, innumerable, infinitely numerous, which is the last word of the poem and apparently, or figuratively, describes that which, like tracks or the humid thing (*Feuchtes*), is buried in the bog. . . . "Todtnauberg" remains thus to be read, to be received—as gift or forgiveness themselves, a gift and a forgiveness which are the poem before being, possibly, its themes or the theme of the poet's disappointed expectation.

2. The other, *the second* reference that I mentioned, involves an exchange of letters that took place in 1980 and 1981 between a young German and Jankélévitch following the publication of *L'imprescriptible*.[14] The young German who writes to Jankélévitch places in epigraph to his moving and troubling letter the words of Jankélévitch ("They killed six million Jews. But they sleep well. They eat well and the Mark is doing well."), and the long letter begins painfully as follows:

> I myself have not killed any Jews. Having been born German is not my fault, or my doing. No one asked my permission [thus is posed from the outset the immense question, which will remain with us, the question of guilt or forgiveness according to the legacy, the genealogy, the collectivity of a *we* and of which *we*]. I am completely innocent of Nazi crimes; but this does not console me at all. My conscience is not clear, and I feel a mixture of shame, pity, resignation, sadness, incredulity, revolt. I do not always sleep well. I often remain awake at night, and I think, and I imagine. I have nightmares that I cannot get rid of. I think of Anne Frank, and of Auschwitz and of *Todesfuge* and of *Nuit et Brouillard*: "*Der Tod ist ein Meister aus Deutschland.*"

"Todesfuge" is the title, as you know, of another of Celan's poems clearly referring to the death camps and in which the line "Der Tod ist ein Meister aus Deutschland" comes back four or five times; guilt without fault and repentance or forgiveness asked for a priori, infinitely, in the name of the other. Mixture of a "pardon beseeched," without the word "pardon" but this amounts to the same, of a pardon beseeched and a protest against what condemns one to admit and to ask forgiveness in the name of the other, for a fault that one has not oneself committed; as for the nightmare, it alerts us to the guilt, and the scene of forgiveness, and the mourning that is inseparable from it; when he says that he does not have a "clear conscience," Wiard Raveling no doubt knows that he is addressing the author of a book called *La mauvaise conscience*, which includes an entire chapter on "The Irreversible" and some very fine subsections on regret, the irremediable, remorse, and repentance. *La mauvaise conscience* is a book whose first edition dates from 1933 and of which the book *Le pardon*, in 1967, given all that you know, is a kind of sequel.

This young German also invited Vladimir Jankélévitch to visit him, thus offering him hospitality (hospitality, gift and pardon, tears: the gift is always insufficient, thus pardon, or else ghost [*revenant*] and mourning): "If ever, dear M. Jankélévitch, you pass through here, knock on our door and come in. You will be welcome. And be assured [this is the painful irony of the entire letter]. My parents will not be there. No one will speak to you of Hegel, or of Nietzsche, or of Jaspers, or of Heidegger or of any other of the great Teutonic thinkers. I will ask you about Descartes and Sartre. I like the music of Schubert and Schumann. But I will play a record of Chopin, or if you prefer Fauré and Debussy. [. . .] Let it be said in passing: I admire and respect Rubinstein; I like Menuhin."

Following this long letter, which, once again, I cannot read to you here, and which is both a pathos-filled complaint, a protest, a confession, a plea, and a summation, Wiard Raveling received two responses, both of which are also published in the *Magazine Littéraire*. The first from Fr. Régis Bastide, on July 1st, 1980, from which I will cite several lines:

> Dear Sir, I cannot tell you for lack of time, the degree to which I was
> moved by your letter to Vladimir Jankélévitch. [. . .] I am an old friend
> of Vladimir Jankélévitch. But his attitude shocks me profoundly. This
> non-forgiveness is dreadful. It is up to us, to us Christians (even non-
> believers!) to be different. The fanatical Jew is just as bad as the Nazi.

But I cannot say this to Vladimir Jankélévitch. [. . .] You are no doubt a French teacher to write so well and so powerfully. I agree absolutely with all the words of your letter that my friend will surely judge too sentimental, tinged as it is with the awful *Gemütlichkeit* that must seem to him the greatest of vices. But you are right. Do not judge all French Jews by the terrible words of my friend. [. . .] What is the origin of your last name, and your first name? Hungarian? Viking?

The other response came from Vladimir Jankélévitch himself. The word "forgiveness" is not uttered. But it clearly says that what was awaited (You remember these words: " . . . to ask for forgiveness! We have long been waiting for a word, a single word, a word of understanding and sympathy . . . We have hoped for it, this fraternal word!") has finally arrived:

Dear Sir, I am moved by your letter. I have waited for this letter for thirty-five years. I mean a letter in which the abomination is fully assumed and by someone who has had no part in it [*n'y est pour rien*]. This is the first time I have received a letter from a German, a letter that was not a letter of a more or less disguised self-justification. Apparently, German philosophers, "my colleagues" (if I dare to use this term) have nothing to say to me, nothing to explain. Their good conscience is unperturbable. [Injustice or ignorance of Vladimir Jankélévitch: as if a letter addressed to him personally were the only reparation possible.] You alone, you the first and no doubt the last, have found the necessary words outside the political commonplaces and the pious clichés. It is rare for generosity, spontaneity, and a keen sensitivity to find their language in the words we use. And such is your case. There is no mistaking it. Thank you [pardon beseeched: a gift that calls for thanks]. No, I will not come see you in Germany. I will not go that far. I am too old to inaugurate this new era. Because for me it is a new era all the same. For which I have waited too long. But you are young, you do not have the same reasons as I. You do not have this uncrossable barrier to cross. It is my turn to say to you: When you come to Paris, do as everyone does, knock on my door. . . . We will sit down at the piano.

I underline this allusion, on both sides, on the part of both correspondents, to music, to a musical correspondence, to music played or listened to together, a sharing of music. I underline it not only because Vladimir

Jankélévitch was, as you know, a musician, an interpreter of music and a music lover, but also because between a certain beyond the word required, perhaps by forgiveness (a theme to which I should return later—the theme of verbal language, of discourse as the disastrous condition of forgiveness, which makes possible forgiveness but which also destroys it), between a certain beyond the word required, perhaps by forgiveness, and music, and even wordless song, there is perhaps an essential affinity, a correspondence which is not only that of reconciliation.

And in fact, Wiard Raveling recounts that he visited Vladimir Jankélévitch only once, that everything took place very cordially but that Jankélévitch always "systematically avoided" returning to these questions. Even in the correspondence that followed. But you will have remarked in Vladimir Jankélévitch's letter that I have just quoted and which speaks of a "new era" for which "I am too old" ("You do not have this uncrossable barrier to cross": "the uncrossable to cross"), Jankélévitch, in a way which is exemplary for us, causes two discourses to cross each other [*croise entre eux deux discours*], two logics, two axiomatics, which are contradictory, incompatible, irreconcilable, one of which is, precisely, that of conciliation or reconciliation, the other that of the irreconcilable. On one side, he welcomes the idea of a process, of a history that continues, of the passage from one generation to the other, and thus of the work of memory, as the work of mourning that makes what was not possible for him, forgiveness, possible in the future. Forgiveness will be good for you, for the next generation, the work will have been done, the work of mourning and memory, history, the work of the negative that will make reconciliation possible, and expiation, and healing, and so forth. But at the same time, he makes it known, more than he says it, that if this barrier—which will perhaps be crossed by new generations—remains uncrossable for him, this is because it must and can only remain uncrossable.

In other words, history, as the history of forgiveness, has stopped and it has stopped forever, it will have to have remained stopped by radical evil. It has stopped forever. And one feels this double conviction, both sincere and contradictory, self-contradictory. He does not doubt, he even hopes, and sincerely, that history will continue, that forgiveness and reconciliation will be possible for the new generation. But at the same time, he does not want this, he does not want this for himself, thus he does not want what he wants and what he accepts wanting, what he wants to want, what he would like to want, he believes in it but he does not believe in it, he believes that this reconciliation, this forgiveness will be illusory and false; they will not be authentic forgivenesses, but symptoms, the symptoms of a work of mourning, of a therapy of forgetting, of healing away, of the passage of time; in short, a sort of narcissism, reparation and self-reparation, a healing that re-narcissizes (and we would have to study in the Hegelian problematic of forgiveness this logic of the identification with the other that is assumed by the scene of forgiveness, on both sides, of the forgiver or the forgiven, an identification that forgiveness assumes but which also compromises and neutralizes, cancels out in advance, the truth of forgiveness as forgiveness from the other to the other as such). The uncrossable will remain uncrossable at the very same moment it will have been crossed over. Forgiveness will remain im-possible and with it history, the continuation of history, even if it becomes possible one day. What is it one senses at the heart of Jankélévitch's letter—and that I call to your attention because it should remain a great paradigmatic lesson for us? One senses the unaltered conviction, unalterable, that even when forgiveness of the inexpiable will have taken place, in the future, in the generations to come, it will not have taken place, it will have remained illusory, inauthentic, illegitimate, scandalous, equivocal, mixed with forgetting (even when its subjects are and believe themselves to be sincere and generous). History will continue and with it reconciliation, but with the equivocation of a forgiveness mixed up with the work of mourning, with forgetting, an assimilation of the wrong, as if, in short, if I can summarize here this unfinished development in a formula, tomorrow's forgiveness, the promised forgiveness will have had not only to become the work of mourning (a therapy, a healing away, even an ecology of memory, a manner of better-being with the other and with oneself in order to continue to work and to live and to enjoy) but, more seriously, the work of mourning forgiveness itself, forgiveness mourning forgiveness. History continues on the background of [*sur fond de*] an interruption of history, in the abyss, rather, of an infinite wound, which, in its very scarring, will have to remain an open and unsuturable wound. In any case it is in the zone of hyperbole, of aporia and paradox that we should often have to stand or move in this reflection on forgiveness.

Before leaving, at least provisionally, these texts of Jankélévitch, I would like to return to another of the paradoxes of the "inexpiable," of the logic of the "inexpiable" that he puts to work under this word in *L'imprescriptible*. The word "inexpiable" is used at least twice in a disturbing face-to-face.[15] You will remember that Jankélévitch said, I quoted it earlier, that "what happened [namely the Shoah, which defies all judgment, all logic, all logic of punishment, and so forth] is literally inexpiable." Before this, he has already described the will to exterminate the Jews as a singular, exceptional, incomparable movement of hatred against an existence, the existence of the Jew insofar as this existence is felt to be an "inexpiable" sin of existence. In this context, it is more particularly a matter of the human, anthropocentric dimension that structures the problem—and which will interest us precisely when it becomes a problem, a problematic, contestable and contested by the very idea of forgiveness.

A little earlier in his text,[16] in fact, precisely at the beginning of the chapter that bears the title "The Imprescriptible" (at the very moment of the vote in France on the imprescriptibility of crimes against humanity), Jankélévitch reminds us that these crimes are aimed at the essence of the human, "or, if one prefers, the 'humanness' ['*l'hominité*'] of man in general."

> The German [he says, hypostasizing in turn, in a way that is problematic, something like the essence of Germanity], the German did not want, strictly speaking, to destroy beliefs judged to be erroneous or doctrines considered to be pernicious: it was the very being of man, *Esse*, that the racist genocide attempted to annihilate in the suffering flesh of these millions of martyrs. Racist crimes are an assault against man as man: not against this or that man (*quatenus* . . .), not against man insofar as he is this or that, for example, communist, Freemason, or ideological adversary. No! the racist was truly aiming at the ipseity of being, that is, the human in all men. Anti-Semitism is a grave offense against man in general. The Jews were persecuted because it was they, and not at all because of their opinions or their faith: it is existence itself that was refused them; one was not reproaching them for professing this or that, one was reproaching them for being.[17]

Here, through some gap in the argument that does not explain why an aggression against the humanity of man is aimed at the Jew alone (and even Israel, for he extends the same reasoning to the existence of the

State of Israel, in a way that is even less convincing), Jankélévitch goes so far as to reverse, in some sense, the logic of the inexpiable. What becomes inexpiable, and this is Jankélévitch's word for the Nazis, is the very existence of the Jew. For the German, the Germans, the Nazis (and Jankélévitch passes easily from one to the other or others), "it is not obvious that a Jew must exist: a Jew must always justify himself, excuse himself for living and breathing; his arrogance in fighting for subsistence and survival is in itself an incomprehensible scandal and there is something outrageous about it; the idea that *'sub-humans'* [my emphasis] may defend themselves fills the *superhumans* [my emphasis] with indignant stupefaction. A Jew does not have the right to be, existing is his sin."[18]

I take up and underline the expression, polemical here, "sin of existing," removing it a little from its context: "A Jew does not have the right to be, existing is his sin." Implicit is: for the German. I am taking up the expression, I am exporting it out of its context and I am indicating in it a horizon of possible generality in order to point out one of the paths of the problematic of forgiveness—which will, furthermore, be illustrated quite strongly and classically by thinkers as powerful and as diverse as Kant, Hegel, Nietzsche, Heidegger, Levinas, and others, no doubt: It is a matter of forgiveness—asked for, granted or not—a priori, and always asked for, whose request is originary and without end, because of a guilt or a debt, an original liability or imputability, infinite and indeterminate, in some sense, such that existence, or consciousness, or the "I," before any determined fault is at fault and in the process, consequently, of asking at least implicitly for forgiveness for the simple fact, finally, of being-there. This being-there, this existence, would be both responsible and guilty in a way that is constitutive ("sin of existing") and could only constitute itself, persevere in its being, sur-vive by asking for forgiveness (knowing or without knowing of whom or why) and by assuming forgiveness to be, if not granted, at least promised, hoped for, enough to be able to continue to persevere in one's being. And along with forgiveness, reconciliation and redemption, atonement for this "sin of existing"—which would not be reserved for the Jew here, unless the Jew, what one understands by this word, is once again interpreted as exemplary of the humanity of man, with all the problems that this claim to exemplarity would engender and on the subject of which I have often questioned myself. In all of these cases, forgiveness can be just as constantly hoped for, assumed to come, as desperately deferred, for if the sin is the sin of existing, if guilt is originary and attached from birth, stained by birth, so to speak, forgiveness, redemption, expiation will remain forever impossible. We would all be in that inexpiable state of which Jankélévitch speaks regarding the Jew for the German: if the fault consists in being-there, only death, only annihilation can put an end to it and feign salvation, mimic atonement or redemption, silence the plaint or the accusation. Naturally, the problem is enormous and we should return to it more than once, for we would have to ask ourselves what relation there may be among all these determinations of the "sin of existing," of an originary scene of "forgiving," first among them, between, let's say, a Hegelian type, a Heideggerian type, or a Levinassian type in the description and interpretation of this structure, and what relation there might be between this general structure, universal and supposedly originary, aneventful, pre-eventful, and on the other hand determined faults, crimes, events of malice or viciousness, effective perjury for which I must accuse myself and for which I could ask for forgiveness.]

I am closing my digression here on the expression "inexpiable" I noted earlier. On the next page, in the spirit of the same logic, one thus finds this word "inexpiable" again, this time not to describe the crime of Hitler's Germany but the being-Jew as being-human for the Nazis. For the latter, Jankélévitch says, and I quote, "the crime of being a Jew is inexpiable. Nothing can erase that curse: neither political affiliation, nor wealth, nor conversion."[19]

Conveyed by the same word, "inexpiable," (and it is to an entire history of this word and to the expiatory that we are summoned here: what does "to expiate" mean?), we have two antagonistic and complementary movements: as if it were because the Nazis treated the being of their victim, the Jew, as an *inexpiable* crime (it is not *forgivable* to be Jewish), that they behaved in a way that was itself *inexpiable*, beyond all possible forgiveness. If one takes account of these two occurrences of the word "inexpiable" in Jankélévitch's text, and of their logic, one will say that the crime of the Nazis seems inexpiable because they themselves considered their victims to be guilty of the (inexpiable) sin of existing or of claiming to exist as men. And this always takes place around the limit of man, of the human figure. This is why I emphasized the words *subhuman* and superhuman a moment ago. It is because they have taken themselves to be superhuman and have treated the Jews as sub-human, it is because from both sides the Nazis believed they could pass over the limit of man that they committed these *inexpiable* crimes against humanity, that is, *imprescriptible* crimes—according to the juridical translation and the human right, according to the right of man which is here at the horizon of our problem.

I insist on this point for two reasons, two programmatic or problematic reasons, two ways of announcing today what should subsequently give us steady pause. Thus two questions.

1. *First question.* Is forgiveness a thing of man, something that belongs to man, a power of man—or else is it reserved for God, and thus already the opening of experience or existence onto a supernaturality just as to a superhumanity: divine, transcendent, or immanent, sacred, whether saintly or not? All the debates around forgiveness are also regularly debates around this "limit" and the passage of this limit. Such a limit passes between what one calls the human and the divine and also between what one calls the animal, the human, and the divine. In a moment, we will perhaps say a word about "animal" forgiveness.

2. *Second question.* Because this limit is not just a limit among others, everything that depends on it will also affect it, as it will affect this difference—or distinction—that we have already recalled more than once today, between pure or unconditional forgiveness and these related and heterogeneous forms of remission, heterogeneous among themselves and heterogeneous to forgiveness and that are called excuse, regret, prescription, amnesty, and so forth, so many forms of conditional forgiveness (hence impure), and sometimes juridical-political forms. We thus dissociated *on the one hand* unconditional forgiveness, absolute forgiveness—I am not saying absolution in the Christian sense—absolutely unconditional forgiveness that allows us to think [*donne à penser*] the essence of forgiveness, if there is such a thing—and which ultimately should even be able to do without repentance and the request for forgiveness, *and on the other hand* conditional forgiveness, for example, that forgiveness which is inscribed within a set of conditions of all kinds, psychological, political, juridical above all (since forgiveness is bound up with the judiciary as penal order). Yet the distinction between unconditionality and conditionality is shifty [*retorse*] enough not to let itself be determined as a simple opposition. The unconditional and the conditional are, certainly, absolutely heterogeneous, and this forever, on either side of

a limit, but they are also indissociable. There is in the movement, in the motion of unconditional forgiveness, an inner exigency of becoming-effective, manifest, determined, and, in determining itself, bending to conditionality. In such a way that, for example, and I am saying it too quickly for the moment, phenomenality or juridical or political conditionality is both outside and inside the motion of forgiveness—which will not make things easy. Even if the "imprescriptible" does not mean the "unforgivable," the contamination of the two orders will not be an accident that is itself reducible; and this will be valid of all the distinctions we will have to make.

We started by considering cases in which the noun "pardon" belonged to a performative utterance (Pardon! I ask your pardon [*je te demande pardon/je vous demande pardon*], We ask your pardon [*nous te demandons, nous vous demandons pardon*]). You will note that in French it can only be used alone (*Pardon!*) in an act of performative language in the sense of "pardon beseeched," never in the case of forgiveness granted or refused. Is it true that for forgiveness to be granted or even only envisaged, it must be asked for and asked for on the basis of [*sur fond*] confession and regret? In my eyes, this is not a given and might even have to be excluded as the first fault of anyone who grants forgiveness; if I grant forgiveness on condition that the other confess, that the other begin to redeem himself, to transfigure his fault, to dissociate himself from it in order to ask me for forgiveness, then my forgiveness begins to let itself be contaminated by an economy, a calculation that corrupts it.

As soon as the word "pardon!"—the performative of forgiveness as speech act—is uttered, is there not the beginning of a reappropriation, a mourning process, a process of redemption, of a transfiguring calculation which, through language, the sharing of language (see Hegel on the subject) rushes toward the economy of a reconciliation that causes the wrong itself to be simply forgotten or annihilated, and thus this unforgivable as well, this unforgivable that is the only possible correlate of a forgiveness worthy of the name, of an absolutely singular forgiveness as unique event, unique but necessarily iterable, as always? The result of this law of iterable unicity, promised to repetition, divided by the promise that haunts all forgiveness, the result of this law of iterable unicity is that at the same time there is no sense in asking for forgiveness collectively of a community, a family, an ethnic or religious group—and at the same time multiplicity and the third and the witness are involved from the outset [*d'entrée de jeu de la partie*]. This may be one of the reasons, certainly not the only one, why forgiveness is often asked of God. Of God not because he alone would be capable of forgiveness, of a power-to-forgive otherwise inaccessible to man, but because, in the absence of the singularity of a victim who is sometimes no longer there to receive the request or to grant forgiveness, or in the absence of the criminal or the sinner, God is the only name, the name of the name of an absolute and nameable singularity as such. Of the absolute substitute. Of the absolute witness, the absolute *superstes*, the absolute surviving witness. But inversely, if the address of forgiveness (I say the *address of forgiveness* to designate both the act of asking for forgiveness, of addressing a request for forgiveness, and the place from which forgiveness, once the request is received by the addressee of the request, is either granted or not granted), if the address of forgiveness is always singular, singular as to the fault, the sin, the crime, the harm, and singular as to the perpetrator or his victim, nonetheless it calls forth not only repetition but, through or as this repetition, a disidentification, a disseminating multiplication, all of whose modes we would have to analyze.

Three suspension points before concluding.

1. Why did I begin with the single word "pardon," with the noun "pardon" about which it was impossible to know, to decide at the beginning, out of context, whether I was quoting, whether I was mentioning a noun, a theme, a problem or whether I was asking your pardon, performatively, not by mentioning but by using the noun (mention/use distinction in speech act theory)? I began in this way not only because I have an infinite number of reasons for asking your forgiveness (and in particular for keeping you too long: this is always the first fault of anyone who asks forgiveness: to think he has the right to interest the other and to keep his attention—"Listen to me, I am begging your pardon; wait, don't leave, I am begging your pardon; pay attention, pay attention to me, I am begging your pardon"—this can become an odious strategy or an odious and ridiculous calculation of false mortification that can go as far as tears; and we are very familiar with situations in which the person who does this is a pain in the neck and you pretend to forgive him or her in order to change the subject and to interrupt the conversation:

"OK, give me a break, I am not even accusing you, enough already; OK, I forgive you but I don't want to see you again . . . my mind is elsewhere, let's talk about something else, I don't even take you seriously enough to be accusing you").

No, I began in this way to quote a performative (neither to *mention*, nor to *use*, but to mention a use) in order to draw your attention to the question of the word, the performative word as speech, as verb (pardon, I ask your [*te-vous*] pardon). Like everyone, like all those who wait and think, they must wait for forgiveness to be asked for; it is a *word* of forgiveness, a verb, a verbal-noun that Jankélévitch was waiting for ("I have been waiting for this letter for thirty-five years . . . , Have we ever been asked for forgiveness?") and even, according to his interpreters, it was a word that Celan was waiting for (*von / einer Hoffnung, heute, / auf eines Denkenden / kommendes / Wort / im Herzen*). Must forgiveness pass through words or must it pass [beyond] words? Must it pass through word-verbs or must it pass [beyond] them, these word-verbs? Can one only forgive or ask forgiveness when speaking or sharing the language of the other, that is to say, by already identifying sufficiently with the other for this, and, by identifying with the other, making forgiveness both possible and impossible? Must one refuse the experience of forgiveness to whoever does not speak? Or, on the contrary, must one make silence the very element of forgiveness, if there is such a thing? This question is not only that of music, which I alluded to earlier; it is also, even if it is not only this, the question of the animal and of that which is said to "belong to man." Does forgiveness belong to man or does it belong to God? This question seems to exclude the animal, that which one calls by this confused general term "animal" or the animality of the beast or of man. Yet we know that it would be very imprudent to deny all animality access to forms of sociality in which guilt, and therefore procedures of reparation, even of mercy—begged or granted—are implicated in a very differentiated way. There is no doubt an animal thank you or mercy. You know that certain animals are just as capable of manifesting what can be interpreted as an act of war, an aggressive accusation, as they are capable of manifesting guilt, shame, discomfort, regret, anxiety in the face of punishment, and so forth. I am sure you have seen shameful animals, animals giving all the signs of "feeling guilty," thus of remorse and regret, and animals fearing judgment or punishment, animals hiding or exposing themselves to reproach or chastisement. One also knows that in the often-overloaded symbolism of combat or war, of fights between animals, well, that movements and even rites of reconciliation, of the interruption of hostility, of peace, even of mercy, of mercy begged and granted, are possible. The moment an animal is, I would say, at the mercy of another, it can admit to being defeated and make signs that put it at the mercy of the other who then sovereignly grants it its life unharmed as a sign of peace. Certain animals make war and peace. Not all, not always, but neither do men. So, without confusing everything and without erasing all sorts of ruptures that arise with the articulation of a verbal language, one cannot deny this possibility, even this necessity of extra-verbal forgiveness, even un-human [*an-humain*] forgiveness.

2. We constantly struggle in the snares of an aporia whose abstract and dry form, whose logical formality is as implacable as it is indisputable: There is only forgiveness, if there is such a thing, of the un-forgivable. Thus forgiveness, if it is possible, if there is such a thing, is not possible, it does not exist as possible, it only exists by exempting itself from the law of the possible, by im-possibilizing itself, so to speak, and in the infinite endurance of the im-possible as impossible; and this is what it would have in common with the gift; but besides the fact that this enjoins us to try to think the possible and the im-possible otherwise, the very history of what one calls the possible and "power" in our culture and in culture as philosophy or as knowledge, we must ask ourselves, breaking the symmetry or the analogy between gift and forgiveness, if the urgency of an im-possible forgiveness is not first what the enduring and non-conscious experience of the im-possible gives to be forgiven, as if forgiveness, far from being a modification or a secondary complication or a complication that arises out of the gift, were in truth its first and final truth. Forgiveness as the impossible truth of the impossible gift. Before the gift, forgiveness. Before this im-possible, and as the impossible of this latter im-possible, the other. The other im-possible. You understand that this lecture could also have been a lecture on the possible and on the "im-" that comes in front of it, of an im-possible which is neither negative, nor non-negative, nor dialectical.

3. Finally, perjury. Today I must justify the articulation (proposed as the title of this seminar) of pardon and perjury. Pardon/Perjury: As you can imagine, if I associate these two nouns, it is not because

"[parleying] with the syllable *par* thus begin these words [*par la syllabe par commencent donc ces mots*]," as a certain Ponge would have said, Ponge's "Fable" which I am parodying here (*Par le mot par commence donc ce texte / Dont la première ligne dit la vérité* [With the word with thus begins this text / Whose first line tells the truth]), *Fable* which would not be without relation, nonetheless, to the scene of forgiveness, since it revolves around a judgment, on the one hand, and on the other, of the breaking of a mirror, of the interruption of a specular identification: "(*Par le mot par commence donc ce texte / Dont la première ligne dit la vérité / Mais ce tain sous l'une et l'autre / peut-il être toléré? / Cher lecteur déjà tu juges. Là de nos difficultés . . . /APRES sept ans de malheurs / Elle brisa son miroir* [With the word with thus begins this text / Whose first line tells the truth / But this silvering under one and the other / can it be tolerated? / Dear reader, already you judge. There as to our difficulties . . . /AFTER seven years of bad luck / She broke her mirror.])"[20]

The reader, apostrophized as judge ("you judge": performative and constative), is being asked to forgive—and this is perhaps the truth of which the text speaks as the truth of any scene of writing and reading: to ask the reader's pardon by confessing. One always writes in order to confess, one always writes in order to ask forgiveness; I wrote something like this somewhere, forgive me for quoting myself. No doubt one always teaches, also, in order to ask forgiveness; this is perhaps why I think I will no longer change, henceforth, the title of this seminar, for as long as it may be destined to last. If I have associated pardon and perjury, it is thus not to begin with words that begin with *par*. . . . But for a reason that here again I will state dryly, I will lay out abstractly, before returning to it later. I will draw a broad outline of it in two strokes.

1. Any fault, any crime, anything there might be to forgive or for which one might have to ask forgiveness is or assumes some perjury; any fault, any wrong, is first a perjury, namely the breach of some promise (implicit or explicit), the breach of some engagement, of some responsibility before a law one has sworn to respect, that one is supposed to have sworn to respect. Forgiveness always concerns a perjury—and we will (would) then have to ask ourselves what in fact perjury is, what an abjuration is, what it is to break a vow, an oath, a conjuration, and so forth.

And thus first what it means to swear, to take an oath, to give one's word, and so forth.

2. The second feature, even more aporetic, more impossible, if this is possible. Perjury is not an accident; it is not an event that happens or does not happen to a promise or to a prior oath. Perjury is inscribed in advance, as its destiny, its fatality, its inexpiable destination, in the structure of the promise and the oath, in the word of honor, in justice, in the desire for justice. As if the oath were already a perjury (something of which the Greeks, as we will see, had more than a premonition). And this, I have already spoken of this in the wake [*sillage*] of Levinas but by dangerously complicating the trajectory of this Levinassian path [*sillage*], from the moment that in the face-to-face there are more than two, from the moment that the question of justice and law arises. From the moment there is law and three. And there are at least three from the first dawn of the face-to-face, from the first look [*regard*], from the crossing of the first look that sees itself looking. Then it is justice itself that makes me perjure myself and throws me into a scene of forgiveness.

I must ask forgiveness—*pour être juste* [*for* being just/*to be* just]. Listen carefully to the equivocation of this "*pour.*" I must ask forgiveness in order to be just, *to be* just, with a view to being just; but I must also ask forgiveness for being just, for the fact of being just, because I am just, because in order to be just, I am unjust and I betray. I must ask forgiveness for (the fact of) being just. Because it is unjust to be just. I always betray someone to be just; I always betray one for the other, I perjure myself like I breathe. And this is endless, for not only am I always asking forgiveness for a perjury but I always risk perjuring myself by forgiving, of betraying someone else by forgiving, for one is always doomed to forgive (thus abusively) in the name of another.

Forgive me for having taken so long, and without mercy [*merci*], so much of your time, thank you [*merci*]. When one says "thank you," does one say "thank you," I am thanking you for what you give me and what I acknowledge with gratitude? Or else "mercy," I ask for your mercy, I ask you not to be "merciless," I ask your forgiveness for what you give me, I give you thanks [*grâce*] for mercy [*grâce*], for the forgiveness that I am still asking you to give me, and so forth. In short, you will never know what it is I am saying to you when I say to you, to conclude, as in the beginning, pardon, thank you/mercy [*merci*]. In the beginning, there will have been the word "pardon," "thank you/mercy [*merci*]."

Translated by Elizabeth Rottenberg

NOTES

This essay first appeared in English as Jacques Derrida, "To Forgive: The Unforgivable and the Imprescriptible," in John D. Caputo, Mark Dooley, and Michael J. Scanlon, eds., *Questioning God* (Bloomington: Indiana University Press, 2001), 21–51. Copyright © 2001 Indiana University Press. Reprinted with permission.

1. Jacques Derrida, *Given Time, I: Counterfeit Money*, trans. Peggy Kamuf (Chicago: University of Chicago Press, 1991).

2. Vladimir Jankélévitch, *Le pardon* (Paris: Aubier-Montaigne, 1967), 165. See also the little book that was published shortly after Jankélévitch's death under the title *L'imprescriptible: Pardonner? Dans l'honneur et la dignité* (Paris: Seuil, 1986), which brings together essays and talks from 1948, 1956, and 1971.

Le pardon is also available in Vladimir Jankélévitch, *Philosophie Morale*, ed. Françoise Schwab (Paris: Flammarion, 1998), 991–1149. The articles "Should We Pardon Them?" and "Do Not Listen to What They Say, Look at What They Do" are translated by Ann Hobart in the journal *Critical Inquiry* 22 (Spring 1996): 549–72, which also contains brief "Introductory Remarks" by Arnold Davidson (545–48). There is also a translation of "Irony: A French Approach" in the *Sewanee Review Quarterly* 47 (1939). See also Emmanuel Levinas, *Outside the Subject*, trans. Michael B. Smith (Stanford: Stanford University Press, 1993), especially "Vladimir Jankélévitch," 84–89.

3. Jankélévitch, "Should We Pardon Them?" 553 (translation modified).

4. Ibid.

5. Ibid., 567 (translation modified).

6. This is cited by Alain Gouhier in an article entitled "Le temps de l'impardonnable et le temps du pardon selon Jankélévitch" (The Time of the Unforgivable and the Time of Forgiveness According to Jankélévitch), published in the proceedings of a remarkable colloquium devoted to forgiveness, Michel Perrin, ed., *Le Point Théologique, Forgiveness: Proceedings of the Colloquium Organized by the Centre Histoire des Idées*, Université de Picardie (Paris: Beauchesnes, 1987).

7. Jankélévitch, "Should We Pardon Them?" 558 (translation modified).

8. In a passage in Hannah Arendt, *The Human Condition* (Chicago: University of Chicago Press, 1958), 241.

9. Jankélévitch, "Should We Pardon Them?" 558.

10. Ibid. (modified).

11. Jankélévitch, "Should We Pardon Them?" 567 (translation modified), *Le pardon*, 51.

12. For example: "Robert Minder forcefully asserts that Heidegger is responsible not only for everything he said under Nazism but also for everything he

abstained from saying in 1945." Jankélévitch, "Should We Pardon Them?" 568 (translation modified), *Le pardon*, 53. See Robert Minder, "Hebel et Heidegger: Lumière et obscurantisme," in Pierre Francastel, ed., *Utopies et institutions au dix-huitième siècle* (Paris: Mouton, 1963).

13. Paul Celan, "Todtnauberg," in *Poems of Paul Celan*, trans. Michael Hamburger (New York: Persea, 1989), pp. 292–93.

14. This exchange is too long for me to cite here, but it was published in an issue of the *Magazine Littéraire* devoted to Vladimir Jankélévitch in June 1995 (no. 333), and it can be consulted there.

15. *L'impréscriptible*, 24, 29, and again 62; English translation: 554, 558.

16. Ibid., 22 ff.; English translation 554ff.

17. Ibid., 555 (modified).

18. Ibid., 23; 555 (modified).

19. Ibid., 24; 556.

20. See Jacques Derrida, "Psyche: Inventions of the Other," trans. Catherine Porter, in Lindsay Waters and Wlad Godzich, eds., *Reading de Man Reading* (Minneapolis: University of Minnesota Press, 1989), 30–42.

THOUGHTS ON LOVE

Sari Nusseibeh

As a wheel turns smoothly, free from jars,
my will and my desire were turned by love
the love that moves the sun and the other stars.

—Dante Alighieri, *The Divine Comedy*

IF MUSIC SPEAKS TO THE HEART, then imagine how much farther
and deeper must its reach be when its very theme happens to be love, the
heart's core passion. The Star of the East, as Umm Kulthoum, arguably
the Arab world's best-ever singer, came to be known, could keep millions of men and women in the grip of her words and sound as people
became glued to their radio sets listening to her latest operatic release.
So mesmerized by her was the Arab world that Cairo's streets would
come to a standstill on the first Thursday of each month during the sea-
son as the Lady was about to perform. While her concert hall would be
packed to the brim with Cairo's elegantly dressed elites, her voice and
music would beam live across Egypt and the rest of the Arab world and
be heard by the rich and poor, in houses and cafés and street shops, reso-
nating in the hearts of everyone who listened. "Sirat al-Hubb" (Love's
Tale) is just one of her many songs about love.[1] "Lo, how beautiful the
world is in the eyes of lovers." *Ya Salaam . . . Ya Salaam.* How is this word,
originally meaning peace as well as a name of God, translatable in this
context? What Magnificence! What Glory! By God Almighty! Behold
How Glorious the world becomes when viewed with the eyes of love,
with the eyes of lovers! One could say the same, *Ya Salaam,* about Um
Kulthoum's own magical power: she seems to have found the secret of
how to open hearts, how to speak to peoples' deepest personal emotions,

how to bring alive in them that primal passion, drawing them in as if by a magnet, transforming a multitude of human beings into a single symphony, a symphony whose theme is love, a passion experienced or longed for by each, as strongly and as sympathetically as it is also experienced by everyone else.

Odes to love abound wherever human beings have discovered how to express or to respond to the finer and the more beautiful aspects of themselves. I chose to begin with Umm Kulthoum (rather than with, say, "All You Need Is Love") only as one example among many of how, even in an Arab milieu drowning in poverty, wars, and economic backwardness, at one fell swoop, literally millions simply swooned at a musical celebration of love, sharing together the same joyous moment, putting behind them for a brief spell all the world's worries. For such is love's insuperable power.

But it is well to keep in mind that—and to ponder why—a passion awakened this way cannot be aroused by reason or by a rational discourse. It was in the midst of a post-9/11 atmosphere, and a Huntington-projected future of inevitable cultural collision, that a group of Muslim leaders, responding to the Regensburg speech of Pope Benedict XVI, in which he seemed to be talking down to Muslims, published in October 2007 their open letter, "A Common Word Between Us and You," in the *New York Times*. In that letter—which really was more a kind of declaration—these Muslim leaders appealed to the Christian world to heed the common religious message of love and neighborliness. Only that way—they argued—could world peace (and justice) be achieved. Not long after, a group of Christian leaders published a response, "Loving God and Neighbor Together: A Christian Response to 'A Common Word Between Us and You,'" in which they underscored the Christian double commandment of loving God and one's neighbor. Soon, Muslim and Christian leaders joined hands, widened their respective circles of support, and embarked on a campaign in their respective communities to propagate this message of love and peace. A whole book (prefaced, unfortunately, by none other than the six-figure-salaried peace envoy Tony Blair), in which scholars and religious leaders highlighted what is common between Christians and Muslims, especially on the theme of love, was published in the United States.[2] But, just a few years on, prospects of a nuclear war to be unleashed in the Middle East, involving a Muslim state, a Jewish state and the United States, seem far more of a reality than an impending assemblage of human hearts. And it is not at all clear that the growing religiosity on all sides is accompanied by growing toleration by each side of the other.

So, one wonders, what happened to love? Put differently, why is the primal passion of love, or for love, not there in the forefront of world human affairs? Is its power not insuperable after all? Has it disappeared from our lives?

I WISH HERE TO INVOKE Ibn Khaldun, that fourteenth-century Arab sociologist, and his concept of compassion, or solidarity (*'asabiyyah*). Ibn Khaldun proposed solidarity as that quintessential glue that binds human beings together, gives rise to authority, and explains its rise and fall, as well as that of the polity more generally. How does he ultimately explain or define it? Significantly, as being that primal instinct a mother has for her loved one or that someone has for a blood relative—the instinct that explains that person's readiness to put him- or herself in harm's way lest that harm reach their beloved. Note that this is not a rational calculation. There is fear, but it is less a fear for oneself; it is, primarily, a fear for the other. Rather than fear being a reason for bringing about security through an authority in whom or in which can be vested the right of self-defense, and through whom, therefore, and on the basis of which, a relationship is entered into between oneself and the other—a social contract, so to speak—it is an instinct that already presupposes a more primal instinct that binds people together in the first place. This is the instinct of love, or of caring for another. Let me put it another way: in a classical, Hobbesean model, a human association is presupposed by authority, whose function is to provide security. In a Khaldunian model, authority is presupposed by human associations. Here, the authority exercised is motivated by love, or compassion.

I would argue that it is in this primal love (compassion, concern) for the other that we can find the seed of real peace, and justice. But there is, pitted against this, sometimes in a way that is argued to displace it completely, and sometimes in a way that projects it as the junior partner in the equation, that directionally opposite force or instinct of loving or favoring oneself. That one is prejudiced in favor of oneself is not surprising. But when it is taken to its extreme, as some political models are wont to do, this instinct of self-favoritism or selfishness—an extension, one might argue, of the fear for oneself—is then used as a basic building-block in justifying a political system in which peace is viewed defensively, essentially as a security structure. In this perspective, there is a tendency to think that, left to our own devices, or viewed at the ground-level, so to speak, we human beings are essentially self-seeking and aggressive, that our primal instinct is our unbridled love and fear for ourselves rather than for others. This being so, and the world being so made up, this line of thinking tells us, it becomes necessary to devise a mechanism whereby essentially conflicting selves or wills should optimally be made to reach a point of stability, or peace. Whether at the level of individuals, or nations, this point is simply the maintenance of order. In this view, the calculative imperative of self-interest compels us to temper our selfish desires so that we may enjoy those of them we can. But once again, our primary motivation is the satisfaction of our own desires. Note that, in this view, it is our calculative faculty that is called upon to explain human associations, and to justify the state of peace and stability we should pursue and maintain. Political orders structured in this way are thought to be both natural as well as the best of possible worlds. Umm Kulthoum has no role to play here, nor doess the call to heed the double commandment!

There is also a corollary to this: if asked to explain the love (and the host of compassionate passions that are akin to this) we may feel for our families, or countries, or nations—a love which might make us defend them to the death—someone upholding this view would respond by saying that this love is simply an enlarged projection of self-love. It is not, typically, an example of a love we as human beings have for people or objects we look upon as *others*. Rather, we see these simply as enlarged or projected versions of *ourselves*. In other words, our sense of compassion for those near us, or our caring for them and looking after them, can be explained precisely in terms of our love for ourselves, zoomed out, so to speak, so as to cover a larger human landscape. In this way we manage to explain our feeling of love for the other as simply a case of self-love on a wider scale.

But let us consider whether we are right to do this: is our love for those around us an expanded version of our love for ourselves, or is it different in kind, truly a love for someone other than ourselves? A Khaldunian would have it that it is different, while a Hobbesean, say, would have it be the same or, if not quite the same, less dominant than self-love and, in any case, derived from it. On the first view, love is the essential ingredient of human association; on the second, fear for oneself is.

But what difference does this distinction make to the world, one might ask. The difference is so fundamental that it might well be revolutionary. In our continual pursuit to make our lives better, working toward a new political model rooted in and extracted from love and compassion would serve us far better than one we convince ourselves must be self-serving and based on a looming shadow of fear for ourselves, fear of others. Seeking this new order, we have to reeducate ourselves—to accept that our reverence for human values is not a cosmetic addendum to our political selves but is its basic glue: that the foundation of polities is love, just as it is in the most fundamental relationship that ties couples together. Returning to the Muslim/Christian initiative of "A Common Word," its working assumption is that since both religions exhort us to love God and our neighbors, all that is needed for achieving peace and justice in the world is to make sure that adherents of these religions heed this call. But how does one make sure that adherents of the two religions come to heed this call? It is hardly likely this can happen through a declaration, let alone through a scholarly discourse. Indeed, the call religious adherents heed more often than that of love is that of hate. On the other hand, a cold-blooded survey of the state of the world may encourage us to think that what *peace* there is in the world is based upon balances of power—that is, on a Hobbesean calculation rather than a religious calling. And *justice*, let it be noted, is often absent in this kind of peace.

That justice is absent is perhaps more established than why peace exists. Can love possibly help us understand why justice is absent or why peace truly exists? Let us begin with peace. One could perhaps make out a distinction between positive peace and negative peace. By the former may be meant that peace whose foundation is our love and care for others—what Gandhi might have had in mind when he referred to the power of the soul—and by the latter may be meant the kind of peace that is engaged in to *stay* any possible deterioration of an existing situation or relationship and allow for advantageous benefits that may accrue from such a situation. Negative peace, in the first instance, is there to prevent harm to oneself, often, and without contradiction, at someone else's expense, which immediately explains to us why justice may be absent. Positive peace, in the first instance, is that based on loving others and caring for them, which is why we cannot envision justice being absent from such peace or why, where it is absent, as when it is so in the same family, it is an anomaly. Negative peace, by definition, flouts a basic Kantian rule for guaranteeing permanence. Positive peace, on the other hand, is fully transparent, embedding no concealed time bombs. And so, as we seek to make peace, it is clearly better if we seek that peace which is the natural partner of justice and, therefore, better to seek positive rather than negative peace.

Ibn Khaldun, we said, invokes as a primary instinct to which one could reduce societal motion the love we innately bear, paradigmatically, for our children. From such love he moves on to authority and from authority to kingships and states, at every juncture specifying the characteristics associated with each phase of a society's development, its rise, its apex, and its fall.

Classically, love has also been featured as a final cause, explaining individual but thus also even planetary motions. In his Princeton and then London lectures on the subject, Harry Frankfurt outlines the clear borders setting apart an instinct like love, which is volitional, from both rational as well as cognitive faculties.[3] But although it is volitional, in being instinctive, love constrains. One does not choose whether to love one's children or with whom to fall in love. One *finds* oneself in love. Frankfurt adds three more "conceptually necessary" features that define love: it consists in a disinterested concern for the well-being of the person who is loved; its object is a particular, not an exemplar; and it is desired for its own sake and not as a means. One way or another, love is what makes the world go round—as ends in themselves the things we love constitute our purpose in life. But, though loved ones or objects constitute purposes in life, they are not, *for that reason*, loved. Nor, not having—as loved objects—intrinsic values in themselves to make them loved by us, should we assume that pursuing them makes us *better* persons: their pursuit gives *meaning* to our lives, but such meaning is morally neutral.

Love makes the world go round, we understand Frankfurt as saying, but it does not, as Plato would have it, approximate, in its motion, the Good. Another breach he makes is with Kant. Kant expressed concern with the "dear self" or with our never being able to determine whether an act in accord with duty or the moral imperative was one that was done out of a moral motive—if it was not, in other words, done for some hidden ulterior selfish motive. One could never tell, Kant was supposed to have thought. Frankfurt here questions the meaning of the distinction between self-love and love of others—whether, in fact, self-love is in any way nefarious. And he argues, bravely, both in favor of viewing self-love as a form of proper love—indeed, as the purest form of love—and in distinguishing it from self-indulgence. Even if one were to act morally out of self-love, then, this need not mean that one's act can be, in the Kantian sense, unwholesome. Frankfurt can reach this conclusion—perhaps, he is compelled to reach it, given how he has defined love. But, having reached it, he has to argue his way out of a logical maze. To love oneself, first of all, seems to presuppose two selves, the lover and the loved. And if a conceptually necessary feature of loving the other is selflessness, or holding a concern for the other above that for oneself, then would not self-love be reduced to an unfathomable unconcerned concern? Would we not find ourselves in the horns of a two-wills dilemma? Even more pointedly, would such a thesis not simply destroy the foundation for distinguishing between positive and negative peace or pull the rug from under the notion of justice?

Frankfurt manages to lead us out of *his* maze. But he leaves us in a maze of our own. He rearticulates self-love as loving the things one loves. And he unties the inconsistency knot by positing a third *person*, one that sides with either one or the other of two conflicting desires or wills. Well and good, we might say. But surely, by so conflating such directionally opposite loves, we risk losing its real meaning—what is aroused in us as we listen to Umm Kulthoum—do we not? However noble, or pure, our self-love is, surely it is not *that* which Umm Kulthoum arouses but a love for a specific other, and that specific other is *specifically not* ourselves. We can admit to a certain self-indulgence as we (some of us) listen to her, as we undergo experiencing a mixture of perhaps even conflicting sensations, but this experience simply taps into our reservoir—memory and/or capacity—of love for someone other than ourselves whose love we place even above the love we have for ourselves.

Why might one raise concerns about conflating the love for another with self-love or about giving self-prejudice or selfishness a more dominant role than compassion or love for the other? The reason, simply, has to do with how we then come to view the world. If we recognize the first brick in the structure we are about to build as that of love and compassion (rather than self-seeking), we are more likely to iterate this application wherever we come across the possibility of adding another brick or of setting up a new structure. And if it turns out to be true that it is through such a procedure of building up a positive peace that justice can be assured, simply on account of the fact that it is not order per se that would be being sought but a compassionate peace, then we would also be assured of seeking a permanent peace and not one that will change as soon as the balance of power shifts.

Not so long ago, I was witness to two unsavory manifestations of religion, the Shi'ite celebration of the birth of Ali, which I watched on an Iraqi TV channel, and the Friday sermon from the mosque next door. In both cases what I saw was incitement to hate the other, couched and ornamented with boundless self-adulation. Passion was being aroused, but it was a passion unlike that of Umm Kulthoum's song of love. And it claimed to hail from religious sources, but its reach was clearly much farther than that of "A Common Word." I could not help feeling that the crowds filling the mosques were not by nature different from those listening to Umm Kulthoum and therefore that—given love's borderlessness—people must be by nature more inclined to love than to hate. If any conclusion is to be reached from these observations, then it is that what really keeps the peace in the world is love, just as Gandhi thought, and this in opposition to those forces that portray the human landscape as a jungle and arouse the passions of hate, based upon self-adulation and other-hate. It is true that such passions could be contained, or tamed, under a wise leadership or given wise opinion makers. But these are not always in abundance, and the passions typically aroused (religious, jingoist, ideological) in the context of a Hobbesean world unfortunately more often reinforce this self-centered worldview rather than that of Umm Kulthoum. And yet, paradoxically, we find that in many parts of this self-centered world human values are flagged that are more properly rooted in a positive view of human nature. But is it not a glaring contradiction for us to treat the world as being, at its most basic, "an other" to be guarded against in protection of ourselves, or even as prey, economic or political, while at the same time upholding and espousing universal principles of human equality?

I BEGAN WITH A LOVE SONG, but I would like to end with a rational discourse. Here I cite the work of Prince Ghazi bin Mohammad, the man behind the "Common Word" initiative, and who devoted a whole work to the theme of love in the Qur'an.[4] He explains that there is God's love for us, defined by the kind of people we are, and then there is our love for him, toward which we are exhorted. One of the seven categories of people singled out for love by God is the category of those who act justly. Our love for him, on the other hand, is manifested through our *acting justly*. But has it not now become clear that it is only through love—in the form of a positive peace—that justice itself can be brought about?

NOTES

1. http://www.youtube.com/watch?v=qSPHGsO28uU&feature=youtu.be.

2. Miroslav Volf, Ghazi bin Muhammad Bin Talal, and Melissa Yarrington, eds., *A Common Word: Muslims and Christians on Loving God and Neighbor* (Grand Rapids: Eerdmans, 2009).

3. Harry G. Frankfurt, *The Reasons of Love* (Princeton: Princeton University Press, 2004).

4. Ghazi bin Muhammad, *Love in the Holy Qu'ran* (Cambridge: Islamic Texts Society, 2013).

THE PASSIONATE UTTERANCE OF LOVE

Hent de Vries

For one must speak of love in the same way as one must love—in the first person.

—Jean-Luc Marion, *The Erotic Phenomenon*

The most global event joins the most intimate event; they are collapsed into each other . . .

—Jean-Luc Marion, *Being Given*

THROUGHOUT HIS MULTIFACETED WRITINGS, whose wide arches span three triads of studies of a very different nature and style—covering the history of modern philosophy, especially since Descartes; the recalibration of phenomenological method, notably in Husserl and Heidegger; and the pursuit of theology proper, that is, in its nonidolatrous, mystical adoration of a God who "doesn't even need to be" (or among whose proper names "Being" does not centrally figure)—Jean-Luc Marion offers an intriguing rejoinder to the contemporary revaluation of love as an important philosophical concept with relevant moral and political implications. The two essays included in this volume aptly restate Marion's overall views, and in the following I would like to summarize the crucial features of the at once simple and elegant argument that leads up to his reappraisal of the age-old idea and theologoumenon of love, while drawing out some first conclusions for a deeply pragmatic outlook that would heed its deepest call.

In the present essay I undertake an attempt to sound out the wider ramifications of this overall argument, approaching the phenomenon of love, as Marion discusses it, once more from a slightly different angle, emphasizing the ways in which he, with the help of Stanley Cavell's original work, succeeds in giving new meaning to love's so-called passionate element in speech act–theoretical or, rather, deep pragmatic terms. The "passionate utterance" reveals love's pivotal expression not so much as irrational and optional or volitional, in other words as a gesture and practice to be tempered and mastered (as the Western tradition mostly defined and treated it), but as imbued with a proper reason and inescapability, at times tragic fatality, if not comedy or even banality, of its own.

Marion's 1997 magnum opus, *Étant donné: Essai d'une phénoménologie de la donation* (*Being Given: Toward a Phenomenology of Givenness*), together with the publications that prepared for and followed upon it, ultimately circles around what is, in his view, the most concrete and intimate as well as the most widespread—indeed, global—of all genuinely given phenomena: the *concretissimum* of love. It is this phenomenon, whose so-called iconicity and saturation, but also aporia and ultimate ordinariness—or, as he will come to say, banality—are shown to be revelatory, emblematic, and demonstrative of the impasse and future of philosophical thinking, coming at the end of especially modern Western metaphysics and the death of its God (the highest Being, substance, and *causa sui*, to cite His most technical names), that Marion has increasingly taken as his philosophical, theological, and, now, also political lead. Indeed, the significance of love, like that of forgiveness, is presented in his writings as the old-new Archimedean point and conceptual as well as practical lever with which the metaphysical fixation on knowledge, objects, and beings, as well as on the whole historical series of so-called first or determining, efficient and final causes (from cosmos and nature to subject and life), comes unhinged in light of "another, more radical meaning" of the name and concept, method and practice of philosophy, which has been largely forgotten and repressed throughout the ages—nowhere more than in the modern era of globalized commerce and ever newer technological media of communication whose universal equivalents of exchange (of money and bits) produce a de facto, material, and functionalist idolatry, nothing less, nothing more. As a counterpoint to this rampant, rule-governed naturalism, utilitarianism and instrumentalism, together with the often empty, formalist representationalism that accompanies and enables it, distorting philosophy's first and ultimate ambition, inspiration, and driving force, Marion reminds us that this permanently updated and upgraded *mathesis universalis* nonetheless does not suffice itself as it lacks the sole explanatory—if, incalculable, measureless, infinite, and infinitizing—instance that makes it work in the first place but also shows it its insurmountable limits, call it its finitude.

Interestingly, then, what Marion seems to combine in his overall analysis is the importance of two distinct intuitions that we have taken as our epigraphs for this chapter: one singular (i.e., first-person) and one general (i.e., global) observation that serves as its corollary and that resumes, recapitulates and expands on its meaning and its peculiar force without power:

> For one must speak of love in the same way as one must love—in the first person.

> The most global event joins the most intimate event; they are collapsed into each other . . .

In his study, entitled *Le phénomène érotique* (*The Erotic Phenomenon*), the series of "six meditations" (from which the first quote is taken) and that elaborate the central intuition underlying *Being Given* (from which the second line stems), Marion puts things as follows:

> philosophy defines itself as the "love of wisdom" because it must in effect begin by loving before claiming to know. It order to comprehend, it is first necessary to desire to comprehend; put another way, one must be astonished at not comprehending (and this astonishment thus offers a beginning to wisdom); or one must suffer at not comprehending, indeed fear not comprehending (and this fear opens onto wisdom). Philosophy comprehends only to the extent that it loves—I love to comprehend, therefore I love in order to comprehend. I do not, as one might prefer to believe, end up by comprehending enough to dispense forever with loving.[1]

The prominence given to love by Marion—moreover, his insistence that we return to "the erotic origin of "*philo*-sophy" and its corollary disposition of "powerlessness [or lack of power, perhaps, unpower; here: *impuissance*, not *impouvoir*],"[2] countering its apparent demise, already in the classical and, increasingly, in the medieval, Scholastic turn to Aristotle's metaphysics and ontology, not to mention its modern substitutions by epistemology and axiology, and, ultimately, ideology and technology—all by itself already merits a succinct discussion of this neglected motif, its different motivations, variable modalities and modulations, in his expansive, at once historically reconstructive, innovatively phenomenological, and apophatic as well as post- or, rather *ana*theistic theological oeuvre.

In that still growing body of work at least three triadic elements and structures can be discerned, while different, if related, strands of a more visually or pictorially oriented and, more recently, political project are being developed that illustrate its overall impetus in parallel registers (from the early *La croisée du visible* to the recent *Courbet ou la peinture à l'oeil* and the essay on power, translated in this volume). Yet all of them revolve around a simple, if quite devastating, question that turns the twentieth-century destruction or so-called deconstruction (*Destruktion* or, later, *Verwindung*) of the whole of Western metaphysics—first presented by Martin Heidegger in his 1927, epoch-making *Sein und Zeit* (*Being and Time*)—even somewhat further upside down, putting this author's fleeting early and later references to "love [*Liebe*]" and "liking [*Mögen*]," each of them exemplifying the possibility (*Möglichkeit*) and general possibilism of Being's and beings' structural features (that is, not so much "categories," which are reserved for the order of things that are merely ontic, but "existentials" that characterize *Dasein* as the very being the we are as humans, and, eventually, the human as the sounding board and "shepherd" of Being's sendings) centerstage, as it were, such that agapaic as well as erotic love, the *ego amans*, now comes first.

As Marion puts it succinctly: "Doesn't the history of philosophy's divorce from the love within it merit at least as much attention and effort as the history of being and its retreat?"[3] With this laconic and rhetorical question, the stage for Marion's wider and deeper inquiry into the more and other than ontological primacy and prevalence of love over and against "Being" in *both* its metaphysical determination *and* its eventual (and, presumably, "evental") overcomings (*Überwindung, Verwindung*) is set once for all, inaugurating and enabling yet another "turning" and latest chapter in the modern history of phenomenological thought.

That this chapter also includes a critical engagement with yet another contemporary French thinker, namely Jacques Derrida, I only note here in passing. As a matter of fact, Marion's deliberate attempt to investigate the apophatic or, in his preferred terms, *mystical* discourse of love—beyond the languages of "saying" and "unsaying" of so-called positive (or kataphatic) and negative (or what is traditionally understood to characterize apophatic) theology, both of which remain steeped in the regimes differentiating "truth" and "falsity"—is to circumvent a presumed radically deconstructive program: the demonstration, put forward in Derrida's Jerusalem lecture, entitled "How to Avoid Speaking: Denials," and published in his volume *Psyche: Inventions de l'autre* (*Psyche: Inventions of the Other*), according to which the third path of mystical theology does not escape the pitfalls of metaphysical thinking as it would seem to remain privy to a *hyperessentiality* in and beyond its "denials" (*dénégations*). On Marion's view, the *via eminentiae* that supplements both the *via affirmativa* and *via negativa* and whose "prayer" or "praise" (also called the *encomium*) is neither true nor false (as also Aristotle and especially Heidegger all too well knew), eludes the predicament of predication that Derrida, for his part, sees as its *unavoidable* fate, reverting so-called hypertheology to the assumption of hyperessentiality, as we said. As I have discussed these matters elsewhere and continue to think that this debate is, at the very least, inconclusive, I will not return to it here.

THE THIRD REDUCTION

It can hardly be a surprise, at least to those who have attentively followed Marion's writings over the years, that love has become the central focus in his massive attempt to redraw the traditional map of metaphysical, in particular, ontotheological thinking that has dominated the Western tradition of philosophy in its theoretical preoccupations with objects (things) and beings (or Being) for far too long, steadfastly ignoring the other voices (but also icons and prayers, faces and passions, revelations and other historical events, revelations and hierarchies) at or near its origins. Nor should we forget, from a repeatedly safeguarded methodological distance, that the legacies, namely the archives and apparatuses of biblical and patristic theology, together with the more or less elusive, if not less rigorous, traditions of mystical rather than negative theology, form a constant source of inspiration and orientation that accompany Marion's philosophical writing, just as they trigger, if not dictate, its privileging of some themes and topoi over and against others. This is certainly the case with his studies of Descartes and then of Augustine, but also with his phenomenological studies, especially those following up on *Réduction et donation* (*Reduction and Donation*) that leave exposition

and commentary more and more behind in favor of a resolutely constructive, at times deconstructive recasting of the phenomenological project,
both in its method and aims (as those who previously had taught him,
notably Emmanuel Levinas, Jacques Derrida, and Michel Henry had
already boldly attempted, with partial success).

With the help of a phenomenological procedure, which he terms the
"erotic reduction" (to be distinguished from the previous two reductions
Edmund Husserl and Martin Heidegger introduced and operated),
Marion portrays "love" as the very heart, constitutive force, and original intention or intentionality of reason and everything for which it
stands (to wit, human agency, moral, aesthetic, and political judgment,
the wish to know, the know-how to do, and so on and so forth). With a
seemingly anti-Cartesian twist (seemingly, because a more recent study,
entitled *Sur la pensée passive de Descartes*, shows a possibly different take
and appreciation of this author as well)—undoing the modern philosophical requirement of epistemic *certainty* and replacing it with a demand or, rather, desire for so-called assurance by an anonymous or spec-
ified, even special other, the difference matters little—Marion bases
knowledge's principle, beginning and foundation, if one could say so,
upon a simple intuition whose acknowledgment takes a far more passionate and, as we will see, deeply pragmatic form. In it we are dealing
not so much with a speech act–theoretical situation in which utterance
is governed by linguistic contexts and social conventions, but a disposition and dispossession in which such criteriological determinants have,
precisely, fallen away (thus unsettling the very self-identification that
Descartes's famous *dubito, ergo cogito, ergo sum* [I doubt, therefore I think,
therefore I am] in one of its renderings and in its reigning interpretation, at least, would have seemed to allow):

> In order for me to appear as a full-fledged phenomenon, it is not enough
> that I recognize myself as a certified object, nor as a certifying *ego*, nor
> even as a properly being being; I must discover myself as a given (and
> gifted) phenomenon, assured as a given that is free from vanity. . . . It is
> a question of assuring against the vanity of my own given (and gifted)
> phenomenon by responding to a new question: no longer "Am I cer-
> tain?" but "Am I not, despite my certainty, in vain?" Now, asking to as-
> sure my own certainty of being against the dark assault of vanity comes
> down to asking to nothing less than "Does anybody love me?"[4]

Of this "erotic reduction" and its correlative "phenomenology of eros," a terminology first introduced by Levinas, that other great phenomenologist of love, in his 1960 classic *Totalité et Infini* (*Totality and Infinity*), it must first of all be observed that Marion—unlike his predecessor—refuses to formally distinguish its guiding concept (*eros*) from that of *agape*, the fundamentally Christian concept of a noncarnal brotherly or sisterly love. By the same token, one would be hard-pressed to delineate the phenomenology of the "erotic phenomenon" from that of the concept and practice of "charity" (*charité*), which Marion's *Prolégomènes à la charité* (*Prolegomena to Charity*) presents in great depth.[5] Undercutting further Levinas's distinction between "need" (*besoin*) and "desire" (*désir*), Marion insists that "love," precisely by its very concept and meaning, is "univocal, love is only told in *one way*."[6] In this sense, love's original concept and practice directly challenges yet another central premise of Western metaphysics and all ontology, explicit at least since Aristotle and reigning virtually unchecked from the Scholastics up until German Idealism and early twentieth-century phenomenology. After all, with a locution that is reiterated by Thomas of Aquinas, Hegel, and Heidegger alike, "Being is said in multiple ways [*to on pollachôs legetai*]." On Marion's more radical and far-ranging view, love, for its part, is not; nor, for that matter, is love one of the ways in which Being expresses itself, first and foremost or even at all: love, like God, does not even need "to be" for it—and its practice or "making" (as in the "making of truth," the *veritatem facere* of which Augustine spoke so fervently in the *Confessions*, book 10, I, I, 14, 140)—to live up to its very concept.[7]

THE MYSTICISM OF LOVE'S SPEECH

The "one way" in which love pronounces itself is neither that of affirmative predication nor that of its parallel—and, often, all too abstract—negation, as in the positive and negative, kataphatic and apophatic, theologies of old. Neither of these speaks of love in adequate—or, rather, practical—ways, as both remain steeped in and, hence, fail "moving from a constative (and predicative) use of language toward a strictly pragmatic usage."[8] Instead, love's mode of speech is "mystic" and its direction is that of a spiral upward, as in the superlative motif, mode, and mood of the third way of so-called *via eminentiae*, whose rhetorical and figural archive and apparatus—like that of the *encomium*, next to the *kenosis* of discourse, both of which I explored in more detail in a different context[9]—Marion views as an immense resource and repository for redescribing and reinterpreting the phenomenon of love (its very concept and practice) in the current day and age. Indeed, he views it as the *via regia* for investigating the very paradox of which St. Paul (referencing Isaiah 64:4, cf. 52:15) speaks in the biblical text: "What no eye has seen, nor ear heard, nor the human heart conceived . . . God has prepared for those who love him" (I Corinthians 2:9).

Now, if mystical rather than negative theology is seen as exemplifying the "radical pragmatic (perlocutionary) use" of language of which Marion will come to speak, just as speech act theory and ordinary language philosophy, as understood by J. L. Austin, especially as read by Cavell, find a significant and, as it were, "lateral confirmation" in the hyperbolic modality of erotic discourse and its ancient, at least Christian, hypertheological counterparts, then this has important consequences for our view of the broader legacy of this particular form and format of apophatic speech in its historical, modern, and contemporary roles. The legacies of a finely, indeed deeply, attuned pragmatism, of the "special" and "general theory" of "action"—of "speech acts"—of which Austin muses in the last of his lectures on *How to Do Things with Words*,[10] can then be seen as latter-day echoes of a much earlier intuition and insight, one that Michel de Certeau, in his *La fable mystique* (*The Mystic Fable*), with explicit reference to this thinker, has described in terms of a *modus loquendi* and *modus agendi*.[11]

It is in this sense, then, that the pragmatics of mystical theology finds a surprising

> lateral confirmation in the perlocutions of erotic discourse. In both cases there is a pragmatic use of language, in the form of three privileged perlocutions (and all of their variations which could be itemized): "I love you!" and "Do you love me?" and their repetition, corresponding to kataphasis, apophasis, and hyperbole. In this sense, mystical theology would no longer constitute a marginal and insignificant exception in language theory but, on the contrary, would indicate a much more central and vast domain, where pragmatics, perlocutions, and what they render utterable unfold, among other things. It is no longer a question of a discourse about beings and objects, about the world and its states of affairs, but rather the speech shared by those who discourse about

these things when they no longer discourse about them but speak to each other. The suspicion that modern philosophy has bred of the encounter with theology in general and mystical theology in particular differs little from its disinheritance of the question of love in all its forms. One could then interrogate the dimensions of encounter between erotic discourse and mystical theology. Are we dealing with a formal similitude, limited to linguistics, or a deeper univocity?[12]

Marion leaves the question open in this context. Yet what is important is to begin to ask it and to envisage a discourse—or, at least, two parallel types of discourse—in which the fixation on "objects," "beings," the "world," and its "states of affairs" (everything that Austin condemned under the heading of "descriptive" or "constative fallacy") no longer delimits the range of philosophical-phenomenological or, for that matter, theological inquiry. The "passionate utterance" of love, like mystic speech, is not of this world, but, paradoxically, prepares us all the more for it.

THE UNIVOCITY AND POWERLESSNESS OF LOVE

According to Marion, desire, in its post-, pre-, para- and, perhaps, ultra- or quasi-metaphysical definition—much of which survived or announced itself at the margins of major philosophical texts (and therefore could be restored to greater prominence)—would not need to be distinguished from the satisfaction of needs (as, again, Levinas had urged in his "phenomenology of eros"). "Eros" or "the erotic" retain, for Marion, all of their spiritual and corporeal aspects. In its broadest possible definition, then, erotic love signifies the "vital" aspect, the "flesh" (a term whose ontological significance Marion adopts from the later Maurice Merleau-Ponty no less than from Michel Henry, each of whom, next to Levinas and Jacques Derrida, influences his phenomenological writings in important, alternative and recognizable ways).

It is the very assumption of love's "univocity," Marion suggests, that allows and obliges us to develop "a philosophy that means to think after and thanks to the end of metaphysics."[13] The latter's long tradition— together with its "conceptual idolatry," as Marion adds in *L'idole et la distance* (*Idol and Distance*)—has blocked and distorted our view on the most original of all phenomena, which love "is" or for whose actualization love calls. And "love," Marion leaves no doubt, in its very concept and practice, requires a certain back and forth, to and fro, which is not necessarily the same as reciprocity but presupposes distance and the primacy or prevalence of some other—some other mind and/or body—as its very condition or, rather, lack thereof: its lack of self-sufficiency and auto-foundation, its "unpower" (*impouvoir*), as it were.

Being Given portrays the "event of love" as the, perhaps, most concrete example of the "saturated phenomenon," which is the given and gifted as such. Indeed, Marion's *magnum opus* claims that the phenomenon of givenness (*donation*), more generally, has not only been ignored by classical phenomenology insofar as Husserl's *Logische Untersuchungen* (*Logical Investigations*), as is well known, fixated on "objects" whereas Heidegger's *Being and Time* singled out "beings" (in what might be called the "first" and "second" methodic "reduction" that we owe to these works). The phenomenon of givenness has been rendered secondary—indeed, conceptually and practically irrelevant—by virtually all of the tradition of Western metaphysics as it has suppressed and sublimated its originally instigating and driving weak force or *eros* in its very definition and exercise of what (all the more surprisingly) was nonetheless called *philo*sophy.

According to the ancient, medieval, and modern tradition of metaphysics, it is as if "love" or "to love" ought to be based, first of all, on self-knowledge or self-certainty or at least on some preliminary awareness of the world and others as well as oneself placed in it. As Spinoza's *Ethica* had systematized through and through, it as if "love" or "to love" presupposed a prior tendency of all beings to persevere in their being (the so-called *conatus essendi*), a motif that (unattributed) would still seem to resonate in Heidegger's claim, in *Being and Time*, that human existence or *Dasein* is the sole being concerned with its very own being (and, *a fortiori*, with the utmost possibility of its existing, which is the possibility of its impossibility, of its death or, rather, being-toward-death). And, with no *eros*, *agape*, or, for that matter, sex discussed in the otherwise phenomenologically rich pages of that book or anywhere else, for that matter, Heidegger thereby only confirmed a general tendency within ancient, medieval, and modern metaphysics, which consists in relegating love to the realm of sentiment and mere passion alone: that is to say, to moods and modalities of human existence whose proper direction cannot be generated from within the self's most rational, most proper resources, by its own enabling and driving force (its being "thrown" yet "projecting" itself forward) or, indeed, on its ownmost existential terms (its *Eigentlichkeit*, insufficiently rendered as "authenticity," or its *Entschlossenheit*, aptly translated as "resoluteness").

This forgetting of love, which, Marion claims, equals a forgetting of the very heart of theoretical and practical reason, of *logos* and rationality, has been suppressed, perhaps, most visibly in the work of René Descartes, with whose *Metaphysical Meditations* Marion contrasts his own (indeed, as in Descartes, exactly, six) "erotic meditations," which are likewise guided by a seemingly deeply personal spiritual exercise just as much as they stand out by a rigorously intellectual quest, punctuated by the voice of the first person singular, the "I," whose call and, presumably, calling this pursuit of *philo*sophy proper it first of all is. In Descartes's classic work, the ego had been defined as a thinking thing (*res cogitans*) that must first of all "be" in order to be good for anything else at all, and this according to an "order of reasons" (to echo Martial Gueroult's famous commentary on this author) that Marion—who had first established himself as one of the most prominent scholars of the genesis and structure of Descartes's overall oeuvre in its ontotheological borrowings and limitation—will increasingly come to challenge in the most consequential of ways.[14]

EGO AMANS

In *The Erotic Phenomenon*, Marion privileges the *ego amans* over and against the *ego cogitans*, echoing an old Christian, more precisely, Augustinian theme, according to which I must first "love" in order to know (or even to be). Marion recalls that the modern, Cartesian thinking thing (*res cogitans*) "established itself only in opposition to and by repressing the erotic instance," that is to say, by deriding it as a "passion, and therefore as a derivative modality, indeed as optional to the "subject," who is defined by exercise of the rationality exclusively appropriate to objects and to beings."[15] In claiming as much, Descartes would have epitomized an all too common metaphysical dogma. In fact, in his work more clearly than anywhere else in modern philosophy, "the concept of love succumbed" and did so, precisely, "because philosophy simultaneously refused love's unity, its rationality, and its primacy (and to begin with, its primacy over being)."[16] But what, then, is implied in a concept and practice whose supposed referent—"love"—does not even need to "be" or whose substance, if one could still say so, does not find in "being" one of its predicates, much less its condition of possibility, its *transcendens*, as such, or whose meaning and force does not let itself by grasped by ontological as well as logical categories, attributes, to say nothing of the modes, moods, and existentials (*Existenzialien*) that Heidegger discovers in the being (*Dasein*) that "we" are.

It is in our renewed meditation upon the concept and practice of love—more precisely, its utterance and passion and the more than simply rhetorical and visual, if special, effect they cannot but produce—that the whole edifice of Western metaphysics and ontology thus becomes unhinged. Love thereby serves as a central focus in what Marion considers the urgent need for a more general philosophical and, possibly, theological task, namely that of "rethinking the classic operation of reduction as no longer dedicated only to securing objects (as in Husserl) or disclosing being (as for Heidegger), but more radically to opening a still more originary determination of the phenomenon—the given."[17] Indeed, he goes on to argue, not only is love a most telling figure of the "saturated phenomenon," the "given par excellence,"[18] it is *the* privileged figure of givenness as such, of its purity and nakedness, if we can say so (rivaled in this only by Revelation, it would seem, but let's leave that even thornier subject aside for now). But in what sense, exactly? How can one phenomenon and, especially, one single saturated phenomenon—univocal in its very meaning, as it is said or, as we will see, "uttered" (and, if not "done," then also "made")—hold sway over all equally relevant others?

LOVE AS EVENT

This question, I think, offers a key to an aspect of Marion's thought that strikingly parallels Alain Badiou's undertaking at specific points, notably as it similarly thinks of "love" as an event (albeit it here a "truth-event" and one among three others—those in science, art, and politics). It further speaks to their common focus on what is alternatively called "the gifted" (*l'adonée*), which is the "figure of 'subjectivity' granted to and by givenness,"[19] as Marion has it, or on the "militant" of love, "the lover whose world is enchanted," the lover who, together with his/her beloved is "deliciously isolated by amorous constructions," with love, "if it exists," as Badiou says.[20] For it is here, perhaps, that the question of truth and truthfulness will be decided, if ever it is.

Does one—do we, do I—choose love or hate, even if these alternatives are not simply optional, that is, purely arbitrary or decided "at will," steeped as they are in necessary contingencies or, we should rather say, contingent necessities whose more than historical, psychological, or even ontological—and, in fact, virtual, if massive—weight we, most of the time, hardly fathom and often fail to live up to? And that not least because the weak, if pervasive, force of love's appeal on us has nothing "objective," nothing "subjective," but instead retreats into a strange dimension of anonymity and heteronomy that we can neither master nor will into existence, no matter how often we "declare" (or "make") love as, we think, we do all the time? But how, then, can love claim its phenomenological primacy (as Marion suggests), or acquire its eventlike quality (as Badiou, for his part, insists), if its givenness or gift, its "truth-procedure" or "Subject," is, well, all but a given, all but decided, and, indeed—in the traditional philosophical and modern set-theoretical jargon—an indiscernible or undecidable, from beginning to end? The answer must lie in the peculiar structure of the call received that shows itself nowhere but in the response it is given, in the calling one finds oneself following (to summarize Marion), in the fidelity with which one keeps going on (as Badiou, speaking of "ethics," will put it).

Limiting ourselves further to Marion's project, we can conclude that not only does a focus on love allow a "revival" of phenomenology by "freeing" it from the horizons of "objectness" and "Being"—whose limits, he argues, have become more and more "obvious"—it also invites phenomenology to articulate the novel contours of the subject, or gifted, whose testimony to the event (here to the "event of love") may be the *sole criterion* or *warrant*, indeed, *visible sign* of its eventual occurrence, of its perception and proper effect, if and when it so happens that love does take place (i.e., is "made" even more so than "said"). In any case, the latter's only modality of manifestation or revelation is the nonepistemic and deeply problematic claim or proclamation of which the declaration "I love you!" is the "passionate utterance" and taking effect par excellence.

In the remainder of this chapter, I will examine its logic and referent (or lack thereof) and ask to what extent it indeed opens up a new type of inquiry that eludes traditional and modern semantics and semiotics, and one that Marion ties in with the performative utterance that, follow-ing Austin's *How to Do Things with Words*, he calls "perlocutionary" and, with Stanley Cavell, "passionate," while insisting, for his own part, that the analysis of these "speech acts" (as Austin called them) yields a "radically pragmatic" vision and use of language, including that of non-verbal expression, for which the erotic phenomenon and, more broadly, apophatic mysticism offer the prime historical and contemporary examples.

THE UTTERANCE "I LOVE YOU!"

As Marion points out, neither Austin nor one of his main interpreters, John Searle, seem much troubled by the fact that the most quotidian—perhaps "banal"—utterance ("I love you!") functions, on closer scru-tiny, as a perlocutionary speech act that defies all conditions and conven-tions, that is to say, all those instances listed by *How to Do Things with Words* as the very criteria to establish whether a performative speech act has in fact taken place and been "felicitous." The perlocutionary utter-ance "I love you!," Marion explains, further lacks transparency, com-pletion, verifiable intention, and determinable referent, all of which would seem to disqualify it as a meaningful speech act altogether. Nor is the one who emits the utterance in question (the "I") easily identifiable, thus undermining the privilege of the first singular present indicative active tense that Austin reserves for his examples of the performative in question. In sum, who says what to whom here, where "love" is the issue, as we say, "at hand"? Sender and addressee (must) remain in the dark, with plausible deniability for each pole of this relation (a "relation without relation," strictly conceived, as the two terms absolve themselves as they speak and respond).

Hence the inevitable "apophasis" of at least part of its "discourse"; hence also the "aporia" of the very "sincerity" that it would seem to pre-suppose and that forms part and parcel of its enigma, of its appeal. To this circumstance *The Erotic Phenomenon* alerts us early on:

> "Love"? It resonates as the most prostituted word there is. . . . To declare
> "I love you" sounds, in the best of cases, like an obscenity or a derision,
> to the point where, in polite society (that of the educated), no one dares
> *seriously* to utter such nonsense. Nor to hope for any substitute for this

bankruptcy, not even the least note of credit. Thus the word "charity" itself is found to be, if possible, even more neglected; ... even charity's magnificent name is snatched away, and it is covered by rags deemed more acceptable such as "fellowship," "solidarity," "humanitarian aid."[21]

We will leave charity, discussed at length in Marion's *Prolegomena to Charity*, for another moment and concentrate more specifically on the concept and practice of love. Where love or the expression "I love you!" is at issue, we will never know as a matter of fact—with certainty or without any need of further assurance—whether its event actually took place, whether it did not mistake its mere appearance for its putative essence. We simply lack the criteria to make such a determination and settle the matter once and for all.

What, then, is the speech act, the required "speech tact,"[22] perhaps—at any rate, the passion and, at times, tragedy—of love, of saying "I love you!"? And what does it mean, for our purposes, that, as Cavell writes, "in perlocutionary acts, the 'you' comes essentially into the picture," while, as Marion adds, "in illocutionary acts everything depends on my capacity, as the speaking 'I,' to perform what I say"?[23]

We cannot simply think the event, notably the "event of love," "starting from itself."[24] We should also acknowledge that we have no other starting point in these matters than those of "first-person" discourse.[25] Love, as Cavell was the first to have taught, is "my call," which, again, is not to say that it is, thereby, a matter of subjective "will," nothing more. In love, willing and wanting to say count for so little that another beginning must be made. Marion circumvents this difficulty by resorting to a deeply pragmatic—in fact, simple pragmatist—argument that one of his commentators aptly captures as follows: "A significant general point about saturated phenomena is that they can only be recognized by the effect that they produce in their witness."[26] This cannot merely mean that their appeal originates in the one who makes it his or her call and responds to them accordingly, claiming and proclaiming an acclamation, as it were. More precisely, as Marion himself puts it in one of his chapter's subheadings, in *Being Given*, the phenomenon and what it requires demonstrates itself only or first of all in the pragmatic effect that it takes, in the very impact it makes on the life, that is to say, faith and fidelity, of the hearer (the beholder, the witness, martyr or saint): "The Call [*L'appel*] Shows Itself in the Response."[27] We alluded to this cardinal ·

point in what we said previously, but it cannot be stressed here enough. That the call is "heard only the response and to its measure" is a paradoxical insight that contemporary thinkers have rightly and consistently insisted upon. Marion mentions Emmanuel Levinas and Jean-Louis Chrétien as two main advocates of this consequential—indeed, strangely consequentialist, if anything but utilitarian—view.[28] But there are others as well (again, Badiou's aforementioned work comes to mind).

All this—the call, requiring *our* call, *our* calling, which it "follows" (finding no ear and acquiring no actuality "before" it)—makes saturated phenomena (love most prominently among them) and the performative utterances they elicit or by which they are expressed, peculiar instances of the given, of the ordinary and the everyday. Moving well beyond the phenomenological idiom and its methodological reduction, in this particular context, Marion clarifies their nature by referring to Austin's vocabulary of the perlocutionary speech act. By this type of performative Austin means "an act that we instigate or accomplish by saying something: to convince, persuade, frighten, etc."[29]

What would be an example of such a speech act? Cavell, in "Passionate and Performative Utterances" (the essay from which I have taken my title and on which Marion bases a large part of his argument), suggests that to make someone "green with jealousy" (as Iago does Othello in Shakespeare's tragedy, a constant reference in Cavell's own work) is an instance of such a "perlocutionary effect." To this, Marion adds that the attempt to make someone love you—precisely by saying "I love you!"—is yet another (love and hate revealing a terrifying similarity, in the formal structure of their linguistic or performative utterance at the very least):

> When I say "I love you!," I try . . . not necessarily to perform the love that I speak but to move, to influence, and, at the very least, to summon my listener to consider my declaration. I declare my love as one declares war: it is not yet to engage in it, but already to oblige my adversary to mobilize him- or herself, and thus to determine him- or herself in relation to me. . . . By saying "I love you!" I do not love for all that, but I in effect ask the other to love me or at least to answer me sincerely. I thus accomplish neither a locutionary nor an illocutionary act, but rather a perlocutionary act.[30]

Like Levinas before him, Marion thus respects a remarkable parallel between the enunciation or performative utterance of love, seduction, and erotic desire, on the one hand, and that of the military strategizing of the most worldly, down-to-earth—now banal, then catastrophic—realms of political rhetoric, of diplomacy, indeed, of the language of war, on the other.[31] It is no accident, therefore, that the main protagonist of the novel that offers Marion's prime example here, namely Stendhal's 1839 *La Chartreuse de Parme* (*The Charterhouse of Parma*) lives through the same ambiguity of love and war, of the seducer and the diplomat. Fabrizio del Dongo, who—unable to say with certainty whether he witnessed the battle of Waterloo or not, nor, indeed, whether it took place or not—also makes his appearance in the phenomenology of that other event that interests Marion, notably in *Being Given*, namely the historicity of war.[32] I will return to Stendhal, but suffice to note here that it is as if Marion were suggesting that as to the possibility—in metaphysical parlance, the transcendental condition of possibility—of the very best (love) and the worst (hate and worse) the manifestation of their event is, formally, virtually, at times phenomenologically, absolutely indistinguishable, is as if, therefore, the same.

Moreover, in suggesting that the expression "I love you!" is neither a descriptive statement (a constative) nor a performative pure and simple but a "performative utterance of the perlocutionary type," Marion sees himself as "justifying," against its omission by Austin and Searle, what Cavell specifically calls a "passionate utterance,"[33] while inscribing its register in a much older and broader tradition of apophatic, more precisely, mystic speech. Like Cavell, Marion goes far in his willingness to stress the analytical distinction between the locutionary, illocutionary, and perlocutionary, even noting that the last must be seen as severing its ties from the fact and content of linguistic utterance and its determining context itself. For one thing, the often quite special effects of the perlocutionary utterance—the "responses" to its call and calling, if you like—whether they consist in "emotions, thoughts, reactions, etc.," stand somewhat on their own with respect to linguistic practice, rules and conventions, insofar as they "can be accomplished additionally or entirely by non-locutionary means."[34] For another, they lack normal—normative and normalizing—reference, just they seem to dispense with (their) enabling criteria as they drive home their point.

This is not to deny that our verbal and nonverbal ways of responding, the effect speech has on us (and, indeed, first of all on me, as a singularized addressee) may very well be prefigured by the options and examples that we have encountered or have been taught and shown since our earliest childhood. Long before highlighting the importance of the passionate utterance, Cavell explains as much. In the beautiful "Excursus on Wittgenstein's Vision of Language," which all but sums up the central intuitions guiding his *magnum opus*, *The Claim of Reason*, throughout, we find the following passage that is relevant for our purposes as the apparent corrective or contrast of the view we have propounded so far:

> When you say "I love my love" the child learns the meaning of the word "love" and what love is. *That (what you do)* will *be* love in the child's world; and if it is mixed with resentment and intimidation, then love is a mixture of resentment and intimidation, and when love is sought *that* will be sought. . . . In "learning a language" you learn not merely what the names of things are, but what a name is; . . . not merely what the word for "love" is, but what love is. In learning language, you do not merely learn the pronunciation of sounds, and their grammatical orders, but the "forms of life" which make those sounds the words they are, do what they do.[35]

Cavell continues by reminding his readers that Wittgenstein "sees the relations among *these* forms as 'grammatical' also" and, further, that there is no other way of inaugurating ("initiating" and "gathering around" are his terms) children in the concept and practice of love than to "make ourselves exemplary and take responsibility for that assumption of authority," just as the child, for its part, "must be able to follow us, in however rudimentary a way, *naturally* . . . and must *want* to follow us (care about our approval . . .)."[36] This is, no doubt, all true and necessary, an essential part of the analysis and phenomenology of love one would need to begin by offering, taking it as our acquiescing in the language game and form of life, first of all.

But does this picture capture the more *deeply pragmatic* dimension or aspect of the "passionate utterance" that the declaration as well as acceptance of love—the mystic or, more broadly, apophatic speech of "I love you!"—must also require or, indeed, call for? Indirectly, Cavell seems to acknowledge that there is more to it: "'Teaching here would mean something like 'showing them what we say and do,' and 'accepting what they say and do as what we say and do,' etc.; and this will be *more than we know, or can say.*"[37] There is a "mystical postulate" of "authority," then, for Cavell as well, even in the early excursus. And it, in return, invites us to think of a performative or perlocution that is absolute in that it *absolves* itself from determining contexts, just as much as it eludes the very criteria that seemed (or must have) enabled it. Or so we assume.

MARION ON STENDHAL

Marion establishes that the utterance "I love you!" (*je t'aime*) has a peculiar logic and "radical pragmatic use." He introduces the words, using or mentioning them not so much as a line spoken by an actor on the stage of a theater play, to which Austin might or might not have objected (depending on who one is inclined to follow here, Jacques Derrida or, indeed, Searle), but as a citation from literature nonetheless. Once again quoting the final chapter of Stendhal's *The Charterhouse of Parma*—the author's final novel, often credited for its breaking away from romanticism and its exploration of realism and invoked by Leon Tolstoy and Bernardo Bertolucci as a decisive influence on the former's 1869 *War and Peace*, notably its battle scenes, and the latter's 1964 film *Prima della rivoluzione (Before the Revolution)*—Marion recalls how the novel's hero, the aforementioned Fabrizio, responds to an invitation by his beloved Clélia, extended by letter, to come at midnight to "a small door . . . in the via San Paolo." I cite the new translation by John Sturrock: "Fabrizzio entered cautiously and found himself . . . in the orangery, but facing a heavily barred window raised three or four feet above the ground. The darkness was total. Fabrizzio had heard a sound in the window and was reconnoitering the bars with his hand when he felt a hand that had been passed through the bars take his and carry it to lips that bestowed a kiss on it. 'It's me,' said a beloved voice, 'I've come here to tell you I love you, and to ask you if you're willing to obey me.'"[38]

Love is an important theme throughout Stendhal's work and this not only in his 1821 publication *De l'amour* (*Love*), itself an extensive meditation sprung from the obsession with—and, as it turned out, unhappy because unanswered love for—one woman in particular, Mathilde Visconti Dembowski (Méthilde, as Stendhal would call her). But what happens, exactly, when an utterance such as "I love you!," as in "I've come here to tell you I love you," does not reach its destination or, upon arrival, is not received, such that it "misfires" or is "infelicitous" (rather than "true" or "false" as constatives would be) in speech act–theoretical terms? And also, conversely, we might be tempted to ask, what if the "same" utterance fires and hits without interruption, as it were (as would seem to be the case in Jane Birkin's and Serge Gainsbourg's well-known 1969 duet *"Je t'aime . . moi non plus,"* the infamous song, written originally for Brigitte Bardot in 1967 and long banned in several countries because of its sexual overtones, to put it mildly)?[39] Is there a little and too much of love's succeeding to address itself to a beloved one that may cause it to miss out on what, presumably, is its target? Yet how would we ever be able to tell whether that is what has happened?

For one thing, we know that the utterance to which we can "reduce" Clélia's words—that is, its "central nucleus," "I love you"—cannot be rendered (understood or paraphrased) in terms of some descriptive content. It is not a constative statement, but rather falls "in the domain of pure private language":

> Neither Fabrizio nor anyone else can understand what Clélia is saying. . . .
> I could conjecture that she is describing her subjective attachment to
> the person of Fabrizio. Yet one cannot exclude that she may be pretend-
> ing or lying, either to Fabrizio (to seduce him), to a possible witness (to
> embrace her standing), or even to herself (to love loving, without lov-
> ing anyone in particular). In order to defend the constative character of
> Clélia's utterance, one can also reduce her sentence, "I've come to tell
> you that I love you" to a quasi-predicative proposition in the style
> "Someone exists—X, me, Clélia—such that she is in love with another—
> Y, you, Fabrizio" . . . What signification does this utterance offer? One that
> is revealed by its method of verification.
> (105)

Indeed, if this route is taken, Marion assures us, it quickly becomes clear that no strict verification can ever be found or even hoped for. Aside from some Augustinian truth making (*veritatem facere*), no empirical observation and, definitely, no introspection of even the most serious—indeed, purests of—motifs will reveal that what was meant was real, that what was said was heard and understood as it should be (and how and what, exactly, could that be)? As Marion goes on to note, "reduced to behaviors and states of affair, the declaration 'I love you!' remains ambiguous, precisely because it doesn't describe anything with precision" (106). True enough, it may still be possible to simply "trust Clélia's sincerity." But then, Marion rightly asks,

> how is one to recognize and prove this sincerity? All the facts and actions that one could inventory belong to the world. They cannot say anything, nor can they determine the validity of someone's sincerity, which in principle remains both out of this world and absolutely foreign to things. At its best, sincerity pertains to the private sphere and thus cannot be described or verified any more than lying can. One cannot even invoke private language in this situation, because the private language is precisely deprived of it. What is more, as soon as someone claims to speak and prove his or her sincerity by speaking utterances of the type "I am sincere," "you can trust me," experience has taught us that we should rather hear an indication of deceit. . . . Thus Clélia is saying nothing about nothing to Fabrizio when she says "I love you!"
> (106)

But, with this, not all is said. As Marion goes on to explain, if Clélia's "'I love you!' perhaps states nothing at all . . . this utterance nonetheless speaks this nothing *to* someone, Fabrizio, and it speaks *on behalf of* someone else. . . . Especially if Stendhal is saying nothing about nothing, it is clear that he insists on the speakers and the person spoken to, to the point of saturation. . . . Clearly, predication and proposition fade away, leaving the naked intrigue of the two speakers, that is to say, the interlocutors, in the foreground" (106). Having established this "intrigue," however, Marion does not hesitate to question that its nature must be that of a "strict dialogue, without an object but perfectly intersubjective."[40] On second glance, it is not.

Again, Marion finds support for his analysis in Cavell's essay on "Passionate and Performative Utterance."[41] There Cavell *does* discuss the enunciation "I love you!" (the reference in this case is not to Stendhal's *The Charterhouse of Parma* but to the French composer Georges Bizet's opera *Carmen*), even though he seems unwilling to push the analysis of this utterance in the tripartite direction of the kataphatic, apophatic, and hyperbolic or eminent and, hence, more pragmatic modes of discourse Marion spells out in the mystical register that eludes and dissolves positive and negative, natural and so-called ontotheologies alike—all of which are privy to the descriptive (or constative), representationalist fallacy, as Austin would have said, or, indeed, are idolatrous and blasphemous, as Marion elsewhere will add.

THE APORIA OF INSINCERITY

Nor does Cavell accept Marion's assessment of an inevitable "aporia of sincerity," the fact that it is "a totally private mood, ineffable in everyday language" ("What Cannot Be Said," 109), which not even the hyperbolic "redoubling" of speech and gestures can undo once and for all, although it loosens the knot between words and world implicitly, surreptitiously, now and then, here and there, and entices the lover—and, potentially, lovers—to utter and express (if not necessarily speak, intelligibly, discursively, or directly) more. After all, *je t'aime*, "I love you!," is neither a locution nor an illocution but a performative of the perlocutionary type, *indeed*, "the perlocutory [utterance] par excellence" (134), whose sole proof and success is the effect taken, the call followed up, the response—acknowledgment or avoidance—given or received. Again: "By saying 'I love you!' I do not love for all that, but I in effect ask the other to love me or at least to answer me sincerely. I thus accomplish neither a locutionary act nor an illocutionary act, but rather a perlocutionary act" (111).

Marion reminds us that, according to both Austin and Cavell, "in the case of a perlocutionary act, one does not consider *what* is said but the fact *that* it is said, the effect it has on the listener," but he immediately supplements this view by claiming (what certainly neither Austin nor Cavell would be willing to accept per se) that "this effect belongs unambiguously to apophasis" (109–10). Hence, the enunciation remains "aporetic" in that—whether it is put casually or emphatically—saying "I love you!" (or anything else of this nature and, indeed, come to think of it, virtually everything one meaningfully and forcefully can say)

> guarantees my sincerity [including my own understanding of my deepest motives] no more than it presumes the acceptance (or refusal) of the other or, for that matter, his or her own sincerity [and, we might add, self-transparency]. Following Cavell once more, one must next recognize that the freedom and fragility of "I love you" have no ambition to be of any value for anything other than "now," certainly not "in the fu-

ture": How can I guarantee to someone that I love him or her, if I myself have no certitude? One could answer that I can very well promise to love someone in the future, in spite of the fickleness of my heart and my moods. Of course, but then one is dealing with a promise ("I promise to love you"), and thus with a completely different act from "I love you!" The promise is, in fact, the perfect illocutionary act, even the epitome of the performative, satisfying all conditions, precisely those that "I love you!" does not satisfy (conventional procedure and effect, fixed circumstances, formal and complete fulfillment, guarantee of reciprocity and the future, etc.). Thus, the promise differs essentially from "I love you!"; it can only be added on, and this supplement confirms that by saying "I love you!" I do not perform an illocutionary speech act.

(109)

As in Cavell's discussion of Austin's reference to Euripides' tragedy *Hippolytus*, made in passing in the third lecture of *How to Do Things with Words*, which cites the tragic hero's line on stage—"My tongue swore to, but my heart did not"—the given promise promises forever; its temporality brings in an aspect of infinity, perhaps eternity, such that *"our word is our bond."* But, as Marion wants to make us believe, no such dimension fits for the format of love, that is, its utterance and act. There would thus an interesting conversation to be had as to how Marion and Cavell understand the "supplement" of love that is marriage or remarriage (one is reminded of the latter's works on Hollywood cinema, whether those focusing the "melodrama of the unknown woman" or, indeed, the "comedies of remarriage").

Whereas for Cavell there is always the chance that I might yet make myself intelligible—to the other, even if not necessarily to myself—and that, hence, I might discover myself to be known and acknowledged rather than ignored or avoided, for Marion the ontological or, at least, phenomenal (linguistic, gestural, or expressive) fragility of saying "I love you!"—and everything that it stands for and makes possible—holds no such hopes. Hence the "apophatics of the discourse of love" (*discours amoureux*), as the very title of one of Marion's most relevant essays, in this context, aptly expresses it. And, as we have now established, in the broadest and narrowest of terms, this amorous discourse is a fundamentally "erotic discourse" (*discours érotique*). Its conceptual and practical implication extends, therefore, to the whole analysis of the erotic phenomenon given and, extrapolating even further, to the wider assessment of the very epistemology and ontology, ethics and politics that must necessarily build—depend and follow—upon it as well.

THE PRAGMATIC DIMENSION ONCE MORE

All this is not to deny that the passionate utterance has a "radically pragmatic" (and this means, in Marion's view, an essentially "dialogical" and quite practical) dimension and function in the lives that we lead. Love, its saying and, we said, "making," has unavoidable effects, regardless of—or, precisely, due to—its "aporetics." As we saw, the apophatic utterance of love is uncertain as to both sender and addressee; it lacks descriptive content and clear reference, and these necessary omissions mark the amorous or erotic discourse's most fateful, tragic, comic, and, hence, memorable infelicities, just as they alone enable its success, its happiness, when and wherever it blissfully happens that things come to pass and we stand transfigured.

And yet, some caution is here in order. Since, in *speaking for love*, rather than, say, *out of love*, we're not dealing with performatives utterances of the illocutionary kind and force, but, instead, with perlocutionaries whose effects are much less controllable than the "misfires" and "abuses" (including "insincerities") Austin lists under the heading of "infelicities," properly speaking, a different—more or, perhaps, less stringent—term and designation for their failures, imperfections, or perversions ought yet to be found. Unless, that is, their very failure (which, again, is everything but a "falsity," a lack of description or even of reference) is their success (which, again, is everything but their "truth"). We realize once more that the conceptual, speech act–theoretical, and, more broadly, pragmatic distinctions and terminologies break down one by one (and, we now suspect, were never quite up to the task in the first place). The "revolutionary" and "salutary" contribution that the new philosophy of so-called ordinary language makes (and these words are Austin's own characterization for the "phenomenology" that he undertakes in the lectures in question) consists in bringing out the horror *and* sublimity that *passively* rather than actively governs our speech.

Still, one wonders: is there, on the basis of this analysis, any room for the passionate utterance "I love you!" ever to be felicitous, that is to say, if not sincere and assured, then at least somehow genuine and effective? As Marion shows, the most one can say is that, for all its "categorical and affirmative" nature, the seemingly positive enunciation "I love you!" reverts almost immediately into its opposite, its negation and unsaying, without therefore reducing itself to nothing, as if nothing *was* said:

> No affirmation can impose itself as powerfully as "I love you!" but, paradoxically, it imposes itself as a question whose contours are almost impossible to trace, as the most radical question one can perhaps ever ask. Put otherwise, if my affirmation *that* I love him neither promises nor teaches him anything, it nonetheless forces him to answer a question, a question that is formulated from my point of view as "Does he love me?" while he hears it as "Do you love me?" It follows that the initial affirmation "I love you!" as categorical and affirmative as it remains ends up producing the effect of a "Do you love me?"—a question that leaves room for doubt, for choice, and for a possible refusal. Affirmation thus elicits negation in and of itself; kataphasis becomes apophasis [*la cataphase tourne en une apophase*]."
> (113)

Likewise, when it comes to the question of

> deciding whether or not (referentially) I am sincere, or whether or not I understand (semantically) what "to love" means, neither she nor I know anything at the moment [*l'instant*] of the declaration—hence the apophasis. One might answer that what is at stake is not our sincerity but our concrete behavior and coherence: each of us will learn more about the intention of the other over time, which means that if I ask "Do you love?" at a particular moment t_1, I can hope to obtain the beginning of an answer at moment t_2 or t_3, etc. This, in its turn, implies that the answer to the question is reached, in the best of cases, only in the moment that follows after. Yet, if precisely only the *following* moment can affirm something in response to what I asked only the moment *before*, the temporal gap between doubt and confirmation cannot be abolished and will extend from question to response, endlessly. Thus, even in the case of a happy confirmation, the temporal delay and lateness maintain a différance. With all other questions about states of affairs or objects that are in principle characterized by a certain permanence, this

différance does not seriously compromise the answer. But in the case of the erotic relation where the fickleness of the heart holds sway even with no intention of lying (and this is precisely why I cannot stop asking "Do you love me?"), différance disqualifies the answer, even when it is positive.

(114)

Sincerity and seriousness, then, are apophatic, hence aporetic, like the discourse on love, in its phenomenology of eros no less than in that of agape or charity. Indeed, the same predicament haunts the situation of two lovers whose "*jouissance* can only speak its own repetition, operating it without syntax and managing its temporality," and the New Testament episode, "near the end of the Gospels, in which Christ asks Peter three times, 'Do you love me?' (John 21:15–17)" (117). There is nothing "surprising," Marion suggests, about this parallel and the need for repetition that it expresses, "inasmuch as between God and humans everything remains ambiguous except, precisely, love"(118). The desire to be loved, to love, is absolute, but it is only its reiterated utterance—three times over in the biblical example given—that conjures a potential assurance that is, as such (or otherwise), not to be found given.

None of this implies, therefore, that the discourses of love—or of passionate utterances in general—are doomed to failure or, more precisely, that, if they necessarily fail, this means that we should or could refrain from entertaining such conversation at all. On the contrary, Marion's whole project is based on the premise that for us to say and mean or do and feel anything genuinely (if not truthfully or sincerely—which would be the felicities of locutionary and illocutionary performatives rather than of perlocutionaries, strictly speaking), we must, first of all, love, call for love, make love our call. Love, before thinking, acting, or judging, is the object and objective of the very wisdom whose love philosophy—the *philein* of *sophia*—once sought, well before metaphysics and its vain overcoming, destruction, or deconstruction, condemned its eros and agape to the periphery as irrational passion, to be ruled by reason and norms, or disputed its proper logic.

The exposition of this theme—which, we now understand, subtracts itself from all thematization and tends toward the apophasis of *both* its origin *and* referent—has a *visual* in addition to narrative, poetic or rhetorical, dimension or aspect as well. In the citation from Stendhal, the female character Clélia says (but do we know this to be true or sincere or genuine?) that she has vowed to the Virgin Mary never to lay eyes on the person (she says) she loves: the male protagonist Fabrizio (who therefore does not get to see much of her, either). Marion does not elaborate on this important motif in the novel, even though it would seem to offer a striking corroboration of the apophatics and aporetics of love and its passionate utterance, as he presents them.

What, exactly, might Clélia's words ("I've come here to tell you I love you, and to ask you if you're willing to obey me") signify,[42] given that her utterance—after the "first transports" are "over"—is immediately followed by the confession of a peculiar proviso: "I have made a vow to the Madonna, as you know, never to set eyes on you, that is why I am receiving you in total darkness. I want you to know that, were you to force me to look at you in broad daylight, everything would be over between us."[43]

One rubs one's eyes: can one love with "eyes wide shut" (to cite Stanley Kubrick's uncanny title for his cinematographic investigation into the pitfalls of love or what goes under its name)? But also, conversely, can one love with eyes wide open? Seeing nothing or seeing everything, like saying all or saying nothing—do not these extremes meet in the end? Or, to ask a different question these pages impose: could one love—and live—by touch (for there's some of that in *The Charterhouse of Parma*, a kiss on a hand, the birth of a child) alone? The peculiar phenomenology of, say, the caress (known from a remarkable chapter in Levinas's *Totalité et infini* (*Totality and Infinity*) and taken up by Marion in *The Erotic Phenomenon*) would prove far too elusive to warrant such a claim, as the invisible in all seeing, in particular in setting one's eyes on someone, finds its echo and parallel in the untouchable—and, indeed, inviolable—as well.

Stendhal's novel's end suggests that none of these options—at least for these protagonists—are sustainable, indeed, livable. The heroine Clélia dies, heartbroken by the death of their son, and so, soon after, does the hero, Fabrizio, who literally retreats from life into the "Charterhouse of Parma" (which gives Stendhal's novel its name). Again, their love remains an apophatic utterance, a form of mystical speech, with no union in sight, and one of the greatest love stories in modern literature all the same.

ÉTANT DONNÉS AND THE STRUCTURE OF CALLING, ST. MATTHEW'S TO BEGIN WITH

There is more direct proof that, in the themes and arguments Marion pursues, the visual and the philosophical or theological reflect—indeed, mirror—each other. Text and image blend into each other as he seeks confirmation and, indeed, further depth and perspective for his phenomenology of eros in classical and modernist paintings whose practices of "absorption" rather than "theatricality," to cite Michael Fried's well-known oppositional pair,[44] reveal the very structure and event of the call for—more precisely, the being first called by—love.

Not only is the saturated phenomenon taken to be obliquely and, as it were, negatively evoked by Albrecht Dürer's *Melancholia* as it presents "vanity," the hither side of the iconicity of grace; it is also evinced by the paintings of cubists, which, precisely, leave no hither side to be suspected and, hence, offer the phenomenon as *too much to take in*. In short, the saturated phenomenon has, so Marion, left its indelible mark in a diversity of works such as the paintings of Raphael and Caravaggio, Cézanne and Kandinsky, Rothko and Pollock, not all of which have love or its opposites and analogues as their explicit theme.

Marion's study *The Crossing of the Visible* makes this case most directly, but throughout his other writings references to the immersion of text and image in each other abound. The prominence and strategic role of these analyses of images in Marion's work should not surprise us and not be taken as ornamental illustrations or accessory visual proof of an insight that could, in principle, be demonstrated by discursive—i.e., textual—means alone. The reason for this is surprisingly simple. If, as Marion claims, "philosophy today has become, essentially, phenomenology" and phenomenology, now defined as a phenomenology of "givenness" or "donation," in its saturation, "no longer pretends to return to the things themselves, because it has undertaken the task of seeing what gives itself [*ce qui se donne*]—what gives [*ce que cela donne*]," then the "exceptional visibility" of images, notably paintings, turns into a "privileged case of the phenomenon" and hence into "one possible route to a consideration of phenomenality in general."[45] Further, one could easily imagine what repercussions there must be in a visual culture that is diffused or disseminated by ever newer technological—digital and mobile—media in the exponential growing of markets and networks of communication around the globe.

For present purposes, however, let me recall only a remarkable reading of Caravaggio's *The Calling of St. Matthew* toward the end of Marion's *Being Given* and also, to begin with, a modernist artwork that is subtly invoked by the very title (in French) of his magisterial book. Both works can serve as illustrations and evocations of the apophatic, perlocutionary problematic of the erotic phenomenon, of agapaic as well as sexual love, including everything that mimics its formal structure as well as its deformalizing tendency, geared as it is toward singling out the "I" whose very call and calling it will and must be.

Étant donné, perhaps not accidentally, echoes the title of Marcel Duchamp's last creation, the mixed-media assemblage or "tableau-construction," *Étant donnés*, exhibited in the Philadelphia Museum of Art, whose title, of course, adds an *s* to *donné* (as in Marion's *Étant donné*) and, in full, reads: *Étant donnés: 1° la chute d'eau / 2° le gaz d'éclairage*, translated as *Given: 1. The Waterfall, 2. The Illuminating Gas*.[46] Through the wooden door's peepholes one sees a nude woman with her face hidden, holding up a gas lamp.

Much could be said about the relevance of this particular work for Marion's overall conception—the secrecy, hence invisibility, not only in which it was prepared over a twenty-year period (from 1944–1966), in New York, in Duchamp's studio at West 14th Street, but also the fact that its installation controls the conditions under which only one spectator can experience the feminine figure stretched out in three-dimensional space through two small holes (the "peep-holes," as Thierry de Duve writes) in an old Spanish door, as well as, perhaps, the reminiscences of a work of another of Marion's heroes, the painter Gustave Courbet's *L'origine du monde*, to whom Marion devotes one of his most recent books.[47]

For one thing, one might be tempted to speculate about the meaning of the words that Duchamp jotted down in a 1934 manuscript note in *The Bride Stripped Bare by Her Bachelors, Even (The Green Box)*.[48] For another, one might want to rethink Marion's persistent use of the concept of the so-called ready-made and *objet trouvé*, both of which reveal or recreate not so much this or that element of the seen or unseen reality that surrounds us but something altogether different still, in the

FIGURE 12.1. "Étants donnés: 1° la chute d'eau, 2° le gaz d'éclairage . . . (Given: 1. The Waterfall, 2. The Illuminating Gas . . .)" (exterior) by Marcel Duchamp. Philadelphia Museum of Art: gift of the Cassandra Foundation, 1969. Copyright © Succession Marcel Duchamp / ADAGP, Paris and JASPAR, Tokyo, 2013.

"blink" of an eye: "*Monstrum*, the presentable par excellence, the brute unseen, the miracle. *Miraculum*, the admirable par excellence. The painter of miracles is made to blink when encountering the visible too much foreseen."[49]

In a similar vein, Marion argues that the central theme of Caravaggio's *The Calling of Saint Matthew*, which it shares with his *Conversion of St. Paul*, is the silent, near invisible incursion of "the miraculous" into the course of ordinary life, unperceived by bystanders and all those who are not concerned—surprised and called—by it directly. Only Matthew seems to heed the call, just as only Paul is blinded on the way to Damascus. Marion uses the painting to illustrate that the address of the call can be noticed only in the response given to it (with the refusal to respond being no less a response). In fact, he suggests, we see the call—*l'appel*, the *Ruf*, the appeal and, perhaps, sex appeal, the difference (as between *agape* and *eros*) mattering little—"appear in Matthew's gaze infinitely more than we do in Christ's gesture" (284).

FIGURE 12.2. "Étants donnés: 1° la chute d'eau, 2° le gaz d'éclairage . . . (Given: 1. The Waterfall, 2. The Illuminating Gas . . .)" (interior) by Marcel Duchamp. Philadelphia Museum of Art: gift of the Cassandra Foundation, 1969. Copyright © Succession Marcel Duchamp / ADAGP, Paris and JASPAR, Tokyo, 2013.

Following "the clues laid down by the painting" (283) carefully, Marion analyzes the enormous difficulty Caravaggio confronts, namely, "the fact that he must show in silence a call that is invisible," which is something he can do only "without making anything heard, by means of the only phenomenality available, that of the silence of the forms, colors, shadow and light" (283). What Caravaggio gives to be seen is that

FIGURE 12.3. "The Calling of Saint Matthew" by Caravaggio (Michelangelo Merisi da). Contarini Chapel. S. Luigi dei Francesi, Rome, Italy. Photo credit: Scala/Art Resource, NY.

Matthew sees Christ's gaze and is, as it were, absorbed by it more than by anything else—the whole theater of human commerce and chatter, which continues around him. His response—the gestured "Who? Do you summon me?"—reveals "not Christ as another spectacle to be seen, but Christ's gaze as a weight that weighs on his own gaze and holds it captive" (284).

In his *The Moment of Caravaggio*, Michael Fried emphasizes the "momentary character of the event," which is known only from a single sentence in the gospel of Matthew (9:9): "Jesus saw a man called Matthew at his seat in the custom-house, and said to him, 'Follow me'; and Matthew rose and followed him" and points out that the calling takes place "in passing," with virtually no time elapsing, such that "Christ's summons and Matthew's 'conversion,' being virtually simultaneous, cannot be understood in terms of ordinary relations of cause and effect."[50] And yet the painting raises serious questions as to who is who and who does what exactly. Long debates have ensued as to who is Matthew in the painting (the traditional reading, with which Fried sides, being that it is the bearded man with the hand pointing to himself, as if in response) and the "summoning gesture" that Christ makes toward him is, Fried writes, "curiously unenergetic, not exactly limp but almost so" (196). For the first detail, Fried claims, speaks the fact that "the bearded man's right knee is raised and his right foot has already left the ground," which might well mean that "Caravaggio wished to signal that without being aware of what he is doing or even that he is doing anything at all, the bearded man has already begun to follow Christ" (198). We would be witnessing a "spontaneous, unreflective obedience to Christ's summons" (199), which makes all the more clear that Christ's and Matthew's gestures almost coincide. With this interpretative tour de force, Fried adds that the weak gesturing of Christ's hand invokes a theologically profound and potential heterodox view that "Christ's exemplariness is associated with a determined renunciation of physical force or even command; the hand's extraordinary efficacy functions in another register—a mimetic register . . . mimesis in this context bearing connotations of something like hypnotic rapport between Christ and Matthew" (199). The call, like the love it inspires, that is to say, requires and summons, is based on a certain powerlessness (Marion might have said *impouvoir*) whose effect and impact is all the more striking.

If the call, as Marion suggests, can be seen or heard only in the response, does Christ merely hold up a mirror or sounding board, then? Can Matthew *project*—see, hear, or respond—in any way he wants, any way he sees fit or opportune? Obviously, he cannot. The analysis leaves no other conclusion than that Matthew's gaze—or, more broadly, the amorous-erotic gaze (which is not entirely absent here)—cannot anticipate nor experience the object to which it directs itself. The revelation, the call or appeal, of the amorous object does not exist *before*, *outside*, and *beyond* the response that is given (i.e., that Matthew gives) to it and that alone is able to call it into existence, phenomenologically speaking.

Put differently, the miracle of calling—or, indeed, the call of the miracle, of its belief and making (doing, performing), I would like to say—resembles the very structure of the perlocutionary in Austin's *How to Do Things with Words* as well as that of the passionate utterance in

Cavell's reformulation. Miracle belief, like professing love, is not so much a belief *in* (this or that being the case) as it is a spiritual and affective, indeed, corporeal disposition and positioning to take or to leave, to acknowledge or to avoid. In other words, it is the way in which we call certain things and events by their name and into existence, viewing them under this and no other aspect and *only thus making them so:* seeing and setting them right in one single gesture whose "word" is our "bond."

THE SPONTANEOUSNESS OF MY CALL

The call is, as Cavell might have said here, "my call" (just as "I am the scandal of skepticism" such that every attempt and imperative to respond if not put an end to it relies on me).[51] By the same token, Levinas once said that the Infinite does not and cannot, must not and ought not, exist first, so as to reveal itself in a second instance or instant. Its signification signals and has no being or value, sense or reference, before or beyond, such that its transcending gesture never comes to rest in a transcendental signified of sorts.

In Marion's excursus on Caravaggio, he likewise leaves no doubt that "the painter's gaze saw (and now shows us) that the call gives itself phenomenologically only by first showing itself in a response. The response that gives itself after the call nevertheless is the first to show it."[52] *There is* what we might call "the real" of the call. Yet in the world as we know it, that of phenomenal and sensuous appearance—and this, quite literally, is all we could *care* about (since *Sorge*, as Heidegger aptly defines it in the first division of *Being and Time*, reveals our "being-in-the-world," including our being in it "with others," in *Fürsorge*, nothing else)—the call's origin and further or ultimate meaning and sense (or is it nonsense?) only come second.

But then, could we not have made this all up? Could we not have misdirected our gaze or even possibly have seen nothing at all? Might our response not be mere whistling in the dark, a narcissistic response to the infinite spaces around and within us, whose hollow resounding we merely wish we could fill up with infinite objects (if not with God, as Pascal wagered, then with love)? The truly and truthful other, after all, resides well beyond the screen of my possible projections, behind "a heavily barred window" and in "total darkness" (as Stendhal writes of Clélia in *The Charterhouse of Parma*) or behind a door that, as a "given," never opens (as is the case in Duchamp's *Étants donnés*) or also behind the uncertainty of the "Who, me?" with which Caravaggio paints us the apostle to be.

For all I know—though I may not be able to bring myself to *acknowledge* (in Cavell's term) as much—the loved and desired one is and was all along *on this side* of my projection, my screening, right in front of me, in the very nudity of her face, but, in that sense, also as somehow too much, too saturated a phenomenon, for me to take in and to process, much less to live up to and be faithful to. Which is, precisely, why acknowledgment tips so easily over into *avoidance*, love into indifference or even hate.

In conclusion, then, could I not have made this all up, with a misdirected, misfired, feigned (hence, abused) acknowledgment, one that effectively "annihilates" the genuine other and encapsulates me even more firmly in my ever expanding, imperialist vanity or, for that matter, in my increasingly narrowing, maddening "privacy" (which, as Cavell demonstrates in *The Claim of Reason*, is the genuine possibility Wittgenstein's *Investigations* may have allowed and explored or touched up on, rather than excluding it as an epistemological and psychological, linguistic and pragmatic impossibility that only philosopher-skeptics envision while in their study)?

To this, the only sincere answer is: yes, indeed, there is no way we can tell with certainty or even in good faith whether we are "called" or "loved" and "love" ourselves, in turn, or not. No epistemic (perceptual, linguistic, or ontological) criteria are available other than the *noncriteriological* persistence and consistency of our "fidelity" to this purported "event" together with our practical investment in it. Its taking effect, and our taking its consequences, are an integral part not just of promises and "words" that are "bound" but of perlocutionary utterances and performances far less conventional and rule bound (or, indeed, obeying no conditions, conventions, and rules at all).

Reading Marion with Badiou here seems, once again, only appropriate, however much as these thinkers differ in intellectual background, argumentative style, existential as well as political commitment, and make only sparse reference to each other, if at all. This is clear when, in *Being Given*, Marion notes: "One could almost accept Alain Badiou's formulation: 'If there exists an event, *its belonging to the situation of its site is undecidable from the standpoint of the situation itself.*'"[53] But we could just as well add that we can read Marion here with Cavell, who in *The Claim of Reason* demonstrates that the call—as in "What a Thing Is Called"[54]— is, well, first of all, "our call," more precisely, "my call," not least since no one can substitute for me in hearing, seeing, or sensing it.

The "passionate utterance of love"—the very expression and expressiveness of the perlocutionary act of the utterance "I love you" (like "I love you too," "I loved you first," or "more" or "longer") has no other warrant than the speaker's and listener's capacity for responsiveness, for taking these words *to heart*, regardless of the universal import we may (and, indeed, must) thereby, immediately, and subsequently give them as well. Indeed, for all the emphasis on the temporality of the "now," there is no dispensing with the perspective of infinite repetition and duration. The "hyperbolic redoubling" of the *via eminentiae* only underscores this point. Textually and in the realm of images, conceptually or discursively and visually, the very same logic operates in the "apophatics of love" and the "aporetics of sincerity." As Marion writes: "Even if I am sincere in the moment, I know very little about my motivations (desire, the vanity of seduction, fear of solitude, moral altruism?) or about their future (for how long?), such that if I confirm, by answering, 'Yes, I love you!' I know only one thing—that I am stepping out of bounds and that, at bottom, as far as the moment to come is concerned, I know nothing. The question 'Do you love me?' thus effectively establishes an apophasis."[55] In other words, while the mystic speech of love is not that of the *via negativa*, just as it is not that of the *via affirmativa*, its need for eminent hyperbole and the repetition that comes with inscribes a moment of "negative certitude" within itself.

Yet would love's indelibly subjective stance—indeed, the emergence of a subject as the perlocutionary effect of a call that has no determinable reality per se, its response to it—enclose us within the circle of what Marion calls "self-idolatry"? And is this what narcissism is or ends up with? Not necessarily. Narcissism, "the love one brings to one's own image" (as the psychoanalytic dictionary of Pontalis and Laplanche has it), is in fact the perversion of this call, of the response, substituting for an irreplaceable responsibility the projection of a fantasy, namely, of oneself onto oneself. For there is such a thing as the idolatry, as opposed to the iconicity, of love: it is to love someone—or think one does—*in one's own image.*[56]

But then, since we cannot tell love (the icon) from its virtual opposite (the idol) with full certainty, lacking all criteriological means to do so and, hence, we can never know for a fact whether we love or are loved in truth or truthfully—for, say, all the right "reasons" the heart well knows of, but "reason" does not, as Pascal might have said—the very concept and experience or practice of "love" remains fundamentally aporetic and without final result. Far from being merely narcissistic, it is and remains—if it can claim existence and some essence or other subsistence at all—deeply "passionate" in pragmatic, speech-act-theoretical terms or, indeed, apophatic, unsayable, invisible, mystical, nothing short of a miracle, in a different register still. Not even the most emphatic "I love you!" doubling as "I love my love," would do the trick, as it continues to fall short of the mark, saying either too little or, as often, a little too much. Yet in this, "passionate utterance" of love perhaps shares the condition of *all* discourse, not least what Marion calls "the traditional vanity of philosophy, which is always more than it knows—but often less than it thinks."[57]

An all too unmediated—almost blunt or brutal—conclusion proposes itself. Marion draws it, not without irony, provocation, and barely veiled frivolousness: "Love is not spoken, in the end, it is made" (*"L'amour ne se dit pas, à la fin, il se fait"*).[58] One is reminded of a *bon mot* that Levinas liked to repeat (unless he invented it to illustrated one of his most crucial phenomenological insights): *"On s'amuse mieux à deux,"* one has more fun together, that is to say, when not alone.

Such duality and such shameless immediacy can, of course, not have the last word. Or, if it is without words—saying nothing (nothing determinate, that is) or only outrageous or obscene things—it will ask for words, for more and other words, none of them first or last, none of them decent or indecent proposals per se. Not only does the very phenomenon of love require that it overcome its *égoïsme à deux*, the self- or mutual satisfaction of two (one is reminded of Kant's enlightened, even cynical definition of marriage), it is nothing if not universal, addressed to all, to God—for lack of a better name to hint at infinite reference, that is, to the infinity of reference, of all in all. What I am suggesting, then, is that the irreducibly apophatic—albeit, we have seen, not necessarily negative—moment of passionate utterance undercuts any attempt to characterize the discourse of love in strictly or even primarily narcissistic terms; nor, we might add, is it predominantly, let alone exclusively, erotic or agapaic.

Nothwithstanding Spinozistic and Deleuzean claims to the contrary, we seem to know or feel that there is only so much a body can do. Levinas was right, then, to shift his attention from the all too Freudian emphasis on *eros* in terms of sexual desire and satisfaction—the way of the flesh and of death (as Freud might have agreed with Saint Paul)—in the direction of *agape*, while stripping the latter of its Christian connotations. The point is not the prudence or prudishness of old age, moving away from an early phenomenology of the caress, in *Totality and Infinity*, to the "wisdom of love" with which *Autrement qu'être* (*Otherwise Than Being*) concludes. Rather, his insight is above all systematic, based on an implicated horizon and ineliminable indirectness—too little or too much sense, the difference hardly matters—that it is impossible to deny out of hand.

What I have been claiming is, perhaps, this: I cannot *coherently* say "I love you!," though I nonetheless do so *consistently*—and, one hopes, *responsibly*. This circumstance, with its perpetual threat of apophasis and insincerity (regardless of the best of my intentions and escaping my will) forces me to say it more and more, each time anew, stammering things like "Did I tell you today that I love you?" and this ad infinitum, perhaps ad nauseam (the question of, say, well-being, happiness, and feeling good, on the one hand, and that of love, on the other, being fundamentally unrelated, as soon as the latter no longer pertains to the order of, well, "Being" and, thereby, "beings" and their existential modes and moods per se).

Indeed, since I cannot go one further step along this path—and this is the literal translation of the Greek term *aporia*, of there being no way through, no point of entry, no exit—I must go on, go all the way, and almost nonsensically, if not senselessly or insensitively, say ever more. Marion captures this situation, including its temporality—its comedy no less than its tragedy—by claiming that, "despite this apophasis, the erotic dialogue is no less persistent. How is this possible? By means of a third path [beyond affirmation and its skeptical doubts], a hyperbolic redoubling, a sort of eminence. I can really only repeat 'I love you!' precisely because the other repeats ceaselessly 'Do you love me?'; and for her, it is the same."[59]

Molly Bloom's reiterated "yes, yes, yes . . . "—upon which Jacques Derrida famously comments in "Nombre de oui" and *Ulysse gramophone*—says it all. These words are a series and *seriature*, without whose mechanism or quasi automaticity no declaration of love could get off the ground, much less be maintained and sustained. The repetition of the "yes" is love's method of verification, its making itself—oneself—true, no matter how often the skeptical question arises (and it always will or, at least, always can).

Repetition, hyperbole, is the method—the very *way*—of the *via eminentiae*, whose mystical theological model points beyond inevitable impasses of either affirmation or negation, of the *kataphatic* and the *apophatic*, following a logic of exaggeration and excess that spirals upward (and also downward, into banality, indeed, obscenity and blasphemy), without ever securing any firm or firmer ground.

All the reasons of the heart, reasons of which reason (to paraphrase, again, Pascal's *Pensées*) knows nothing, will not overcome this predicament. Ultimately, as in Angelus Silesius's poem "The Rose Is Without Why,"[60] its call, its appeal, whether erotically charged or not, shows itself—phenomenologically and otherwise—merely in the one who responds with "passionate utterance," and does so not unlike the *miraculé*—call him the lucky guy—who is, in Marion's words, "the one in whom or upon whom a miracle, like a healing, has been performed."[61] There is "no suggestion of its cause," but in the "event" (as which) it takes place, the most "intimate" and "global" of aspects and horizons are joined or even "collapsed into each other and, in both cases, described by the same determinations."[62]

THE LOVING ANIMAL

One final question remains. While Marion *denaturalizes* the phenomenon of love, in full phenomenological rigor, as it were (as phenomenology, beginning with Husserl, has sought to expunge the naturalistic fallacy, notably psychologism, from the very description and analysis of the phenomenon in question), just as he takes his meditations to be the "search for a concept" that begins by describing and analyzing the phenomenon "in its own proper horizon—that of a *love without being*," in so doing he nonetheless reinscribes the apophatics and aporetics of love within a larger horizon, not so much that of "being" (or is it?) but of "life":

> Man, as *ego cogito*, thinks, but he does not love, at least from the outset. Yet the most incontestable evidence—that which includes all other evidence, governs our time and our life from beginning to end and

penetrates us in every intervening instant—attests that, on the contrary, we are, insofar as we come to know ourselves, always already caught within the tonality of the erotic disposition—love or hate, unhappiness or unhappiness, enjoyment or suffering, hope or despair, solitude or communion—and that we can never, without lying to ourselves, claim to arrive at a fundamental erotic neutrality. Besides, who would strive for inaccessible ataraxy, who would demand it and boast of it, if he did not feel himself precisely to be, from the outset and forever, wrought, paralyzed, and obsessed by amorous tonalities? Man is revealed to himself by the originary and radical modality of the erotic. Man loves—which is what distinguishes him from all other finite beings, if not the angels. Man is defined neither by the *logos*, nor by the being within him, but this fact that he loves (or hates), whether he wants to or not. In this world, only man loves, for animals and computers, in their own way, think just as well as he, indeed better than he; but one cannot confirm that they love. But man does—the loving animal.[63]

But does the phenomenon of love, even taken in its erotic and not merely agapic dimension, necessarily require us to invoke animality as a concept, especially if neither animals nor machines know anything of love as "we," human animals, supposedly do? Or, put differently, does our animality have a "life" of its own, immanent to the phenomenon of love, as it were? And, if love does not even need to "be"—that is, if it neither requires nor allows "being" among its predicates as its condition and ultimate horizon, so to speak—does love need "life" (or also: does love need "to be lived") so as to come truly into its own? Can it not call for a greater passion, one that sacrifices—phenomenologically reduces—this last among the metaphysical vestiges, namely, the concept of "Life," of the "loving animal," or, at the very least, of its most direct implication, namely the prevalence of the presently living to the potential detriment of all—indeed, everyone—else; indeed, the unquestioned appeal and ultimate value of an all too ordinary and, in that sense, natural, if also somewhat naturalistic, interpretation of quotidian life?[64]

NOTES

1. See Jean-Luc Marion, *The Erotic Phenomenon*, trans. Stephen E. Lewis (Chicago: University of Chicago Press, 2007), 2.

2. Ibid., 3.

3. Ibid.

4. Ibid., 22.

5. Jean-Luc Marion, *Prolegomena to Charity*, trans. Stephen E. Lewis (New York: Fordham University Press, 2002).

6. Marion, *The Erotic Phenomenon*, 5.

7. See Jean-Luc Marion, *In the Self's Place: The Approach of Saint Augustine*, trans. Jeffrey Kosky (Stanford: Stanford University Press, 2012), 132–33.

8. Jean-Luc Marion, "What Cannot Be Said: Apophasis and the Discourse of Love," in *The Visible and the Revealed*, trans. Christine Geschwandtner and others (New York: Fordham University Press, 2008), 101–18, 104.

9. For a discussion, see Hent de Vries, *Philosophy and the Turn to Religion* (Baltimore: Johns Hopkins University, 1999), chapter 2, entitled "Hypertheology" (96–157), and chapter 5, entitled "The Kenosis of Discourse" (305–58).

10. See J. L. Austin, *How to Do Things with Words*, ed. J. O. Urmson and Marina Sbisà (Cambridge: Harvard University Press, 1975), 148.

11. Michel de Certeau, *The Mystic Fable*, vol. 1: *The Sixteenth and Seventeenth Centuries*, trans. Michael B. Smith (Chicago: University of Chicago Press, 1992), 14, 173. For a discussion, see Hent de Vries, *Religion and Violence: Philosophical Perspectives from Kant to Derrida* (Baltimore: Johns Hopkins University Press, 2002), chapter 3, entitled "Anti-Babel: The Theologico-Political at Cross Purposes," especially 256ff.

12. Marion, *The Erotic Phenomenon*, 9.

13. Jean-Luc Marion, *Being Given: Toward a Phenomenology of Givenness*, trans. Jeffrey L. Kosky (Stanford: Stanford University Press, 2002), x.

14. See Jean-Luc Marion, *On Descartes' Metaphysical Prism: The Constitution and the Limits of Onto-Theology in Cartesian Thought*, trans. Jeffrey L. Kosky (Chicago: University of Chicago Press, 1999). It should be noted that a more recent, probing rereading of Descartes, this time starting out from the sixth of the *Metaphysical Meditations* and focusing on the *Passions de l'âme*, uncovers an even deeper-situated stratum in this modern author's pivotal thought, expressing the unity of mind and body, thought and extension, indeed, a mode or way of living before any further articulation of philosophy proper or, at least, of its method and system. See Jean-Luc Marion, *La pensée passive de Descartes* (Paris: Presses Universitaires de France, 2013). In addition to the metaphor of "prism," at least two other among Marion's early titles already alerted the reader to this ambiguity in Descartes' writing, by highlighting its 'grey ontology' and 'white theology' (*Sur l'ontologie grise de Descartes: Science cartésienne et savoir aristotélicien dans les* Regulae (Paris: Vrin, 1975, 2000); *Sur la théologie blanche de Descartes: Analogie, création des vérités éternelles, fondement* (Paris: Presses Universitaires de France, 1981, 1991).

15. Marion, *The Erotic Phenomenon*, 6.

16. Ibid., 4.

17. Marion, *Being Given*, ix.

18. Ibid., x.

19. Ibid.

20. Alain Badiou, *Being and Event*, trans. Oliver Feltham (New York: Continuum, 2005), xiii, xv, and 17.

21. Marion, *The Erotic Phenomenon*, 3.

22. For a discussion of this expression, see my *Philosophy and the Turn to Religion*, 404–18.

23. Marion, "What Cannot Be Said," 112.

24. Marion, *The Erotic Phenomenon*, 9.

25. Ibid.

26. Robyn Horner in her *Jean-Luc Marion: A Theo-Logical Introduction* (Hants: Ashgate, 2005), 124.

27. Marion, *Being Given*, 282.

28. See ibid., 287. Marion's reference is to Emmanuel Levinas, *Autrement qu'être, ou au-delà de l'essence* (Dordrecht: Kluwer Academic, 1991), 190, *Otherwise Than Being, or Beyond Essence*, trans. Alphonso Lingis (Pittsburgh: Duquesne University Press, 1998), 148, and to Jean-Louis Chrétien, *L'appel et la réponse* (Paris, 1992), 42, *The Call and the Response*, trans. Anne A. Davenport (New York: Fordham University Press, 2004).

29. Austin, *How to Do Things with Words*, 109, cf. 110.

30. Marion, "What Cannot Be Said," 110–11.

31. See my *Religion and Violence*, 143.

32. Marion, *Being Given*, 318, cf. 319.

33. Stanley Cavell, "Performative and Passionate Utterance," in *Philosophy the Day After Tomorrow* (Cambridge: Belknap, 2005), 155–91, 180; Marion, "What Cannot Be Said," 112.

34. Marion, "What Cannot Be Said," 112.

35. Stanley Cavell, *The Claim of Reason: Wittgenstein, Skepticism, Morality, and Tragedy* (New York: Oxford University Press, 1999 [1979]), 177–78.

36. Ibid., 178.

37. Ibid. (emphasis added).

38. Stendhal, The *Charterhouse of Parma*, trans. John Sturrock (New York: Penguin, 2006), 502.

39. https://www.youtube.com/watch?v=GlpDf6XX_jo (last accessed March 20, 2014).

40. Marion, "What Cannot Be Said," 106.

41. For a discussion, see Hent de Vries, "Must We (NOT) Mean What We Say? Seriousness and Sincerity in J. L. Austin and Stanley Cavell," in Ernst van Alphen, Mieke Bal, and Carel Smits, eds., *The Rhetoric of Sincerity* (Stanford: Stanford University Press, 2009), 90–118.

42. Stendhal, *The Charterhouse of Parma*, 502.

43. Ibid., 502–3.

44. Michael Fried, *Absorption and Theatricality: Painting and Beholder in the Age of Diderot* (Chicago: University of Chicago Press, 1980).

45. Jean-Luc Marion, "Preface," in *The Crossing of the Visible*, trans. James Smith (Stanford: Stanford University Press, 2003), ix. A difficulty remains. For why should paintings have any privilege over, say, photography, film, video, digital art, and the broadest spectrum of popular visual culture, as Marion seems to suggest?

46. Michael R. Taylor, ed., *Marcel Duchamp: Étant donnés* (New Haven: Yale University Press, 2009).

47. Jean-Luc Marion, *Courbet ou la peinture à l'oeil* (Paris: Flammarion, 2014).

48. Taylor, *Marcel Duchamp*, 284.

49. Marion, *The Crossing of the Visible* 29.

50. Michael Fried, *The Moment of Caravaggio* (Princeton: Princeton University Press, 2010), 196–97. As Fried reminds us (ibid., 195–201, cf. also 284–86), *The Calling of St. Matthew* was unveiled together—and paired—with another picture, namely *The Martyrdom of St. Matthew*, in 1600. The canvases faced each other in the Contarelli Chapel in San Luigi dei Francesi in Rome and still do. As Fried notes, thanks to X-ray photography we know that Caravaggio "began by working on the *Martyrdom*, then broke off to turn to the *Calling*, and only after completing the latter returned to the *Martyrdom*" (ibid., 195).

51. See Stanley Cavell, "What Is the Scandal of Skepticism?" in his *Philosophy the Day After Tomorrow*, 132–54, cf. 151. This, incidentally, is also one of the contexts in which Cavell speaks of "the feeling that the fact of language is like a miracle" (ibid., 139).

52. Marion, *Being Given*, 285

53. Marion, *Being Given*, 356n57 and 358n75. The citation is taken from Alain Badiou, *Being and Event*, 181, who, to my knowledge, "almost" nowhere refers to Marion in turn. See also Christopher Watkin, *Difficult Atheism: Post-Theological Thinking in Alain Badiou, Jean-Luc Nancy, and Quentin Meillassoux* (Edinburgh: Edinburgh University Press, 2011, 2013), 100–2.

54. Cavell, *The Claim of Reason*, 65ff., 170.

55. Marion, "What Cannot Be Said," 115.

56. The most subtle examples seem to be invoked by Marcel Proust, in *A la recherche du temps perdu* (*In Search of Lost Time*). But then again, what Proust renders so compellingly is the *composition*—the copositioning—of constitutive elements of the image of the other, rather than its idealizing constitution, leaving always in suspense our belief in it, our attachment to it. We do not necessarily make the (image of) the other in our own image—at least we do not do so successfully—because this other can continually disappoint, elude, or deceive us. It is just that what gets us hooked in the first placed is not without relation to what we bring to it, whether knowingly, willingly, or not.

57. Marion, "Preface," *The Crossing of the Visible*, x. One is reminded of Cavell's words, in *The Claim of Reason*, which extend this lesson from philosophy into that of learning, beginning with learning a language, as such: "What we learn is not just what we have studied; and what we have been taught is not just what we were intended to learn. What we have in our memories is not just what we have memorized" (Cavell, *The Claim of Reason*, 177). There is such a thing, Cavell seems to say, as "'the spirit'" (ibid.), adding the scare quotes, in which we give and take things. There is calling, in other words, proactively before and beyond any actual (audible, visible, linguistic-discursive) "call," as it were. Not surprisingly *The Claim of Reason* chooses its epigraph from Ralph Waldo Emerson's "An Address Delivered before the Senior Class Divinity School, Cambridge, Sunday evening, 15 July, 1838": "Truly speaking, it is not instruction, but provocation, that I can receive from another soul" (ibid., iv).

58. Marion, *God Without Being*, 107.

59. Marion, "What Cannot Be Said," 115.

60. Marion, *Being Given*, 170.

61. Marion, *The Crossing of the Visible*, 93n4 (translator's note). See ibid., 31 and following. In *Le Petit Robert*, we read the following definition: the *miraculé* is the one "*sur qui un miracle s'est opéré*," as in the expression "*Les miraculés de Lourdes*."

62. Marion, *Being Given*, 170.

63. Marion, *The Erotic Phenomenon*, 7.

64. Returning to Caravaggio's *The Calling of Saint Matthew*, we can, once more, call on Fried's strong reading as he concludes:

> in the *Calling* there is the added suggestion that the depicted scene is on the verge of dissolution: in another moment Christ and Peter will be gone (Christ is as good as gone, the painting implies) and Matthew, gesturing towards himself, his life transformed, will have left with them (he is on his way). His right hand's lingering preoccupation with the coins on the table—in what, anachronistically, may be called the "bad" everyday—delays that outcome, as perhaps does, on a different level of experience, the viewer's uncertainty as to his identity. And we are left to wonder about the probable reaction of the charmed liveried youth at his side, who seems to rest his right arm on the back of Matthew's chair in a gesture of casual intimacy, should the latter in fact rise and leave. But the outcome is not only certain; it has in a sense already occurred. (The youth, we might say, emblematizes in his sheer attractiveness everything that Matthew is in the act of giving up. We should not think of the "bad" everyday as unappealing).
> (Fried, *The Moment of Caravaggio*, 201)

In light of the more recent art historical attempts to identify Matthew with the young man (and not with the bearded one)—a reading Fried ends up disagreeing with—one might feel justified in characterizing the young man as Matthew's *alter ego*, paradoxically, his old self, deeply engrossed in an everydayness that, for all its appeal, is not his true calling, not what really matters.

SUGGESTED READING

The list of books and articles on love and forgiveness emphasizes recent work from across the humanities and social sciences that addresses many of the issues raised in this volume. The collections of essays in particular provide further bibliographical information.

Akhtar, Salman. "Forgiveness: Origins, Dynamics, Psychopathology, and Technical Relevance." *Psychoanalytic Quarterly* 71 (2002): 175–212.

Alam, Edward J., ed. *Compassion and Forgiveness: Religious and Philosophical Perspectives from Around the World*. Beirut: Notre Dame University Press Lebanon, 2013.

Arendt, Hannah. "Irreversibility and the Power to Forgive." In *The Human Condition*, 236–43. Chicago: University of Chicago Press, 2013.

Beckwith, Sarah. *Shakespeare and the Grammar of Forgiveness*. Ithaca: Cornell University Press, 2011.

Bernstein, Richard J. "Derrida: The Aporia of Forgiveness?" *Constellations: An International Journal of Critical and Democratic Theory* 13, no. 3 (2006): 394–406.

Caputo, John D., and Michael J. Scanlon, eds. *Questioning God*, esp. 1–18. Bloomington: Indiana University Press, 2001.

Cavell, Stanley. "The Avoidance of Love." In *Must We Mean What We Say?* Rev. ed. Cambridge: Cambridge University Press, 2002.

Frankfurt, Harry G. *The Reasons of Love*. Princeton: Princeton University Press, 2004.

Fricke, Christel, ed. *The Ethics of Forgiveness: A Collection of Essays*. New York: Routledge, 2011.

Gaita, Raimond. *A Common Humanity: Thinking About Love and Truth and Justice*. New York: Routledge, 2000.

Griswold, Charles. *Forgiveness: A Philosophical Exploration.* Cambridge: Cambridge University Press, 2007.

Griswold, Charles, and David Konstan, eds. *Ancient Forgiveness: Classical, Judaic, and Christian.* Cambridge: Cambridge University Press, 2012.

Jankélévitch, Vladimir. *Forgiveness.* Trans. Andrew Kelley. Chicago: University of Chicago Press, 2005.

Janover, Michael, "The Limits of Forgiveness and the Ends of Politics," *Journal of Intercultural Studies* 26, no. 3 (2005): 221–35.

Kaposy, Chris, "'Analytic' Reading, 'Continental' Text: The Case of Derrida's 'On Forgiveness,'" *International Journal of Philosophical Studies* 13, no. 2 (June 2005): 203–26.

Klein, Melanie. *Love, Guilt, and Reparation and Other Works, 1921–1945.* New York: Free Press, 1975.

Klein, Melanie. *Envy and Gratitude and Other Works, 1946–1963.* New York: Free Press, 1975.

Krapp, Peter, "Amnesty: Between an Ethics of Forgiveness and the Politics of Forgetting," *German Law Journal* 6, no. 1 (January 2005): 185–96.

Levinas, Emmanuel. *Entre nous: On Thinking-of-the-other.* Trans. Michael B. Smith and Barbara Harshav. New York: Columbia University Press, 1998.

Macaleese, Mary. *Love in Chaos: Spiritual Growth and the Search for Peace in Northern Ireland.* New York: Continuum, 1999.

Marion, Jean-Luc. *The Erotic Phenomenon.* Trans. Stephen E. Lewis. Chicago: University of Chicago Press, 2007.

McCullough, Michael E., Kenneth I. Pargament, and Carl E. Thoresen, eds. *Forgiveness: Theory, Research, and Practice.* New York: Guilford, 2000.

Murphy, Jeffrie G. *Getting Even: Forgiveness and Its Limits.* New York: Oxford University Press, 2003.

Nussbaum, Martha C., *Love's Knowledge: Essays on Philosophy and Literature.* New York: Oxford University Press, 1992.

Pettigrove, Glen. *Forgiveness and Love.* Oxford: Oxford University Press, 2012.

Pettman, Dominic. *Love and Other Technologies: Retrofitting Eros for the Information Age.* New York: Fordham University Press, 2006.

Ricœur, Paul. "Reflections on a New Ethos for Europe." In Richard Kearney, ed., *The Hermeneutics of Action,* 3–13. London: Sage, 1996.

Secomb, Linnell. *Philosophy and Love: From Plato to Popular Culture.* Edinburgh: Edinburgh University Press, 2007.

Singer, Irving. *Philosophy of Love: A Partial Summing-up.* Cambridge: MIT Press, 2009.

Tutu, Desmond, and Mpho A. Tutu. *The Book of Forgiving: The Fourfold Path for Healing Ourselves and Our World.* Ed. Douglas C. Abrams. San Francisco: HarperOne, 2014.

Udoff, Alan, ed. *Vladimir Jankélévitch and the Question of Forgiveness.* Lanham: Lexington, 2013.

Ure, Michael, "The Politics of Mercy, Forgiveness and Love: A Nietzschean Appraisal," *South African Journal of Philosophy* 26, no. 1 (2007): 56–69.

CONTRIBUTORS

RANIA AJAMI is the founder and director of Jumping Pages, spearheading the productions of the company's first two critically acclaimed children's book apps: "David and Goliath for the iPad" and "The House That Went on Strike." In addition, Rania is an award-winning film writer and director, garnering awards for her full-length feature *Asylum Seekers* (2009), documentary *Qaddafi's Female Bodyguards* (2004), and short film *Katalog* (2005). Her work in film and app development has been widely acclaimed in the national media. A graduate of Princeton University, Rania Ajami holds an MFA from New York University's Tisch School of the Arts.

SEGAHL AVIN is an American Israeli television writer, playwright, and director. She is the creator and executive producer of several of Israel's most acclaimed telenovelas (*Game of Life, Michaela, Telenovela Inc.*) and comedy series (*Mythological Ex, Irreversible*). In the U.S., Avin has worked with CBS (*The Ex-List*) and is currently working with HBO. Her work for theater includes highly acclaimed plays for children (*How to Make a Boy, A New Friend Shmulik*) as well as plays produced at festivals around the world (*With a Gun and a Smile, Freaks, Taxi*).

LEORA BATNITZKY is professor of religion at Princeton University, where she chairs the Department of Religion and serves as director of Princeton's Tikvah Project on Jewish Thought. She is the author of *Idolatry and Representation: The Philosophy of Franz Rosenzweig Reconsidered* (Princeton University Press, 2000); *Leo Strauss and Emmanuel Levinas: Philosophy and the Politics of Revelation* (Cambridge University Press, 2006); and *How Judaism Became a Religion: An Introduction to Modern Jewish Thought* (Princeton University Press, 2011) as well as of many articles and edited volumes.

Jacques Derrida (1930–2004) was one of the most influential philosophers of his generation. His many publications have broken new ground across the humanities, the arts, the social sciences, and beyond. Derrida taught in France and at universities in Europe and the United States. A dedicated teacher and source of inspiration for a host of scholars and cultural critics worldwide, Derrida was the author of fundamental contributions that probed the presuppositions of Western metaphysics, the phenomenological method, psychoanalysis, visual and media studies, and law and ethics. The topics of love and forgiveness figure prominently in several of both earlier and especially later writings.

Hent de Vries is Professor in the Humanities Center and the Department of Philosophy at the Johns Hopkins University, where he holds the Russ Family Chair and serves as the director of the Humanities Center. Since 2014, he has served as the director of the School of Criticism and Theory at Cornell University. He is currently also a distinguished visiting professor at the Hebrew University, Jerusalem. His principal publications include *Philosophy and the Turn to Religion* (Johns Hopkins University Press, 1999, 2000); *Religion and Violence: Philosophical Perspectives from Kant to Derrida* (Johns Hopkins University Press, 2002, 2006); and *Minimal Theologies: Critiques of Secular Reason in Theodor W. Adorno and Emmanuel Levinas* (Johns Hopkins University Press, 2005). He was the coeditor, with Samuel Weber, of *Religion and Media* (Stanford University Press 2001); the coeditor, with Lawrence Sullivan, of *Political Theologies: Public Religions in a Post-Secular World* (Fordham University Press 2006); and the coeditor, with Ward Blanton, of *Paul and the Philosophers* (Fordham University Press, 2013). In addition, he was the general editor of the five-volume miniseries entitled *The Future of the Religious Past* as well as of its first title, *Religion Beyond a Concept* (Fordham University Press, 2008). Currently, he is completing two book-length studies, "Of Miracles, Events, and Special Effects: Global Religion in an Age of New Media" and "Spiritual Exercises: Concepts and Practices."

Haleh Liza Gafori is a poet, musician, and video artist living in Brooklyn, New York. She has toured throughout the U.S. and in Europe. Haleh has performed at Carnegie Hall, the Mimi Fest in Marseilles, the Bonnaroo Festival, and UNC's Memorial Hall. Her poems have appeared in *Rattapallax* and *Beyond Borders*. In 2011 her band The Mast released the debut album *Wild Poppies,* followed by the singles "Seas Across Your Mind" and "UpUpUp" in 2012. Haleh was part of the editing team for the 2013 relaunch of the poetry and culture journal *Rattapallax*. She holds a BS in Biology from Stanford University and an MFA in Creative Writing/Poetry from CCNY.

Jean-Luc Marion is the Andrew Thomas Greeley and Grace McNichols Greeley Professor of Catholic Studies and professor of the philosophy of religions and theology at the University of Chicago. His has widely published in the history of modern philosophy and contemporary phenomenology and theology, including *The Idol and Distance* (Fordham University Press, 2001); *God Without Being* (University of Chicago Press, 1991); *Reduction and Givenness* (Northwestern University Press, 1998); *Being Given* (Stanford University Press, 2002); and *In the Self's Place*

(Stanford University Press, 2012). In 2008 Jean-Luc Marion received the Karl-Jaspers-Preis and was elected to the Académie Française to take the chair of his mentor, the archbishop of Paris, Cardinal Lustiger.

ALBERT MASON, MB, BS, PsyD, FIPA, is one of the main interviewees in Roger Spottiswoode's documentary *Beyond Right and Wrong: Stories of Justice and Forgiveness* (2012), which explores the relationship between aggressors and the families of their victims in conflicts around the world. Through interviews conducted with those on both sides of the conflict in Rwanda, Northern Ireland, and Israel/Palestine, the film examines the process of learning to forgive in the most difficult of circumstances. *Beyond Right and Wrong* is a meditation on the concept of justice in a troubled world. In this film Dr. Mason brings his profound understanding of unconscious dynamics to bear to illuminate the complex process of forgiveness. Dr. Mason trained at the British Institute of Psychoanalysis and immigrated to the United States in 1969 with Wilfried Bion and Susanna Isaacs to further the work of Melanie Klein. Dr. Mason is a training and supervising analyst at the Psychoanalytic Center of California and the New Center for Psychoanalysis in Los Angeles. He has published and taught extensively both in the U.S. and abroad. He is a founding member and two-time president of PCC, a founding board member of CIPS, and a past member of the House of Delegates of the International Psychoanalytical Association. Dr. Mason maintains a private practice in Beverly Hills.

SARI NUSSEIBEH is professor of Islamic and political philosophy at al-Quds University in East Jerusalem where he was also president from 1995 until 2014. He studied philosophy at Christ Church at Oxford and holds a PhD in Islamic Philosophy from Harvard University. After his studies in Britain and the U.S., he returned to the West Bank in 1978–1988 to teach at Birzeit University. Nusseibeh has written and lectured widely, his focus often being the subject of war and peace in his region of the world. His book on the two-state solution (with Mark Heller, 1991) has been translated into German, Italian, Japanese, Hebrew, and French. Nusseibeh's autobiography, *Once Upon a Country: A Palestinian Life* (Farrar, Straus and Giroux, 2007), one of the most moving and balanced accounts of the Middle East, Israeli-Palestinian conflict in all of its historical aspects and impasses, received numerous positive reviews and has been translated into many languages. It recounts his family history in Jerusalem, which goes back some thirteen hundred years. His ancestors were among the first Muslims to come to the holy city. Since then, the family has been in charge of the key to the Church of the Holy Sepulchre in the Old City. Every day, a Nusseibeh opens and closes the church gate. Nusseibeh has further authored an *Introductory Symbolic Logic*, a work on *Absolute and Restricted Freedom*, and a host of specialized articles on the history of Islamic philosophy. His latest book, *What Is a Palestinian State Worth?* was published by Harvard University Press in 2011. He is currently finishing two books for Stanford University Press: one on the concept of reason in Islamic thought, entitled *The Story of Reason in Islam*, and the other a collection of philosophical papers, to be published under the title *Why Philosophy Matters*. Dr. Nusseibeh was selected to give the much acclaimed Tanner Lectures at Harvard University in 2008 and the

Multatuli Lecture in Leuven, Belgium, in 2009. Over the years he has received several awards, including, most recently, an honorary doctorate from the Catholic University of Leuven University, also in 2009. He was twice selected, in 2005 and 2007, by *Foreign Policy* and *Prospect* magazines as one of the one hundred leading world public figures.

ORNA OPHIR is an Israeli clinical psychologist and a psychoanalyst in private practice in New York. She graduated from the Cohn Institute for the History and Philosophy of Science and Ideas and holds a PhD from the School of History at Tel Aviv University. Alongside her clinical work she is invested in historical research of her field. She is an adjunct associate professor at the Humanities Center at Johns Hopkins University. In addition, she is an associate at the DeWitt Wallace Institute for the History of Psychiatry at Weill-Cornell Medical College in New York City, as well as an adjunct associate professor in the doctoral studies program in clinical psychology at Long Island University. Her past research and publications focused on the history of schizophrenia and psychoanalysis in postwar America. Her current project is entitled "Klein in America: the Marginalization of Melanie Klein's Thought in America, 1924–2010." She is the author of a book, written in Hebrew, entitled *On the Borderland of Madness: Psychoanalysis, Psychiatry, and Psychosis in Postwar USA* (Resling, 2013), which is forthcoming in a revised and an expanded English translation (Routledge, 2015).

NILS F. SCHOTT is the James M. Motley Postdoctoral Fellow in the Humanities at Johns Hopkins University. He is the author of *The Conversion of Knowledge*, and coeditor of Vladimir Jankélévitch's *Henri Bergson* (Duke University Press, 2015). He is also a widely published translator of philosophy, for example of Helmuth Plessner, Lambert Wiesing, François Delaporte, and Henri Atlan.

REGINA M. SCHWARTZ is professor of English at Northwestern University. In addition to numerous articles, her publications include *Remembering and Repeating: Biblical Creation in Paradise Lost* (Cambridge University Press, 1988); *The Book and the Text: The Bible and Literary Theory* (Blackwell, 1990); *Desire in the Renaissance: Psychoanalysis and Literature* (Princeton University Press, 1994); *The Postmodern Bible* (Yale University Press, 1995); and *Transcendence: Philosophy, Literature, and Theology Approach the Beyond* (Routledge, 2004). *The Curse of Cain: The Violent Legacy of Monotheism* (University of Chicago Press, 1997) was nominated for a Pulitzer Prize. Her book *Sacramental Poetics at the Dawn of Secularism: When God Left the World* was published by Stanford in 2008. She has served as president of the Milton Society of America and chair of the Modern Language Association's Religion and Literature Division.

INDEX

RELIGION, CULTURE, AND PUBLIC LIFE
Series Editor: Karen Barkey

The resurgence of religion calls for careful analysis and constructive criticism of new forms of intolerance, as well as new approaches to tolerance, respect, mutual understanding, and accommodation. In order to promote serious scholarship and informed debate, the Institute for Religion, Culture, and Public Life and Columbia University Press are sponsoring a book series devoted to the investigation of the role of religion in society and culture today. This series includes works by scholars in religious studies, political science, history, cultural anthropology, economics, social psychology, and other allied fields whose work sustains multidisciplinary and comparative as well as transnational analyses of historical and contemporary issues. The series focuses on issues related to questions of difference, identity, and practice within local, national, and international contexts. Special attention is paid to the ways in which religious traditions encourage conflict, violence, and intolerance and also support human rights, ecumenical values, and mutual understanding. By mediating alternative methodologies and different religious, social, and cultural traditions, books published in this series will open channels of communication that facilitate critical analysis.

After Pluralism: Reimagining Religious Engagement, edited by Courtney Bender and Pamela E. Klassen
Religion and International Relations Theory, edited by Jack Snyder
Religion in America: A Political History, Denis Lacorne
Democracy, Islam, and Secularism in Turkey, edited by Ahmet T. Kuru and Alfred Stepan
Refiguring the Spiritual: Beuys, Barney, Turrell, Goldsworthy, Mark C. Taylor
Tolerance, Democracy, and Sufis in Senegal, edited by Mamadou Diouf
Rewiring the Real: In Conversation with William Gaddis, Richard Powers, Mark Danielewski, and Don DeLillo, Mark C. Taylor
Democracy and Islam in Indonesia, edited by Mirjam Künkler and Alfred Stepan
Religion, the Secular, and the Politics of Sexual Difference, edited by Linell E. Cady and Tracy Fessenden
Recovering Place: Reflections on Stone Hill, Mark C. Taylor
Boundaries of Toleration, edited by Alfred Stepan and Charles Taylor
Choreographies of Sharing at Sacred Sites: Religion, Politics, and Conflict Resolution, edited by Elazar Barkan and Karen Barkey
Beyond Individualism: The Challenge of Inclusive Communities, George Rupp
Relativism and Religion: Why Democratic Societies Do Not Need Moral Absolutes, Carlo Invernizzi Accetti
Mormonism and American Politics, edited by Randall Balmer and Jana Riess
Pakistan at the Crossroads: Domestic Dynamics and External Pressures, edited by Christophe Jaffrelot
Race and Secularism in America, edited by Jonathon S. Kahn and Vincent W. Lloyd